Alexandria, Virginia City and County Census

1860

Transcribed by

T. Michael Miller
Alexandria Library
Lloyd House

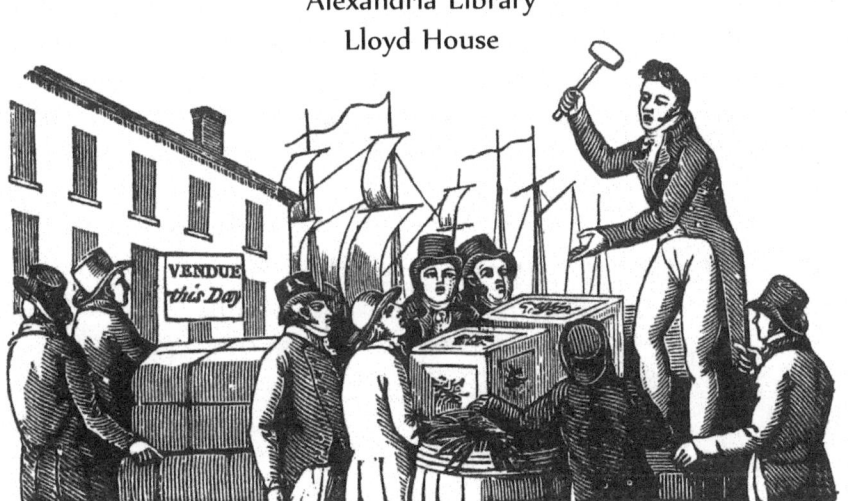

HERITAGE BOOKS
2015

HERITAGE BOOKS
AN IMPRINT OF HERITAGE BOOKS, INC.

Books, CDs, and more—Worldwide

For our listing of thousands of titles see our website
at
www.HeritageBooks.com

Published 2015 by
HERITAGE BOOKS, INC.
Publishing Division
5810 Ruatan Street
Berwyn Heights, Md. 20740

Copyright © 1986 Alexandria Library
717 Queen Street, Alexandria, Virginia 22314

Heritage Books by T. Michael Miller:

*Alexandria and Alexandria [Arlington] County, Virginia:
Minister Returns and Marriage Bonds, 1801–1852*

Alexandria Virginia City Officialdom, 1749–1992

Alexandria, Virginia City and County Census, 1860

*Artisans and Merchants of Alexandria, Virginia, 1780–1820,
Volume 1: Abercrombie to Myer*

*Artisans and Merchants of Alexandria, Virginia, 1780–1820,
Volume 2: Napey to Zimmerman*

Burials in St. Mary's Catholic Cemetery, Alexandria, Virginia, 1798–1983

Murder and Mayhem: Criminal Conduct in Old Alexandria, Virginia, 1749–1900

Pen Portraits: Alexandria, Virginia, 1739–1900

Portrait of a Town: Alexandria, District of Columbia [Virginia], 1820–1830

CD: *Alexandria and Alexandria [Arlington] County, Virginia:
Minister Returns and Marriage Bonds, 1801–1852*

All rights reserved. No part of this book may be reproduced or transmitted in any form or by any means, electronic or mechanical, including photocopying, recording or by any information storage and retrieval system without written permission from the author, except for the inclusion of brief quotations in a review.

International Standard Book Numbers
Paperbound: 978-0-917890-71-0
Clothbound: 978-0-7884-6230-6

SILENT MEMORIES

The 1860s were a time of turmoil and tragedy for the city and county of Alexandria, Virginia. Having recovered from the economic doldrums of the forties, the decade dawned brightly as the building boom of the 1850s and railroad construction provided an impetus for economic recovery and prosperity. Ninety-six firms produced a variety of goods ranging from bark to tinware. The Alexandria Gazette reported:

> business upon change is now quite brisk, and the increased arrival of grain from the country promises of a heavy trade.... The railroads are bringing excellent freight and a very large number of passengers are passing over the routes....[G. Terry Sharrer, "Commerce and Industry," in Alexandria A Towne in Transition, 1800-1900, edited by John D. Macoll & George J. Stansfield, (Alexandria, Va.: Alexandria Bicentennial Commission, 1977)].

Little did the 12,652 inhabitants realize that a conflagrant wave of death and destruction would rend asunder the national body politic. There would be few who would not lose their husbands, brothers or sons to the machinery of war as it tore to bits the fabric of society and their personal lives. The dreams and aspirations of so many young men would die on the battlefields of Frazier's Farm, Five Forks, Manassas, Chancellorsville and the Wilderness. Untold writers, musicians and artists would never have the opportunity to write or compose. Instead their legacy would be mouldering graves nestled amongst the hills and streams of the Virginia country-side. These are the silent memories of a generation which endured a catastrophic civil war and watched as their way of life dissolved before their eyes. Alexandria would be forever changed.

The following enumeration is an alphabetical list of households in the city and county of Alexandria in 1860 arranged according to the name of the head of the household. All persons listed as members of the household are enumerated here with occupation, value of real estate/personal property, age, sex, and birthplace to the extent the data is given in the census records. The slave schedule, however, was not included. Occupations have been abbreviated where necessary because of space limitations using the abbreviations defined below, but are otherwise given just as they appear in the records. Birthplaces have been abbreviated using the standard two letter postal codes where possible and some special codes defined below for foreign locations. Citations to the original records are given in the form "page number-family number" at the end of each entry. These numbers can also be used to determine which residents lived in the city and which lived in the county. The 200 or so households outside the city limits were listed at the end of the census beginning on census page 253 with household number 1968, so households with these or larger numbers were located in the county. Persons whose surname differs from that of the head of the household can be found by means of the cross-index.

Needless to say, any transcription of a large mass of material is fraught with difficulties. In this case the handwriting and legibility of the microfilm copy from which the transcription was made left much to be desired. In addition the original records are frequently incomplete. If the researcher feels certain that a person resided in Alexandria in 1860 and finds no indication of the same, it would be wise to look for variant spellings of their name. Lastly, there undoubtedly were individuals who resided in the area who were simply missed by the census taker for unknown reasons. A supplemental index to the 1859 poll book appears here at the end of the 1860 census as an additional resource to be consulted. It lists eligible white voters 21 years of age or older and specifies what ward of the city they inhabited. Finally, a chart of tithables is given below which mirrors the socio-economic conditions prevalent in Alexandria in 1860.

ALEXANDRIA CITY TITHABLES IN 1860

Free Male persons above the age of 16 2,113
Slaves who have attained the age of 16 485
Total 2,598

	Value	Tax on Value	Total Tax
1865 White males, at 89¢			1,492.00
159 Male free negroes at 180¢			286.20
525 slaves at 120¢			630.00
268 horses, mules, asses and jennets	25,275	101.10	
161 cattle	2,794	11.18	
127 Pleasure carriages, stage coaches	15,880	63.52	
737 Watches	25,057	100.23	
622 Clocks	2,672	10.69	
141 Pianos and harps	17,230	68.92	
Plate and jewelry	13,806	55.22	
Household & Kitchen furniture	186,395	745.58	
30 Hogs	120	.48	
Money, bonds, securities and claims	273,179	1,092.72	
Capital invested in mining or manufacturing	156,125	624.50	
Money, etc. under control of the Court	7,100	28.40	
Capital of Companies which declare no dividend	185,000	74.00	
Personal property etc of internal improvements	300	1.20	
Other articles of personl property	6,376	25.50	
Fees of Office			10.51
Amount of income			1,949.02
Interest or profit at 6 2/3 per cent			1,545.39
Dividends, 6 2/3 per cent			644.89
Toll bridge and ferries, 6 per ct			
Values and tax thereon	750,809	3,003.24	6,558.01
TOTAL			9,561.25
Value of town lots including buildings $3,607,275 at 40 cents			14,420.10
			23,990.35

Source: *Alexandria Gazette*, June 5, 1860, p. 3

ABBREVIATIONS

agr - agricultural
agt - agent
appren - apprentice
asslt & bty - assault & battery
asst - assistant
asym - asylum

(B) - Black or Negro Race
BA - British America
BD - Baden
blksmith - blacksmith
BM - Bermuda, West Indies
BR - Brunswick
brd - boarding
brklyr - bricklayer
btch - butcher
BV - Bavaria

cab mkr - cabinet maker
carptr - carpenter
Cath - Catholic
cgrs - cigars
CH - China
chm - chemist
chr - chair
clk - clerk
CN - Canada
cndl - candle
co - company
coll - collector/collection
comm/cm - commission
confect - confectioner
contr - contractor
ctn - cotton
curr - currier
custm - custom

dau - daughter
dig - digger
dr gd - dry good
drug - druggist
dom - domestic

EG - England
emplr - employer
Epis - Episcopal

FK - Frankfort
FR - France
ftry - factory

gds - goods
genrl - general
gov - government
GR - Germany
gr - grocer/grocery
GT - Georgetown, DC

HC - Hesse Cassel
HD - Hesse Darmstadt
HL - Holland
HN - Hanover, Germany
hotelkpr - hotelkeeper
HP - Hesse Capel
hrdwr - hardware
hrns - harness
HS - Hesse Casad
hs - house
HV - Havana
HY - Hungary

i & b fdr - iron & brass
        foundry
IJ - Isle Juen..
IR - Ireland

JM - Jamica

K - 1,000
kpr - keeper

lmb - lumber

(M) - Mulatto
mat - matress
MC - Mechlenberg
mech - mechanic
merch/mc - merchant
Meth - Methodist
mfg - manufacturer
MH - Masach
mkr - maker
mn - minister
ms - master
mus tch - music teacher

NA - Nassau
NB - New Brunswick
NF - New Foundland
nonpay - nonpayment
NW - Newport

off - office
orp - orphan

plstr/pls grindr - plasterer grinder
PO - Poland
PR - Prussia
pres - president
Pres - Presbytarian
prop - proprietor
prost - prostitution
Prot - Protestant

rm - room
RR - railroad

SB - Saxe Coburgh
SD - Sweden
sdlr - saddler
semstrs - seamstress
serv - service
sh cp - ship carpenter
SL - Switzerland
ST - Scotland
stm - steam

stmb stw - steamboat stewart
SW - Saxe Weymer
SX - Saxony

tabacnist - tabacconist
tanr - tanner
tbco - tabacco
TP - Tin Pan Alley
tr - trader
treas - treasurer

US - United States
undertkr - undertaker

var - variety

WB - Wurtenburgh
wf - wharf
whsale - wholesale
wk - work/works
WL - Wales
WR - Wartenburg
wsh & irn - wash and iron
WT - Wentenburg

ALEXANDRIA CITY AND COUNTY VIRGINIA 1860 CENSUS

ADAM, Wallace, watchmaker 11000/1500	43 m	ADAMS, Mary B	66 f
Hannah	40 f PA	DADE, Jane, 8000/300	71 f
John, clerk	19 m	Eliza	30 f
William, bank clerk	16 m VA	133-971	
Mary H	16 f		
Robt A	12 m	ADAMS, Samuel R, dry good merchant	40 m
Charles	10 m	Theresa 10K/10K	38 f
James	8 m	Frank	12 m
Alice	6 f	William	10 m
Ruth	5 f	Henry C	8 m
Florence	4/12 f	117-864	
117-862			
		ADAMS, Thomas J, physician	39 m
		Hannah	23 f
ADAMS, Ann, -/500	76 f	POWELL, Mary	55 f
Ellen	50 f MD	ADAMS, Clarence	6 f
Margaret	41 f VA	Charles D	4 m
James, h carpenter -/500	34 m	Brook P	9/12 m
Sarah	22 f	POWELL, John, carpenter	20 m
John Thomas (M)	11 m	Sidney	18 m
227-1746		30-192	
ADAMS, Charles, dry good clerk	34 m	ADDISON, A E, 20,000/35,000	55 m MD
178-1332		Mary	35 f
		Walter	16 m
ADAMS, Geo (M)	36 m	Augustus	16 m
Annie (B)	23 m	Jane	11 f
James (B)	6 m	Francis	9 m
Emma (B)	3 f	Elizabeth	7 f
Willie (B)	4/12 m	Joseph	5 m
Annie (B)	40 f	Mary	3 f
282-2157		LAW, Mary, teacher	26 f NY
		275-2118	
ADAMS, George, blacksmith	24 m	ADDISON, Alfred (B)	71 m
Ellen	26 f MD	Harriet (M)	67 f
26-154		167-1255	
ADAMS, J N, clerk	26 m VA	ADDISON, Ed B, 6,000/2,000	65 m
10-47		Elizabeth	27 f
		Catharine	22 f
ADAMS, Jas, bricklayer -/600	39 m	Fanny	20 f
Sarah	29 f	John	24 m
KIDWELL, Harriet, monthly nurse	46 f	Chas	18 m
Jane	23 f	Thomas	16 m
William, printer	21 m	35-223	
Robert, tailor	19 m		
James	16 m	ADDISON, Edward B, agri store -/1500	26 m
Caroline	14 f	Emily W	23 f NJ
135-984		108-801	

ALEXANDRIA VIRGINIA 1860 CENSUS

ADDISON, Fred (M), laborer	36 m		ALEXANDER, Elizabeth 6000/600	65 f	
Louise (B)	28 f		Chas W, grocer 2000/300	30 m	
Cornelia (B)	8 f		John R -/100	27 m VA	
Frederick (B)	4 m		Elizabeth	26 f	
Louise (B)	7 f		James R	1 m	
Mary V (M)	9/12 f		Cecil	21 f	
167-1250			62-435		
AFFEY, Kate, domestic	22 f IR		ALEXANDER, Jane, seamstress	42 f VA	
75-532			124-906		
AGER, Jas B, contractor	46 m		ALLEN, James, house painter	26 m	
Susan	36 f		Mary	26 f	
Wilson	13 m		Annie	4 f	
Marcila	11 f		Charles	2 m	
Kate	9 f		224-1724		
Mercer	1 m				
Jordan (B)	21 m		ALLEN, John, house carpenter -/30	26 m	
PAYNE, John (B)	16 m		Susan	23 f	
276-2120			Sarah	4 f	
AGES, Wm (B)	25 m VA		James	3 m	
Maria (M)	20 f		Maria	5/12 f	
135-986			192-1460		
AGNEW, J T, coal agent	35 m		ALLEN, John (B)	31 m	
8-46			Mary (M)	36 f	
			Harriette (M)	2 f	
AGNEW, James, coal agent -/300	40 m PA		202-1544		
Matilda	37 f VA				
Frank	13 m		ALLEN, Margaret, domestic	35 f	
Leonora	11 f		Florence	16 f	
Rebecca	9 f		210-1606		
May	7 f				
David	3 m		ALLEN, Wm, ship smith 500/500	30 m VA	
CROSSINGER, Mary, domestic	25 f PA		Mary	28 f	
177-1322			William	7 m	
			Ernest	3 m	
			Sally E	2 f	
AHEARN, Bartholomew, laborer -/300	36 m IR		127-926		
Ella	26 f IR				
Mary	5 f VA		ALLISON, Sarah, tailoress	50 f	
Margaret	3 f VA		133-973		
Ellen	9/12 f VA				
BURG, Agnes, nurse	11 f		ALLISON, Thomas D, shoemaker	44 m VA	
158-1172			Ann	35 f	
			James, apprentice	15 m	
AHEARN, John, laborer -/50	52 m IR		May	16 f	
Margaret	45 f		Thomas	13 m	
Mary	17 f		Ellen	11 f	
Michael	13 m		Sarah	9 f	
Patrick	10 m		Margaret	8 f	
150-1104			John	5 m	
			George	4 m	
ALAN, James, coal agent -/300	40 m PA		Charles	2 m	
Matilda	37 f		241-1868		
Frank	13 m				
Leonard	11 f		ALLISON, William, shoemaker 1200/100	45 m VA	
Rebecca	9 f		Matilda	45 f	
May	7 f		Dacie	19 f	
David	3 m		Delphia	16 f	
CUPUYA, Mary, domestic	25 f PA		Emma	2 f	
177-1322			29-184		

ALEXANDRIA VIRGINIA 1860 CENSUS

ALMS HOUSE			McCLUSKEY, J	23 m	
STEPHENSON, John, keeper alms house	53 m		278-79--2136		
Sarah, matron	40 f				
May	14 f		ALWFORD, Jas, restaurant	40 m	PA
John	12 m		Mary	35 f	MD
Emma	6 f		John	12 m	
THROP, Rachael	69 f	NY	James	8 m	VA
NEWFIELD, May	85 f	IR	Parke	5 M	
ATWELL, John, cooper	65 m		McCULLIN, Sarah	68 f	MD
JONES, Sarah	20 f		63-442		
Mary	22 f				
FINNIGAN, Mary	40 f		ALWELL, Ewell, ice merchant 500/250	29 m	VA
BATT..., John	14 m		Julia	25 f	
THOMAS, Charles	12 m		Ella	2 f	
ROACH, Mary	5 f		Infant	1 f	
RYE, Jesse, h carpenter	52 m		THORM, Clay, carter	25 m	MD
Jane	60 f		59-416		
Jane E	16 f				
HICKS, Mary	32 f		ANDERSON, Thomas (M), laborer	38 m	
GALLAHAY, M, laborer	30 m	IR	Louisa (M), chambermaid	35 f	
RILEY, Wm	35 m	VA	36-233		
McGIZZY, J	40 m	IR			
WILSON, John, machinist	30 m	ST	APPICH, David, confectioner 16000/500	61 m	WT
DAILY, John, laborer	26 m	NY	Caroline	27 f	
McDON, Alexander	45 m	ST	Jacob, clerk	23 m	VA
MAY, Alexander, sailor	45 m		Eunice	16 f	
QUISAIL, Chris, silversmith	51 m	GR	Margaret	14 f	
WILLIAMS, Wm	70 m	VA	Anna	6 f	
GERMAN, Michael, laborer	35 m	IR	Caroline	2 f	
COX, Andrew	50 m	IR	Catharine	3/12 f	
BENNETT, Nancy (M)	90 f		WALL, Conrad, journey confectioner	30 m	HD
ALLEN, Jane (M)	45 f		SHUMAN, Franklin	16 m	
BALL, Sarah (M)	88 f		14-78		
BROWN, Wm (B)	109 m				
HATHAWAY, Maria (B)	89 f		APPICH, Gotlieb, confect 20000/1000	58 m	WT
BLACK, Emma (B)	65 f		Catharine	55 f	
THOMAS, Robert (B)	4 m		MITCLIFF, West, railroad construction	25 m	
BENNETE, Barney	7 m	IR	Catharine	20 f	
Catharine	6 f		Catharine	3/12 f	
SIMMS, Louis	27 f		SPICER, James, journey confectioner	35 m	
ELLIS, Ann	22 f		DAVIS, Frank	22 m	GT
HALL, Catharine	40 f		MITZ, Geo, shoemaker	24 m	GR
BLOXAM, Fanny	49 f		17-91		
BENNET, Ann	40 f	IR			
BLOXAM, Levi	45 m		APPICH, Louis, confectioner -/1500	31 m	BD
ADAMS, Mary	50 f		Dorinda	31 f	
WHEELER, Ray (B)	25 f		Kate	5 f	
COLTON, Hanna (B)	30 f		Louis	4 m	
HAWKINS, Eliza (B)	60 f		George	2 m	
GARNET, Laura (B)	30 f		Caroline	69 f	BD
GRIGGS, Frances, laborer	45 m		HESS, Elizabeth	38 f	WT
Michael	7 m		5-34		
ROBINSON, Wm, laborer	65 m	NY			
McCAY, Catharine	84 f	MD	ARCHIBALD, James, laborer	45 m	
HICKS, Mary	18 f		Hannah	40 f	
LUCAS, Ger	8 m		William	10 m	
PAGE, Thomas, laborer	30 m		Fanny	8 f	
JEFFERSON, John	60 m		55-388		
FOX, Mary	43 f	NY			
THOMPSON, Elizabeth	23 f		ARMSTRONG, J T, cooper 5000/-	55 m	VA
FORD, Wm, shoemaker	63 m		Lucy A	45 f	MD
WARD, John, laborer	60 m	IR	Marion	22 f	VA

ALEXANDRIA VIRGINIA 1860 CENSUS

George	19 m	Alice	11 f
Alice	16 f	Albert	5 m
Louisa	16 f	157-1166	
Charlotte	11 f		
Anthony	7 m	ASH, Irael, peddler -/400	40 m PR
58-411		Susan, milliner	37 f
		Michael	15 m MD
ARMSTRONG, Samuel, cooper	50 m VA	Elizabeth	13 f
Lucy	41 f	Frederick	10 f
Carroll	14 m	Julia	9 f
230-1772		124-912	
ARMY, Louis, ale maker -/300	36 m GT	ASHBY, F W, china merchant	41 m VA
Sarah	30 f PA	Margaret J	26 f
Willie	5 m GT	Eugene D	4 m
Chas	3 m	Carroll W	3 m
Eliza	2 f VA	Rebecca	2 f
DENNIS, Mary, domestic	15 f IR	HOOE, Margaret, h house keeper	14 f
125-914		6-44	
ARNELL, Clement L, shoemaker -/400	32 m MD		
Emily	30 f	ASHBY, T W, post master -/2000	47 m VA
Emily	2 f	Elizabeth	30 f
75-529		Edith	4 f
		Janet	2 f
ARNOLD, Jane, -/2000	30 f VA	170-1275	
Henry, apprentice carpenter	19 m		
Julian	14 m	ASHER, Lylla (M), wash & ironing	42 f
Mary	11 f	Jackson (M), white washer	15 m
Ada	7 f	38-250	
53-370			
		ASHFORD, John, house painter	25 m
ARNOLD, John, hatter 15,000/1500	49 m VA	Margaret	24 f
Eliza	42 f	John	4 m
Laura	20 f	Henry	2 m
John, clerk	17 m	Minerva	3/12 f
Arthur, student	21 m	HALLS, Margaret	56 f
Nancy	15 f	80-571	
Georgianna	13 f		
Thos F	11 m		
Ed Taylor	11 m	ASHFORD, John	67 m
Emma	9 f	Chas, house painter	30 m
Betty	7 f	192-1464	
Robert	3 m		
11-55		ASHTON, Jno, shoemaker -/20	37 m
		Emily	25 f
ARNOLD, Wm, tailor	43 m	Emily	10 f
Celcela	31 f	John	6 m
Laura M	20 f	MILLS, Nancy, seamstress	17 f VA
Indiana	18 f	151-1119	
Tradone	16 f		
Viminia	16 f	ASHTON, Lucy (M), wash & iron	35 f
William	11 m	Annabella (B)	19 f
Drucella	8 f	Fenter (M)	18 f
John	3/12 m	Thomas (B), laborer	15 m
ROSE, Drucella	68 f	Ascenius (B), dining room servant	14 m
DUFFEY, Patrick, tailor	22 m	Henry (M)	13 m
172-1290		Victoria (M)	8 f
		Georgia (M)	4 f
ARRINGTON, Cath	42 f	Ruth (M)	1 f
Laura	15 f	Infant (M)	4/12 f
Billy	13 m	86-619	

ALEXANDRIA VIRGINIA 1860 CENSUS

ATKINS, Malinda, 5600/2000	72 f	
Emma	33 f	
Alice	37 f	
Sarah	16 f	
Alice N	15 f	
Geo	10 m VA	
Emma	8 f	
149-1103		
ATKINSON, Isabella 6000/400	48 f MD	
Elenor	35 f	
Williamson, civil engineer	33 m	
Billie, teacher	21 f	
Griffith, appren apothecary	17 m	
Ellen	14 f	
Alfred	12 m	
140-1025		
ATKINSON, Jas W, blacksmith 4300/800	40 m	
Mary	34 f	
James	10 m VA	
Mary	8 f	
Richard	5 m	
Bettie	3 f	
DAY, James, blacksmith	40 m	
TRUMAN, Geo, jr wheelwright	37 m HC	
LI...MCH, John, appren blacksmith	18 m	
REESE, Elizabeth, domestic	41 f	
149-1102		
ATWELL, John, harness maker	26 m VA	
Catharine	29 f	
Isabella	8 f	
Ellen	5 f	
Charles	4 m	
Catharine	1 f	
158-1170		
ATWELL, William, cigar maker -/200	46 m	
Julia	37 f	
Elenor	16 f	
74-523		
ATWELL, Wm E, tailor	38 m VA	
Mary	34 f	
John, tailor	21 m	
William	18 m	
Samuel, printer	17 m	
Sarah F	14 f	
Mary	8 f	
112-832		
AUBINOE, Sommersett, shoemaker -/200	51 m NY	
Charlotte	29 f NJ	
Lonza	31 f VA	
Samuel	18 m	
John	7 m	
Isabella	4 f	
4-25		
AUDISON, Aurelia (B)	27 f	
William (B)	10 m	

Sarah (B)	8 f	
Charles (B)	6 m	
167-1252		
AUSTIN, David, master weaver -/150	40 m IR	
Elizabeth	35 f	
Emma	14 f	
Louisa	12 f	
William	8 m	
Elizabeth	3 f	
45-318		
AUTISELL, Thomas, patent clk -/2000	38 m IR	
Marion	30 f	
Euphasia	16 f	
Elizabeth	13 f	
May	16 f	
Lina	11 f	
Alice	3 f	
Thomas	2 m	
FORSYTH, Monia	55 f	
May	17 f MA	
274-2111		
AVERY, Wesley, collector	56 m	
Mary	43 f	
Wesley	21 m	
Cornelia	19 f	
Mary	17 f	
William	16 m	
Arthur	2 m	
32-207		
AWFORD, Jas A, restaurant	40 m PA	
Mary	35 f MD	
John	12 m	
James	8 m VA	
Parke	5 m	
McMULLIN, Sarah	68 f MD	
63-442		
AXYTOWN (?), Auguston, apprentice	15 m GR	
17-92		
BACKER, Charlotte, 6000/2000	68 f MD	
76-535		
BACON, Ebenezer, canal coll 9000/1000	63 m ME	
Susan	60 f	
ROBINS, Mary	30 f	
John, sailor	33 m ME	
BACON, William, machinist	18 m	
192-1461		
BADEN, Amanda (M), -/600	26 f	
212-1626		
BADGETT, Adama	56 f VA	
Esther	20 f	
PETTY, Mary E	13 f	

ALEXANDRIA VIRGINIA 1860 CENSUS

PRICE, Jas E	1 m		William	2 m
PETTY, Geo	15 m		Lawrence	6/12 f
61-432			242-1881	

BADGETT, John H, butcher 2000/200	57 m		BAGUE, Elizabeth	16 f
Margaret	49 f		Emma	15 f
Ruberta	16 f		Zorra	15 f
Oscar	16 m		219-1691	
Ida	10 f			
WATERS, Helen	27 f		BAILEY, Harvey, farmer 6000/50	30 m
249-1936			Sarah	22 f
			Charles	6 m
			GIBSON, Ellen, domestic	25 f
BAGGETT, Aloysious, baker	50 m		251-1955	
Frances	37 f			
Alexander	15 m		BAILY, Jas	25 m
Mary	11 f		Catharine	20 f
Willie	8 m		Michael	6/12 m VA
GORE, Annie, seamstress	23 f		95-693	
BAGGETT, Ann				
32-202			BAILY, John H, pilot -/30	49 m
			Temperance	49 f
BAGGETT, John C, tailor -/80	44 m		John	13 m
Eliza	39 f		James	12 m
Louise	14 f		ARCHIBALD, Mary	7 f
Wm H	14 m		BUTY, May	5 f NJ
Ann	8 f		198-1510	
Rosalie	6 f			
Ella	5 f		BAINE, M E, -/6000	31 f DC
213-1635			Wm S	6 m
			Geo H	4 m
BAGGETT, John T, farmer 5000/2000	48 m		Marrion	2 f
Virginia	36 f		SPADEU, Marion	50 f EG
Bettie	36 f		Theodore	16 m
197-1500			Ada	10 f
			William, naval store keeper	25 m
			Edgar	23 m
BAGGETT, Samuel, baker 11500/3000	40 m		170-1274	
Elizabeth	67 f			
SMITH, Louise	45 f		BAINES, George, laborer	45 m
William, sailor	55 m		James	16 m
Mary Violett	7 f		Mary	14 f
118-873			Wm	11 m
			262-2030	
BAGGETT, Townson, butcher 10000/1500	49 m			
Catharine	44 f		BAKER, Henry, blacksmith	35 m
James	29 m		Sarah	30 f
Alexander	27 m		William	14 m
Benjamin	22 m		George	12 m
John	16 m		Menerva	10 f
Samuel	11 m		Milton	8 m
Edie	7 m		Mary	5 f
Sarah	26 f		Rosena	2 f
Georgana	24 f		220-1695	
Catharine	13 f			
Eliza	12 f		BAKER, Lucy	45 f
Annie	6 f		Isaac	35 m
COOK, Ann	64 f		273-2105	
156-1160				
			BAKER, Samuel, stm boat capt 1000/300	51 m MA
BAGS, Elias, laborer	24 m IR		Dorcas	51 f
Maria	27 f		189-1451	

ALEXANDRIA VIRGINIA 1860 CENSUS

BAKER, Thos, clerk -/300	26 m EG	BALL, Robert, farmer 10000/600	86 m	
Elizabeth	24 f	Anna	75 f	
Infant	9/12 f VA	Frank	16 m	
82-586		William	15 m	
		Amanda	12 f	
BAKER, William, clk 4000/250	48 m	265-2053		
Julia	40 f			
FITZHUGH, John, farmer	80 m	BALL, Samuel, h carpenter	40 m	
Amily	60 f	Jane	35 f	
195-1480		Henry	16 m	
		Chas	12 m	
BALDWIN, C A, shoe manufactory -/885	33 m	Harriett	10 f	
Maria	27 f	Martha	8 f	
Kate	6 f	George	5 m	
Edith	3 f	Infant	2/12 m	
WEST, Harriet (M), cook	26 f	263-2040		
170-1276				
		BALL, Sarah (B), cook	35 f	
		Fais (B)	4 f	
BALDWIN, George T, iron/steel dealer	25 m	BURLY, Jas (B), laborer	17 m	
Margaret	23 f	WATERS, Daniel (B), tailor	36 m	
Willie	1 m	Adelide (B)	19 f	
112-830		Charlotte (B), domestic	21 f	
		Anthony (B)	5 m	
BALDWIN, Philo, farmer 5000/300	64 m CT	Marjarietta (B)	2 f	
Julia	53 f	COLTONE, William (B), brick maker	21 m	
Frances	17 f	145-1068		
WILSON, Ethan, laborer	50 m			
269-2079		BALL, Susan (B)	30 f	
		Alice (M)	6 f	
BALL, Ann	29 f	Charles (M)	4 m	
George, laborer	37 m	Mary (M)	3/12 f	
187-1419		56-399		
BALL, Ann, 3000/-	50 f	BALLINGER, John, cooper -/873	46 m	
Annie	20 f	Charlotte	45 f MD	
Indiana	18 f	Theophilus	22 m	
BENTON, Virginia (B), domestic	27 f	John T, grocer	19 m	
MORTIMER, Chas, cardwriter	26 m MD	Charlotte	17 f	
44-300		Susannah	15 f	
		Frances	12 f	
BALL, Charles H, govt messenger -/300	22 m IN	Winfield	10 m	
Kate	25 f DC	58-412		
John T, messenger	19 m			
259-2007		BALLINGER, Peyton, shoe merch 15K/16K	46 m VA	
		Jane	44 f MD	
BALL, Horatio, farmer	32 m VA	Clinton P	17 m	
Mary	23 f MD	Thos J	15 m	
Ida	5 f VA	Andrew J	11 m	
Emma	3 f	Anna J	6 f	
Alice	1 f	Julian	1 m	
272-2096		125-918		
BALL, Horatio, 2000/150	75 m	BAMOSS, Margaret, bleuker -/50	63 f NY	
Elizabeth	60 f	Mona	18 f	
Clara	25 f	Charles, appren printer	15 m CT	
Sarah	23 f	174-1303		
Elmira	22 f			
Matilda	20 f	BANE, Patrick, porter	28 m	
Edwin	23 m	Winifried	25 f	
William	17 m	James	2/12 m VA	
263-2039		243-1882		

ALEXANDRIA VIRGINIA 1860 CENSUS

BARKER, W W, lumber merch 10K/10K	36 m		BARROTT, John, laborer	25 m	
Susan	26 f		Catharine	26 f	
Ella	4 f		27-165		
Ada	3 f				
66-465			BARTHOLD, Fred, shoemaker -/25	24 m	MD
			Anna	20 f	DC
BARKINTEN, Ferdinand, mus tch 3K/500	46 m	SX	Anna	8/12 f	
Elizabeth C	40 f	VA	153-1137		
Rheinhart	12 m				
Sarah	10 f		BARTLEMAN, Mrs 20K/1K	85 f	IR
William	8 m		153-1135		
Laura	6 f				
Margrietta	4 f	VA	BARTLEMAN, Samuel, carpenter 1500/100	77 m	PA
Henry	3 m		Susan	67 f	RI
BLACK, Lucy (M), cook	50 f	VA	William, stone cutter	40 m	VA
HENRY, Hugh, teacher	35 m	VA	Ann	30 F	
136-1000			William	13 m	
			Kate	8 f	
BARLEY, William, ice dealer 2K/300	51 m	IR	Mary	4 f	
Bridgete	51 f		WHEELER, Mattie (B), domestic	16 f	
Tarega	18 f		73-510		
John	16 m				
277-2130			BARTLET, Payton C, laborer	45 m	
			Isabella	28 f	
BARNES, Samuel, wood merch 5K/500	67 m	EG	John	7 m	
Hanna	60 f		Fanny	5 f	
196-1492			William	4 m	
			DUNDAS, Diana	47 f	
BARNES, Wm, Bos cotton mill	60 m		164-1222		
Eliza	28 f	MD			
Margaret	15 f		BARTON, Benj, jeweller 13K/25K	50 m	
Joseph	9 m		Elizabeth	34 f	
Theodore	5 m		Mary	14 f	
98-721			Grace	10 f	VA
			Eliza	9 f	
BARNWELL, Charlotte (B), wash & iron	57 f		Fanny	6 f	
Mary J (B)	17 f		AUDISON, Fanny, domestic	20 f	
164-1228			116-861		
BARNWELL, Nan... (B)	20 f		BARTON, Richard C, sumac man	64 m	IR
Robert (B)	1 m		Alice	56 f	VA
247-1918			BEABE, Virginia	10 f	
			BRADFIELD, C H, machinist	33 m	
BARR, Lewis, dry good merch -/2K	28 m	GR	32-204		
Pauline	24 f	HN			
Jophia	2 f	VA	BASSFORD, M, teacher	46 m	MD
Morris	10/12 m		BASSFORD, _	36 f	
BURRIS, Fannie, milliner	26 f	IR	128-938		
HEYMAN, Catharine, domestic	27 f	SX			
CARRIES, Anne, nurse	12 f	VA	BATES, Skinner, RR engineer -/100	40 m	MA
MEYERBURGH, B	70 f	HN	Eliza	34 f	
126-921			George S, machinist	17 m	
			Alice E	4 f	
BARRAGE, Thomas, barber 300/100	48 m	MD	DAVIS, Benjamin, machinist	32 m	
Hannah	48 f		51-361		
John	23 m				
Georgiana	19 f		BATTERMAN, Dennis -/25	28 m	IR
Francis	15 m		Ella	26 f	
Margaret	13 f		162-1203		
Mary	12 f				
Benj	7 m		BAUMGARTNER, Geo, butcher 800/200	30 M	BV
4-26			Sarah	25 f	

ALEXANDRIA VIRGINIA 1860 CENSUS

Georgiana	5 f	Susan	19 f	
Mary	4 f	216-1665		
Virginia	2 f			
Bettie	6/12 f	BEACH, Harrison, laborer -/100	3 m VA	
281-2151		Catharine	29 f	
		George	9 m	
BAXTER, William, pilot -/80	37 m	Elizabeth	10 f	
Mary E, dress maker	30 f	Benjamin	2 m	
Mary W	7 f	JOYEL, Robert, laborer	20 m	
Catharine	6 f	HARRISON, John	22 m	
Mona	5 f	ARRINGTON, Chas	22 m	
Edwin	5/12 m	James	26	
BEACHLAND, Elizabeth, seamstress	16 f	SWAM, Mary	17 f	
83-596		ARRINGTON, Yeaton	65 m	
		88-634		
BAYLESS, George, blacksmith	28 m			
Mary	26 f	BEACH, J C, house carpenter -/50	31 m	
George	4/12 m	Mary	31 f	
247-1925		Adda	8 f	
		Jesse	4 m	
BAYLESS, W H, bricklayer 700/100	36 m MD	Mary	2 f	
Jane M	35 f	228-1752		
Chas R	18 m			
Elizabeth	12 f	BEACH, James, carter	33 m	
143-1052		Jane	25 f	
		William	8 m	
BAYLISS, Daniel, plasterer 900/100	56 m VA	Frank	4 m	
Sarah	44 f MD	Capitola	1 f	
Richard, cabinet maker	25 m VA	45-306		
John D, cabinet maker	24 m			
John D, cabinet maker	24 m	BEACH, Jas C, turner -/40	35 m	
HENDERSON, Wm	27 m MD	Janice	35 f	
Sarah	21 F VA	James	10 m	
HAMILTON, Lydia, domestic	12 f	Elyzia	4 f	
81-577		Roy	1 m	
		226-1740		
BAYNE, James (B), blacksmith	44 m			
Frances (B)	40 f	BEACH, Jas H, laborer	28 m	
Laura (M)	17 f	Margaret	29 f	
243-1889		Thomas	8 m	
		84-600		
BEACH, Alfred, laborer	23 m			
Mary	27 f MD	BEACH, James H, laborer 30/30	32 m	
William	6 m WA	Adaline	31 f	
93-672		Susan	8 f	
		Sarah	5 f	
BEACH, Elijah, cooper -/30	32 m	Frances	3 f	
Susan	26 f	Susan	20 f	
Elizabeth	3 f	Maera, cotton weaver	18 f	
Susan	62 f	HAMRON, Margaret, domestic	16 f	
ARRINGTON, Yeaton, cottom mill	26 m	75-530		
Ellen	20 f			
McELLEGAN, Ominbus driver	25 m	BEACH, Jno	27 m DC	
Margaret	27 f	Rose	29 f MD	
William	2 m	Charles	7 m	
MADISON, A, domestic	18 f	Mary	3 f	
CAWOOD, Robt, carpenter	26 m VA	118-869		
88-635				
		BEACH, John	29 m DC	
BEACH, Ellen, seamstress	48 f	Anna	26 f	
Silas, laborer	22 m	118-870		

ALEXANDRIA VIRGINIA 1860 CENSUS

BEACH, Mary	58 f VA	BECKLEY, William (B), laborer	59 m	
Geo, newsboy	19 m	Nancy	48 f	
Richard	16 m	Sarah (M), domestic	17 f	
Susanna	16 f	John (M) coulter	23 m	
Lucinda	12 f	160-1189		
93-671				
		BEDINGER, Catherine 2500/6K	58 f	
BEACH, Noah, laborer	47 m	BERRY, Mildred	52 f	
Lucinda	37 f	Jane	40 f VA	
Susan	11 f	170-1278		
Ann	10 f			
Hester	7 f	BELL, Ann	29 f	
Laura	6 f	BELL, George, laborer	37 m	
George	3 m	189-1419		
Sylvestr	5/12 m			
109-807		BELL, W Geo, wharf builder -/40	36 m SC	
		Mary	20 f IR	
		230-1774		
BEACH, S C, house carpenter -/50	31 m VA			
May	31 f	BELL, R M, shoemaker -/100	35 m	
Adda	8 f	Sarah	32 f	
John	4 m	Messonoe M	12 f	
May	2 f	John M	10 m	
228-1752		Frances M	5 m	
		Marry E	2 f	
BEACH, S Ferguson, lawyer -/3K	32 m CT	Mary	60 f	
Elizabeth	32 f	ALLEN, Jane, cottonweaver	20 f	
Constance Corgan	3 f	CONWAY, James, shoemaker	25 m	
Infant	3/12 f	HOBSON, Ambler, shoemaker	60 m NY	
MORGAN, Elizabeth	65 f	SMITH, William, shoemaker	25 m MD	
WEBSTER, Caroline (B)	18 f	47-321		
65-457				
		BELL, Robert, bookseller 1300/7500	51 m EG	
BEACH, Samuel, ice dealer 2K/260	69 m	Mary	48 f	
Saml, teacher	24 m	Mary E	21 f	
John	23 m	Robt	21 m	
Mary	22 f	Fanny S	18 f	
Sarah	9 f	Hanson	15 m	
Sanford	8 m	Lewis M	12 m	
COOK, Angela, spinner	24 f	Laura R	10 f	
KIESLING, Noah, cartier	19 m	Edmund O	8 m	
COOK, Enoch	22 m	Charles W	5 m	
86-615		Frank	2 m	
		BELL, Elizabeth	90 f EG	
BEACHAM, Nathaniel	41 m VA	7-45		
Mary	27 f			
Joseph	11 m	BENEDUM, Jas H, tanner -/175	41 m	
213-1643		Sarah	35 f	
		John	18 m	
		James	16 m	
BEALE, Washington F, moulder -/100	26 m	Harriett	16 m	
Margaret	76 f	William	10 m	
244-1896		133-969		
BEARD, Wm	31 m	BENNETT, Jno	26 m IR	
Janie	27 f	Mary	21 f	
233-1802		Alice	6/12 f MD	
		SHIRLEY, Franklin	22 m IR	
BECKLEY, Roger D (M), brickmaker -/60	30 m	96-703		
Ann (M)	24 f			
STRAP, Jackylin (B)	22 M	BENTER, Geo, butcher -/50	43 m VA	
135-988		Mary	43 f VA	

ALEXANDRIA VIRGINIA 1860 CENSUS

Sarah	13 f		John, laborer	19 m		
Mary	12 f		James	17 m		
John	8 m		Richard	15 m		
155-1154			Lewis	12 m EG		
			George	10 m		
BERKLEY, Wm R, dry goods merch 10K/3K	46 m VA		Thos	2 m VA		
Emily W	46 f MD		100-743			
Patterson	18 m VA					
William	14 m		BEVERLY, Jane 17K/2K	60 f GT		
Frank	7 m		Elizabeth	29 f VA		
Harold	5 m		ROBINSON, Mary	35 f GT		
COOK, Willia (B), cook	50 f		84-607			
	1					
180-1344			BIGGS, James H, tobacconist 1500/100	43 m		
			Elizabeth	46 f		
BERRY, Benjamin, clerk court -/300	47 m		Henry, tobacconist	19 m		
Mary G	52 f		James	17 m		
James, medical student	22 m		George	12 m		
Aphilia	19 f		45-311			
Susan	17 f					
Benjamin	14 m		BILE, Emily (B), wash & iron	42 f		
WEST, Fannie	52 f		James (B)	m		
19-107			164-1225			
BERRY, C C, fancygoods store -/300	44 m		BILL, Margaret (B), wash & iron	44 f		
Elizabeth	38 f		Rose (B)	20 f		
Douglas, clerk	18 m		Virginia (M)	8 f		
Rachael	16 f		190-1443			
Annie	14 f					
Alice	12 f		BILLIPS, Sarah, house of prostitution	28 f MD		
Ida	10		Thomas	9 m		
Tenipt	8 f		ROLLING, Julia	23 f		
29-186			SMITH, Josephine, prostitute	19 f DC		
			86-617			
BERRY, Elizabeth	52 f VA					
Thomas, ship carpenter	27 m		BINGHAM, Alfred, cotton mill boss 100	37 m MD		
Emma	17 f		Rebecca	32 f		
Margaret	12 f		Robt	10 m		
103-758			Sally	6 f		
			Avery	2 f		
BERRY, Geo (B)	77 m		WILSON, Kate, roven maker	32 f		
Elizabeth (M), wash & iron	59 f		BROWN, Lizzie, warper	18 f		
George (M), laborer	37 m		BUTLER, Henrietta, weaver	18 f		
William (M), cooper	36 m		BAYLESS, James, cotton bill boss	28 m		
Elizabeth (M), wash & iron	20 f		BINGHAM, David	20 m		
145-1071			73-511			
BERRY, Richard, wood sawyer -/30	60 m		BIRCH, Caleb -/100	28 m		
Betsey (B)	60 f		Sarah	48 f		
Mary (B)	17 f		Martha	22 f		
74-520			Isabella	14 f		
			Manly	10 f		
BEVENS, George, laborer	67 m		Webb, laborer	20 m		
Kitty	65 f		Irving	1 f		
George	22 m		254-1976			
Eddie	11 m					
Ella	7 f		BIRCH, John, farmer	46 m VA		
152-1126			Susan	47 f		
			John	21 m		
BEVERELL, Geo, farmer -/250	50 m EG		William	17 m		
Sarah	46 f		Susan	15 f		
Mary, domestic	22 f		Bertha	13 f		

ALEXANDRIA VIRGINIA 1860 CENSUS

Mary		11 f	BLACKLOCK, D R, merch 10K/8K	31 m VA	
Martha		9 f	Geo W	22 m	
THOMPSON, Bob, laborer		18 m	Kassy	5/12 f	
Millard		7 m	Ann	9 f	
265-2051			CASSEY, Charity	15 f	
			BLACKLOCK, Mary	65 f	
BIRCH, John T, farmer		45 m	1-3		
Susan		45 f			
John		21 m	BLACKLOCK, Fred S, merch 15K/17K	33 m	
Peter		18 m	Julia	26 f	
Alethia		16 f	Infant	1/12 f	
Ruberta		14 f	George, clerk	31 m	
Paulina		12 f	RAMSEY, Jane	58 f	
Sarah		10 f PA	WALLS, Ellen (M), domestic	25 f	
Millard		7 m	20-115		
270-2090					
			BLACKSTON, Susan (B), wash & iron	28 f	
BIRCH, Randolph, gardner -/100		35 m	Ada (B)	9 f	
Mary		31 f	Ann (B)	5 f	
Sarah		4 f	James (B)	5 m VA	
Annie		2/12 f	165-1239		
Wm		8 m			
GLOVER, Thos, laborer		40 m	BLADEN, Charles, carter 1K/250	40 m VA	
BIRCH, John		30 m	Ann	38 f MD	
262-2032			Laura	14 f VA	
			George	13 m	
BIRCH, Samuel, house carpenter		40 m	Florence	8 f	
Jane		31 f	Norman	6 m	
Henry S		13 m	Jennie	3 f	
Chas C		11 m	23-133		
Harriet		7 f			
Martha		5 f	BLADEN, John, carter -125	40 m VA	
George		3 m	Alunia	31 f	
Infant		3/12 m	Ellen	7 f	
262-2035			30-193		
			BLAKE, Mary, house of prostitution	32 f	
BIRCH, Wm, farmer		77 m	John E	5/12 m	
257-1992			HUTCHIS, Catharine, prostitute	33 f	
			NEILSON, Emma	22 f	
BIRKLEY, Edgar (M), brickmaker 650/50		25 m	102-755		
Martha (M)		21 f			
Amanda (M)		2/12 f	BLOUNT, Wm C, Meth minister -/2K	20 m	
243-1884			Julia A	27 f	
			William C	5 m	
BIRMINGHAM, Thomas, laborer		25 m	Mary L	3 f	
60-420			179-1343		
BITTING, C C, Baptist minister -/1K		30 m PA	BLUE, John, house painter -/50	75 m	
Caroline		25 f	Catharine	81 f MD	
William		4 m VA	Alfred	50 m VA	
Chas C		2 m	203-1552		
Infant		8/12 m			
141-1042			BODKINS, Catharine, boarding -/500	39 f	
			Elizabeth	20 f VA	
BLACKBURN, James (B)		27 m VA	Mary C	17 f	
239-1847			Anna	13 f	
			Blanche	11 f	
BLACKBURN, Jas (B), laborer		31 m	Esther	8 f	
Aurelia (B)		22 f	HAMILTON, Mr, insurrance agent	37 m	
Richard (B)		31 m	HAMILTON, Mrs	36 f	
238-1844			Henry	6 m	

ALEXANDRIA VIRGINIA 1860 CENSUS

Chas	4 m	Alexander, sailor	17 m	
Annie	12 f	John	15 m	
Louise	10 f	Larry	12 m	
BENNIX, Mr, machinist	36 m MD	Henry	7 m	
MANKINS, Jno, house painter	24 m	188-1432		
PEYTON, Jas, baggage master	20 m			
141-1043		BOSWELL, Martha -/30	40 f EG	
		181-1372		
BOLES, Hannah	43 f VA			
Mary, weaver	22 f	BOUDERN, Andrian, dyer -/30	38 m FR	
Hannah, spinner	21 f	Harriet	28 f	
John, Bos cotton mill	19 m	Ellen	7 f	
Martha, weaver	17 f	Augustine	4 f	
Louisa	15 f	26-151		
84-608				
		BOURBON, Dennis, ship carpenter -/50	43 m	
BOND, James (B)	76 m	Rachael	36 f	
Cornelia (B)	49 f	Elmira	18 f	
Georgiana (B)	12 f	Oscar, sailor	16 m	
Jimmy (B)	11 m	Dennis	14 m	
Adeline (B)	10 f	215-1656		
George (B)	6 m			
Hannah (B)	17 f	BOUSH, Nathanial, ship chandler 4K/3K	51 m	
200-1526		Jane	43 f	
		Samuel, clerk	19 m	
BONDER, Addison (M), porter	24 m	Fanny	12 f	
Mary (M)	25 f	Effie	9 f	
Maria (M)	30 f	Kate	6 f	
Douglas (M)	2 m	Constance	4 f	
Riverday (M)	2 m	Nathaniel	2 m	
DOUGLAS, Alex (M), ship carpenter	20 m	108-800		
George (M), ship caulker	22 m			
Elizabeth (M)	10 f	BOWEN, J W, physician 15K/16K	49 m VA	
Ellinor (M)	8 m	Elizabeth	43 f	
208-1594		Lucy L	12 f	
		Alfred	10 m	
BONTZ, William, clerk -/150	48 m	LAWS, Laurena, seamstress	21 f	
Ruth A	19 f	255-1986		
Wm H	1 m			
JOHNSTON, Lucinda (B), domestic	18 f	BOWEN, Samuel, steam tug	30 m	
13-67		Agnes	17 f VA	
		BLACK, Sarah (M)	33 f	
BOOTHE, William J, coal agent 3500/1K	44 m	80-1346		
Christina	39 f			
Christina	15 f	BOWERS, Jacob, brickmaking -/50	38 m PA	
Ann	72 f	Eliza	36 f VA	
83-597		BLISH, Henry, bricklayer -/250	33 m	
		37-243		
BOSSART, Michal, confectioner -/260	32 m BD			
Mary	32 f	BOWGER, John S, cooper	39 m	
Catharine	11 f MD	Ann	33 f	
Mary	9 f	Florence	12 f	
George	5 m	Constance	10 f	
ABENSHEIN, Jas	23 m MC	Teressa	8 f	
Christina	21 f VA	Romula	5 m	
HEBNER, Joseph, confectioner	18 m	Silburn	3 f	
119-877		216-1663		
BOSWELL, James, blacksmith	38 m	BOWLING, J W, druggist 3K/10K	29 m MD	
Eliza	39 f	Mary	24 f	
Willie, machinist	19 m VA	Walter	2 m	
Susan	39 f	177-1324		

ALEXANDRIA VIRGINIA 1860 CENSUS

BOYER, George, sail maker	40 m		Infant (B)	4/12 f
Elizabeth	30 f		43-294	
Richard	10 m			
236-1817			BRADSHAW, Hetty (B), huckster	45 f
			HENRY, Wm (M), laborer	16 m
BOYER, Mary J, dress maker -/100	26 f MD		THOMAS, John (B)	16 m
William, cigar shopkeeper -/100	18 m		FRAZIER, Ed (B), laborer	50 m
Mary E, dress maker	20 f		231-1784	
109-813				
			BRADT, Albert, grocer 2K/600	40 m NY
BOYLE, Benjamin F, wheelwright	26 m MD		Susan	34 f
Mary	22 f		Ella	16 f
72-508			George	12 m
			Maria	8 f
BOYNTON, Elijah, RR super	40 m NY		Orlando	6 m
Caroline	32 f VT		80-570	
Clarinda	5 f VA			
Iranins	2 m		BRAGER, Joseph, clothier -/1K	31 m PR
Wells	8/12 m		Isabella	21 f VA
51-365			Sarah	2 f
			Albert	9/12 m
BRADFORD, Jesse D, RR engineer -/50	45 m CT		LEVI, Amanda, domestic	23 f PR
Emily	21 f MD		3-16	
Emily	9/12 f			
NOWLAND, Mary, domestic	22 f VA		BRANAUGH, J C, farmer 7K/7400	39 m
152-1124			May	16 f
			Adaline	12 f
BRADLEY, Bridgett	40 f IR		William	14 m
John	21 m NW		Sally	11 f
Mary	19 f		Tyler	7 m
James	16 m		Emily	6/12 f
Dank	14 m		TAYLOR, Sally	25 f
Andrew	12 m		262-2031	
Sarah	10 f			
Anne	8 f			
Joseph	6 m		BRANDS, John, ship	42 EG
CLARK, Joseph, bricklayer	20 m		Mary	56 f VA
HASIN, Wm, bricklayer	23 m		Willie	14 m VA
Patty, watchman	28 m		Alice	12 f
35-221			WOOD, Ann	50 f
			MILLS, Wm J, printer 600/500	34 m
BRADLEY, C C, cabinet mfg 12K/5K	43 m		218-1683	
Ann E	41 f			
John H	22 m		BRARRINGER, Frances, laborer	31 m
James	12 m		Mary	28 f
Charles	8 m		Patrick	3/12 m
21-116			277-2132	
BRADLEY, Harrison, undertkr 4500/430	68 m MA		BRAWNER, Jas (M), candle maker 800/50	39 m MD
Elizabeth	63 f VA		Louise (B)	36 f
COLE, Mary, domestic	19 f MD		Emily (B)	10 f
Henry H, dry goods clerk	20 m		Harriet (B)	9 f
139-1023			Sarah (B)	7 f
			James (B)	5 m
BRADOCK, Robert (M), carpenter -/100	35 m		Calvert (B)	4 m
Mary (M)	29 f		Annie (B)	1 f
Annie (M)	2 f		236-1820	
DOYAN, Norman (M), plaster	23 m			
38-245				
			BREEN, Joseph, brewer	25 m
BRADSHAW, Chas (B), laborer	25 m		Fannie	17 f
Mary (B)	29 f		38-246	

ALEXANDRIA VIRGINIA 1860 CENSUS

BRENGLE, Henry, confectioner -/300	35 m	Jau..		1 m VA
Emiline	30 f VA	137-1006		
Emily	12 f			
Alice	7 f	BRIEN, John, bricklayer		36 m
Annie	7 f	Catharine		39 f
Ida	2 f	John		8 m
Christian, confectioner -/1K	30 m MD	Stephen		6 m VA
BOOKINE, William, confectioer	19 m	William		3 m
THOMPSON, Sally, domestic	55 f	89-638		
15-79				
		BRILL, Charles, tanner		25 m HN
BRENT, Elizabeth	65 f	Elizabeth		24 f HD
John, blacksmith	30 m	Hannah		3 f VA
George, house painter	28 m	Chas		7/12 m
Andrew J, machinist	22 m	Hannah		60 f HN
Virginia	23 f	26-150		
CLAPDORE, May, steamstress	35 f			
Ada	5 f	BRILL, Lewis, shoemaker -/50		27 m HN
SCOTT, Thomas, house carpenter	30 m	Catharine		25 f HD
May	15 f	Susan		6 f MD
John	12 m	Charles		3 m VA
HALL, William		Lewis		3/12 m
Annie	10 f	MURPHY, Ann, nurse		10 f IR
Mary	11 f	DAVIDSON, Eliza		73 f VA
Frances	16 f	DWYER, Cor H		46 f
234-1808		LEEF, Wm F		25 m MD
		171-1284-85		
BRENT, Geo, lawyer 2K/3600	38 m			
Lucy	31 f	BRISCOE, Richard, sadler		35 m MD
Thomas	8 m	Milla		28 f VA
Lucy	7 f	Zora		4 f
Samuel	5 m	Henry		1 m
Mary	3 f	174-1302		
Guendaline	6/12 m			
Virginia	26 m	BRISNER, John, tailor -/75		45 m
DANIELS, Lucretia, domestic	17 f	Julia		42 f
172-1288		Edgar, turner		22 m
		Cassius, turner		19 m
		Anthony, appren carpenter		17 m
BRENT, John H 1700/7K	62 m	Gertrude		15 f
Lucy	56 f	Peter		13 m
Courtney	19 m	Julia Ann		7 f
Heath	17 m	58-615		
141-1032				
		BROADBECK, William, laborer		56 m
BRETHEAL, John G, cabinet maker	56 m WT	Susannah		38 f
Barbara	60 f	Joseph, laborer		18 m
249-1937		James		9 m
		49-342		
BRIAN, Martha -/2K	60 f			
Eliza	32 f	BROADERS, Jas F, RR agent -/1200		48 m
Sidney, grocer	27 m	Mary		35 f
Dulaney	19 m	Thomas		13 m
Malinda	15 f	Rosalie		5 f
Susan	24 f	Richard		3 m
Ada.ando	2 f	146-1081		
Kate	6/12 f			
MOORE, Roxise	26 f	BROCKETT, Kitty (M), cook		55 f
53-375		180-1371		
BRIEME, Jas	30 m	BROCKETT, Robert		48 m
Ann	26 f	Elizabeth		62 f

ALEXANDRIA VIRGINIA 1860 CENSUS

```
    Franklin, groc clerk         36 m      BROWN, A W, farmer             39 m
    Virginia                     26 f      HAMMOND, John, laborer         47 m
    Caroline                     27 f      277-2128
    Marye                        25 f
    Virginia                     24 f      BROWN, Benj N, Meth minister   50 m
LAWRENCE, Virginia, domestic     17 f         Ellen                       49 f
76-538                                        Maggie                      22 f WA
                                              Fanny                       20 f MD
BRODBECK, May, confectioner -/300  30 f VA    Alphonse                    17 m VA
    Mary                         12 f         Kate                        11 f
    Kate                          9 f      DIXON, Samuel N, Meth minister 26 m
    Alice                         6 f      MITCHELL, Robert (M), domestic 12 m
    Willie                        4 m      196-1496
MOULDER, Christina               20 F DC
SULLIVAN, Edward, baker          19 m VA   BROWN, Emily 600/50            31 f
APPICH, John                     28 m         Eviline                     13 f
121-890                                       Mary                        12 f
                                              Julia                        9 f
                                              Susan                        5 f
BRODERS, George, laborer         25 m MD      Ellen                        2 f
    Eliza                        23 f      231-1781
SNOWDEN, William                 21 m
    Mary                         5/12 f    BROWN, Emma, adopted daughter  16 f
87-630                                     3-18

BRODERS, Joseph, grocer 3000/-   32 m VA   BROWN, Francis (B), wash & iron 49 f
    Alfurna                      29 f      JOHNSTON, Margaret (M)         15 f
    Elizabeth                     2 f      238-1840
61-430
                                           BROWN, G C, comm merch -/1500  37 m
BROOKS, Fred (M), laborer -/30   45 m         Ellen D                     30 f
    Phebe (B)                    28 f MD      Charles                     11 m
    George (M)                    4 m VA      Catherine                    7 f
    Frances (M)                   6 f         James F                      3 m
209-1603                                   104-771

BROOKS, George, plasterer        35 m      BROWN, Jacob, house carpenter -/75  50 m
    Ann                          30 f         Elinor                      42 f
    Mary                         10 f         Lucinida                    19 f
    George                        6 m         Stuart                      10 m
    Emma                          4 f         Ellen                        8 f
    Martha                        1 f         Alice                        6 f
FUGET, Catharine                 97 f      248-1930
68-476
                                           BROWN, John -/100              60 m
BROOKS, George (M), drayman -/20 70 m         May                         30 f
211-1618                                      May                         16 f
                                              Columbus                    11 m
BROOKS, Henry (M), laborer       52 m         Margaret                     8 f
    May (M)                      24 f         Charles                      7 m
    John (B)                      5 m         Alexander                    6 m
217-1671                                      John                         3 m
                                           252-1959

BROOKS, Wm H, machinist -/100    33 m      BROWN, John B, farmer 7K/800   53 m NY
    Mary E                       31 f         Cornelia                    52 f
    Henry                         9 m         Julia                       25 f
    Laura                         6 f         Harriet                     17 f
    William                       1 m         Sarah                       14 f
    Mary                         19 f      LAIN, Abner W, brick mason     28 m
PARSONS, Joseph, blacksmith -/30 25 m         Rosam..ol                   22 f NY
77-546                                     265-2056
```

ALEXANDRIA VIRGINIA 1860 CENSUS

BROWN, Julia W, carpenter -/100	29 m MD	Manadin (B)	4/12 m	
Sarah	26 f	277-2127		
224-1725		BRUIN, Martha, 2K/150	60 f	
		Eliza	32 f	
BROWN, Maria (M), wash & iron -/50	30 f	Sidney, grocer	27 m	
Mary (B)	8 f	Dulaney	19 m	
Alice (B)	6 f	Malinda	15 f	
Mayait? (B)	4 f	Susan	24 f	
13-64		Amanda	2 f	
		Kate	6/12 f	
BROWN, Marline (M), domestic	20 f	MOORE, Roxie	26 f	
Stella (B)	52 f	53-375		
Marcellus (M), laborer	18 m			
Edward (M)	12 m	BRUNER, John, tailor -/75	45 m	
Sarah (M)	16 f	Julia	42 f	
Samuel (M)	21 m	Edgar, tunner	22 m	
Louis (M)	7 m	Cassius, tunner	19 m	
Autophobies (M)	4 m	Anthony, appren carpenter	17 m	
264-2047		Gertrude	15 f	
		Peter	13 m	
BROWN, Robert, grocer -/500	60 m IR	Julia Ann	7 f	
Margaret	55 f	58-413		
Bridgett	15 f			
Catharine	14 f	BRYAN, Ann, shoe bender	50 f	
John	11 m	222-1708		
206-1577				
		BRYAN, Daniel, 7500/1800	71 m	
BROWN, Sanford, restaurant 6K/300	45 m	Mary	65 f	
Rosamah	36 f	LATHROP, J H, naval agent -/500	45 m	
Preston	1 m	Mary	38 f NH	
SMITH, Richard, bar keeper	24 m	Bryan	16 m	
62-436		Barbara	14 f	
		Minnie	3 f	
BROWN, Septimus, farmer	30 m	Florence	2 f	
Amanda	25 f	WILEY, Andrew, lawyer 16K/2000	45 m PA	
Mary	12 f	Mary	34 f VA	
252-1957		Pendleton	m	
		166-1245		
BROWN, Sylvin (B)	63 f			
165-1238		BRYAN, Geo, dry goods merch 12K/10K	36 m	
		Caroline	30 f MD	
BROWN, Thomas, blacksmith	28 m DE	George	9 m VA	
Georgiana	23 f	Edward	7 m	
189-1444		Albert	5 m	
		COATES, Sally (B)	6 f	
BROWN, William, sadler	38 m	TATE, Maj (B)	30 f	
Sarah	27 f	117-863		
Sarah	6 f			
Joseph	8 m	BRYANT, Geo (M), carpenter 600/30	30 m	
Josephene	2 f	Jane (M)	25 f	
155-1146		Joseph (M)	7 m	
		242-1875		
BROWN, William, harness maker	51 m VA			
Ann	50 f	BRYANT, Reuben, sailor	44 m	
Sally	23 f	Elizabeth	38 f	
3-22		John	15 m	
		Elizabeth	9 f	
BROWNING, Monica (M)	35 m	Reuben	5 m	
Sally (M)	31 f	186-1411		
Sally (B)	8 f			
Jane (B)	6 f			

ALEXANDRIA VIRGINIA 1860 CENSUS

BUCHANAN, Robert, master shmkr 800/200 47 m
   Elizabeth 45 f
   Robert, appren carpenter 18 m
   John M 14 m
   Sallie 16 f
   Thomas 12 m
   Eddie 2 m
20-112

BUCKINGHAM, Isaac, tobacnist 15K/1K 61 m MD
   Mary W 59 f EG
6-38

BUCKINGHAM, William, tabacnist 700/1K 26 m VA
   Mary C 23 f
   Thomas 4 m
   Virginia 2 f
HASKEY, Mary A, domestic 21 f DC
6-39

BUCKLEY, John, laborer 40 m
   Catharine 23 f
   Thomas 7 m
CURTINE, Patrick 23 m
MEAGHAN, Ed 22 m
162-1213

BUMBRY, Mariah (M), wash & iron -/30 41 f
   Burrian (M) 12 m
   Ada (M) 10 f
   Richard (M) 7 m
   Infant (M) 6/12 m
NOKES (B), hack driver 25 m
   Mary (M) 20 f
163-1220

BUNST, Barbara 700/100 70 f PA
23-132

BURCH, Wm R, 1500/2500 46 m
   Julia 48 f
   Joseph 20 m
   Margaret 18 f
   Julia 15 f
   Mary E 13 f
   Phebe 12 f
   Emma 8 f
252-1960

BURCHELL, Edward, 10K/50 63 m
SHIRLEY, Chas B, groc emplr 500/150 40 m VA
   Sarah 30 f
   Chas B 11 m
   Anna 9 f
   Edward 7 m
   Noville 5 m
   Minnie 3 f
   Sallie 1 f
FAR, Susan (M), domestic 30 f
125-915

BURKE, Delany, laborer -/20 31 m
   Sally (B) 28 f
   Lydia (B) 7 f
   Julian French (B) 3 m
   John (B) 2 m
207-1584

BURKE, James, laborer 43 m
   Bridgett 41 f
   John 12 m
   Patrick 11 m
   Johana 10 f
   Thomas 9 m
RYAN, James 16 m
55-384

BURKE, Richard, laborer -/40 46 m IR
   Bridgett, domestic 15 f MD
   Mary 44 f IR
   Bridgett, dressmaker 14 f MD
   Agnes 12 f
   Mary 7 f
   James 2 m VA
202-1547

BURLEY, James, grocer 220/500 26 m IR
   Catharine 26 f
   Mollie 1 f VA
BURUS, Biddie, nurse 14 f IR
63-443

BURN, Thomas, farmer 22 m MD
WOODY, John, laborer 40 m VA
   Sally 30 f
276-2121

BURNS, John, laborer 42 m IR
   Mary 40 f
KING, Patrick 28 m
   Annie 21 f
   James 2 m VA
96-696

BURNS, Thomas, grocer 9K/2K 49 m IR
   Elizabeth 50 f
   Isabella 22 f
116-839

BURRELL, John, barber -/25 23 m VA
IKE, Albert, bar keeper 30 m HN
LOCKRELL, J, grocers clerk -/1K 40 m VA
115-852

BURROUGHS, Henson -/100 35 m
   Sarah 25 f
   John 12 m
   Sarah 8 f
260-2018

BUSH, Samuel, farmer 1K/150 46 m
   Richard 50 f
   Margaret 22 f

ALEXANDRIA VIRGINIA 1860 CENSUS

```
    Jane                              19 f    CAIN, Owen                            30 m
    Chas                              16 m        Mary                              26 f
    Caleb H                           21 m        Michael                            9 m
    Richard                            9 m        Ellen                              6 f
260-2017                                           Thomas                             4 m
                                              150-1110
BUSHBY, Wm, miller 1K/50              38 m
    Lucinda                           23 f    CALLIGHAN, Patrick, laborer -/30      28 m IR
    William                            7 m        Catharine                         28 f
    Ella                               5 f        John                               5 m VA
    Charles                            3 m        Mary                               4 f
176-1319                                           Timothy                            2 m
                                                   Ellen                             30 f
BUTLER, Ana, domestic                 55 f    190-1448
249-1938
                                              CALLIN, Thomas, laborer               35 m
BUTLER, Flora (B), wash & iron        55 f        Mary                              33 f
WATSON, James (B), porter             26 m        Daniel                             7 m
BUTLER, Alonzo (B), blacksmith        20 m        Mary                               5 f
WATSON, Sarah (B)                     21 f    56-396
    Matilda (B)                        6 f
    James (B)                          1 m    CALMUS, Joseph, cabinet maker         46 m BV
43-289                                             Phillipena                        48 f
                                                   Fannie                           14 f VA
BUTLER, James A, sailor               40 m VA     Phillipena                        13 f
    Elizabeth                         36 f    62-439
    Elizabeth                          9 f
LOVELACE, Jane                        14 f    CAMPBELL, Betsy (B)                   41 f
183-1399                                           Martha (B)                        22 f
                                                   Frances (M)                     4/12 f
BUTLER, Robert (B), laborer 100/30    43 m    153-1134
    Elizabeth (B)                     38 f
    Clarence (B)                      18 f    CAMPBELL, David, shoemaker 500/40     40 m
    Henry (B)                         75 m        Sarah                             36 f
    Susannah (B)                      14 m        William                           16 m
240-1857                                           Mary                              13 f
                                                   Sarah                             11 f
BUTLER, Thos, pilot 600/50            50 m        James                              8 f
    Mary                              60 f        Julia                              7 f
    Thos, appren plasterer            17 m    241-1867
93-677
                                              CAMPBELL, John W, custom house 1K/150 44 m
                                                   Alanda                           44 f
BUTLER, W, conductor RR -/50          28 m        Thomas                            16 m
    Sally                             21 f        John, appren ?                    14 m
    Susan                             13 f        Landon                             9 m
152-1121                                           Caroline                          19 f
                                                   Edgar                             5 m
BUTTS, N A, house painter 600/1200    34 m VA     Ida                                3 f
    Catharine                         75 f        Mary                               1 f
    Harriet                           40 f    234-1807
    Mary                              36 f
    Edward                            13 m    CAMPBELL, Mary                        57 f
93-673                                        209-1602

BYGESLY, Nimrod, conductor RR -/10K   36 m    CAMPBELL, Milly (M), wash & iron      62 f
    Adaline                           26 f        Becky (B), domestic               17 f
    Robert                             1 m    214-1650
144-1057
CAHOE, Elith, seamstress              26 f VA CAMPBELL, Wm R, house carpenter       47 m
    James                              3 m PA     Julia                             42 f
56-398                                             Henry, appren printer            17 m
```

ALEXANDRIA VIRGINIA 1860 CENSUS

```
    George                           9 m      CARROLL, Owen, carter 500/25     40 m IR
246-1911                                         Bridgett                       40 f
                                                 Margaret                        6 m
CARLIN, James F, hardware mc 10K/1200 40 m VA    Mary                            5 f
    Martha J                        31 f        Elizabeth                        1 f
    Edm B                           13 m      McNENERY, Owen, laborer          35 m IR
    Geo B                           11 f      80-567
    Mary E                           8 f
    Mason W                          2 m      CARROLL, Rosetta (B)             46 f
WHEAT, H K                          42 f        Jane (B)                       16 f
HUNT, Albert L, clerk               21 m MD     George (B)                     14 m
MILLER, Edward S                    18 m DE     May (B), domestic              22 f
6-43                                            May (B)                         3 f
                                                Precilla (B), domestic         20 f
CARLIN, Wesley, farmer 8K/2K        70 m    227-1749
    Catharine                       76 f
    Mary                            40 f      CARROLL, Thomas                  30 m
    Clinton, farmer                 18 m        Margaret                       28 f
    Burnidete                       16 m        Rosana                          7 f
267-2067                                        John                            5 m
                                                Katy                            3 f
CARLIN, Wm H, conductor RR -/400    30 m        Melly                         3/12 f
    Francis E                       30 m    54-379
    Jas                              6 m
    Fanny                            3 f
175-1310                                      CARROLL, Wm, sailor              24 m
                                                Mary                           23 f
                                                Louise                       9/12 f
CARLIN, Wm H, farmer 20K/-          36 m VA 221-1702
    Ann
    Andrew                          27 m      CARSON, Andrew, house carpenter -/75  31 m VA
    Vittie                          63 f        Mary                           23 f OH
    Aurelia                         50 f        John                            6 m
    Albert ..., laborer             18 m        James                           5 m
ROBERTS, Washington (M)             18 m    219-1687
268-2070
                                              CARSON, Daniel (B), wood sawyer  60 m
CARMICHAEL, Daniel (B)              31 m        Nancy (B)                      40 f
    Racheal (B)                     30 f    165-1234
    Mary (B)                         7 f
198-1514                                      CARSON, George, fisherman        47 m
                                                Angeline                       27 f
CARMICHAEL, William (M), drayman    75 m      WINE, Ellen, domestic            19 f
    Mary (B)                        65 f      CARSON, George                   17 m
26-158                                          Edwin                          13 m
                                                Selome                         11 f
CARNE, R L, clerk hardware          61 m      ELKINS, Laura, domestic          14 f
    Cecilia                         56 f    228-1758
    Richard L, teacher              33 m
    William, hardware               37 m      CARSON, Joseph, steam boat capt -/200  54 m NJ
    Mary L                          24 f        Pamelia                        52 f MA
    Susan                           13 f        Edwin, apothecary              26 m VA
112-831                                     67-472


CARR, Edmund, laborer -/30          39 m      CARTER, Ann                      85 f
    Ann                             28 f        James, baker                   45 m VA
    Ann                             11 f    27-167
    Amanda                           6 f
    Mary J                           3 f      CARTER, George (B), tailor -/100  30 m
WATERS, Phebe                       54 f        Jane (B)                       40 f
39-257                                      258-2001
```

ALEXANDRIA VIRGINIA 1860 CENSUS

CARTER, Edward (B), blacksmith	27 m	
Margaret (B)	22 f	
Billy (B)	5 m	
Helen (B)	3 f	
Margaret (B)	2 f	
274-2112		
CARTER, Hanna (B), wash & iron -/200	40 f	
William (B)	10 m	
Sarah F (B)	18 f	
Horace (B)	8 m	
Harriet (B)	20 f	
Mon.. (B)	1 f	
258-2002		
CASSENE, Francis, farmer	29 m	
Rachael	29 f	
Jane	9 f	
Hanna	2 f	
Fred, laborer	19 m	
John	31 m	
265-2052		
CASSENE, Samuel	60 m	
Maria	50 f	
Eliza	22 f	
264-2049		
CASTLEMAN, C M, sheriff 8K/5K	37 m	
Evaline	26 f	
Chas W	5 m	
Eva	3 f	
Elizzie	2 f	
251-1949		
CATHCARL, Thomas, gov clerk	37 m	
Sarah	28 f	
Arthur	3 m	
Emily	1 f	
INS..., May, domestic	25 f	
NUTCH, John, laborer	20 m	
William	19 m	
267-2068		
CATON, Patrick, laborer	37 m IR	
Sarah	19 f NJ	
Caroline	1 f VA	
CATON, Patrick, laborer	50 m IR	
Margary	48 f	
Ellen, shirt maker	21 f	
Mary	19 f	
Margary	17 f	
Katy	16 f	
148-1096		
CATON, Samuel F, negro trades	30 m	
Eliza A	23 f	
Jarres	9 m	
Infant	2/12 m	
BRETT, Sarah	53 f	
30-191		

CAVERY, Patrick, laborer	43 m IR	
Susan	46 f VA	
Jane, matress maker	22 f	
Wyatt	13 m	
Mary	12 f	
Lucretia	8 f VA	
Susan	7 f	
WEBB, Mary, seamstress	36 f	
98-726		
CAZENOVE, Wm G, comm merch 25K/5K	40 m	
Mary	40 f VA	
Anna	6 f	
Constance	5 f	
Charles	12 m	
Fanny	21 f	
Charlotte	18 f	
STEDCROPH, Sarah, housekeeper	29 f EG	
197-1508		
CEASE, Saml, dairyman	30 m NY	
Margaret	28 f	
Henry	8 m	
Henry	7 m	
Mollie	5 f	
Frances	6/12 f	
George, laborer	25 m	
Deancha	20 f	
270-2084		
CHAMPION, Wm A, house carpenter -/20	28 m PA	
Elizabeth	27 f MD	
241-1872		
CHANCEY, James W, lime burner 1300/75	26 m	
Virginia	25 f	
William	2 m	
Thomas, machinist	19 m	
HAMILTON, Isabella, domestic	12 f	
228-1760		
CHAPMAN, George (M), waiter 1550/50	60 m	
Helen (B)	55 f	
DOZMAN, Geo (M)	25 m	
Helen (M)	24 f	
CHAPMAN, Chas (M)	18 m	
CHINN, Emma (B)	11 f	
163-1219		
CARLTON, Jane, seamstress	52 f	
63-448		
CHARLETON, Stephen, ship carptr -/50	48 m	
Jane	43 f	
John	21 m	
Henry	16 m	
Joseph	8 f	
Annie	5 f	
69-483		
CHASE, John, gov clerk -/1K	56 m HN	
Eliza	50 f	

ALEXANDRIA VIRGINIA 1860 CENSUS

Ann	37 f GT	CHESHIRE, Mary	33 f	
Sarah	35 f MD	Henrietta	11 f	
John E, dentist 6K/2K	33 m DC	Mary	9 f	
17-97		Ann	5 f	
		George	3/12 m	
CHASE, Rachel (B), wash & iron -/75	40 f	149-1100		
Henry (M), oyster shop	40 m MD			
Adalaide (B)	19 f	CHESHIRE, Russell, tavern keeper -/50	54 m	
Evaline (M)	16 f	Elizabeth	49 f	
Maria (M)	12 f	Susan	15 f	
Ida (M)	3 f	Rosena	10 f	
21-120		Adaline	8 f	
		Sophia	5 f	
CHASE, Saml (B)	27 m	COGAN, Richard, pilot	32 m GR	
Ann (B)	21 f	Margaret	28 f VA	
Harriet (B)	5 f	Mary	6 f MD	
Charles (B)	3 m	William	4 m	
Rachael (B)	3/12 f	181-1376		
147-1085				
		CHICHESTER, Patsy, weaver	40 f	
CHASE, Sarah (B), wash & iron	45 f VA	TAYLOR, George W, butcher	26 m	
Dinah (B)	8 f	Eliza	27 f	
Wm (B)	5 m	John	4 m	
John (B)	6 m	William	18 m	
Henry (B), laborer	19 m	Sarah	15 f	
202-1543		Josephene	13 f	
		George	14 m	
CHATHAM, Jas, livery keeper 7500/3500	46 m	154-1143		
CHATHAM, Henry, 60K/5K	70 m MD			
William 3K/1700	29 m VA	CHILTON, Harriet (M), wash & iron	35 f	
13-65		William Hohms (M), tailor	17 m	
		Sally (B)	15 f	
		James (B)	12 m	
CHAUNCE, James, laborer	27 m	Edward (B)	3 m	
Ellen	22 f	George (B)	3/12 m	
Richard	2/12 m	54-380		
190-1450				
		CHISMOND, Thos, carpenter	50 m	
		Elizabeth	37 f	
CHAUNCEY, John F, florist -/200	31 m	Mary	12 f	
Mary	29 f	Annie	4 f	
James	8 m	Elizabeth	1 f	
Chas	3 m	138-1009		
281-2052				
		CHURCH, John, sailor -/100	59 m	
CHESHIRE, E, pilot	27 m	Mary A	59 f	
Mary	21 f	John Suit, turner	25 m DC	
Infant	7/12 f	Sarah E	24 f	
184-1401		2-12		
CHESHIRE, James, laborer	49 m	CHURCH, Peter, -/100	29 M HD	
Margaret	48 f	Catharine	31 f PR	
Henry, house painter	26 m	Mary	2 f VA	
Robert, shoemaker	23 m	260-2019		
Andrew, laborer	19 m			
Marshall, laborer	17 m	CHURCH, Wm, wheelwright 1200/100	47 m	
Elizabeth	17 f	Ellenora	47 f PA	
160-1190		William	16 m VA	
		Ariellen	10 f	
CHESHIRE, John R, shoemaker	23 m	Franklin	7 m	
Annie	20 f	158-1175		
69-484				

ALEXANDRIA VIRGINIA 1860 CENSUS

CIUER, Sarah (M), seamstress	25 f		CLEGGETT, H P, bank clerk -/200	50 m MD		
Elizabeth (M)	4 f		Elizabeth	30 f MA		
51-353			Charles	15 m DC		
			Ruth	12 f VA		
CLAPDORE, Henry, ship carpenter	28 m		Kate	10 f DC		
Ann	20 f		Edith	7 f VA		
John	3 m		Elizabeth	2 f		
4-453			FULLER, Ruth	63 f MA		
			BROOKS, Sarah (M)	34 f VA		
CLAPTONE, Jno M	50 m		180-1345			
Elizabeth	47 f					
Mary	21 f		CLEGGETT, Jas (M), plasterer 300/60	24 m		
Sarah J	14 f		Mary E (B)	25 f		
Isabella	11 f		237-1834			
James	5 f					
123-899			CLEMENTS, Martha	29 f MD		
			Agnes	12 f		
CLARKE, Ed	44 m EG		Henry Clay	10 m		
Sarah	42 f		161-1196			
Edward, lock keeper	21 m					
Alice	18 f		CLIFFORD, Geo W, shoemaker	47 m VA		
101-746			Mary	45 f		
			Mary	18 f		
CLARKE, Jas T, gov clerk 4K/600	36 m DC		Irving	15 m		
Cornelia	29 f		Willie	10 m		
Florence	10		ROADMAN, Christian, shoemaker	22 m		
William	8 m		125-917			
Ann	5 f					
Francis	2 f		CLIFFORD, Jas, laborer	26 m IR		
267-2069			Sarah	27 f		
			98-719			
CLARKE, John C, clerk -/3K	42 m EG					
Adaline	36 f VA					
Henry C	7 m		CLIFFORD, Peter S, laborer	23 m		
Mary	5 f		Mary	22 f		
52-362			98-720			
			CLIPSTEIN, Wm B, physician 25K/3000	43 m		
CLARKE, John T, roper -/4K	37 m EG		May	35 f		
Mary	27 f		Rebecca	8 f		
Isaac	13 m		George	6 m		
SHINN, Robert, sailor 1800/1K	53 m EG		CLARK, Esther	17 f		
Elizabeth	45 f VA		Frances	15 f		
130-947			May	16 f		
			Charles	12 m		
CLARKE, Mary 400/50	31 f VA		CHISMOND, Cornelia	15 f		
Elizabeth	14 f		TAYLOR, Chas M, -/7500	45 m		
Alice	9 f		250-1943			
158-1169						
			CLK, Alethia	55 f		
CLARKSON, Chas, shoemaker	54 m MD		Emma, seamstress	25 f MD		
Catharine	54 f VA		FEGUSON, Henry, butcher	31 m VA		
Virginia, tailer	29 f		Catharine	27 f		
Edward, tuner	22 m		Alice	9 f		
Elizabeth	15 f		John	6 m		
193-1470			Ella	3 f		
			154-1144			
CLAUGHTON, Peter, collector	57 m					
Hannah	60 f		CLODWELL, A W, agent	19 m VA		
Elizabeth	28 f		COLEMAN, Ellen (M)	30 f		
Louisa	18 f MD		John (M)	4 m		
24-141			159-1180			

ALEXANDRIA VIRGINIA 1860 CENSUS

CLOUGHTIN, H O, lawyer -/1K	32 m VA		John	3 m	
Jane	26 f		William	2 m	
Randolph	7 m		5-35		
Blanche	5 f				
HEINDAY, Margaret, domestic	14 f IR		COGSWELL, John S, RR agent -/75	27 m	
3-21			Delia	23 f	
			Annie	3 f	
CLOSE, James T, insur agent 7K/900	32 m NY		Infant	8/12 f	
Eliza	28 f CT		203-1558		
Anne	8 f VA				
Ascan	6 m		COHAGAN, John	86 m VA	
Mary	4 f		Elizabeth	64 f MD	
Rosabel	1 f		Mary	60 f	
BLACK, Susan (M), domestic	30 f		163-1214		
142-1044					
			COHEN, Joshua, milliner 300/25	56 f	
			162-1206		
CLUERING, Henry, glue maker -/230	46 m PA				
Jane	46 f NJ		COLE, Jane, seamstress	50 f	
Elizabeth	20 f		Ann	26 f	
Sarah	18 f		13-69		
Benjamin, glue maker	17 m				
Henry	13 m PA		COLE, Jas, jailor	40 m	
Rebecca	9 f		Mary	35 f	
152-1123			Martha	18 f	
			William	13 m	
COAKLY, Catharine 1500/2500	57 f		John	12 m	
Chas R, baggage master	28 m		Edgar	8 m	
CRUPPER, Ellen	31 f		Louis	6 m	
COAKLY, Fanny	20 f		Bella	4 f	
149-1101			Charles	2 m	
			85-613		
COALMAN, Samuel G, shoemaker -/50	39 m MD				
Ruth	39 f		COLE, Jas, plasterer -/50	22 m	
Alice	12 f VA		Malissa	20 f	
Kenny	10 m		79-563		
Saml	8 m				
Charles	6 m		COLE, Jesse (B), laborer	41 m	
George	3 m		Charlotte (M)	30 f	
83-598			Arthur (B)	10 m	
			Edward (B)	8 m	
COBB, Mary, teacher	34 f		229-1766		
Ann	17 f				
Allen	12 m		COLE, Laura (M), domestic	11 f	
Mary	8 f		213-1638		
160-1188					
			COLE, Mary (M), pie baker	35 f	
COBB, Michael, RR engineer -/300	35 f IR		Mary (M)	9 f	
Bridget	25 f		Emma (M)	5 f	
Annie	3 f VA		Henry (M)	3 m	
Lawrence	9/12 m		BERRY, Rebecca (B)	29 f	
CORBEY, Lawrence	15 m IR		Benjamin (M)	3 m	
204-1560			Anna (B)	1/12 f	
			161-1193		
COGAN, John	64 m IR		COLE, Phebe, domestic	50 f NY	
Eliza	57 f		255-1985		
212-1627					
			COLE, Thomas (M), plasterer	62 m	
COGAN, William, gas fitter 4K/500	29 m EG		Jane (M)	51 f	
Virginia	23 f		Elias (M), plasterer	15 m	
Virginia	6 f		38-247		

ALEXANDRIA VIRGINIA 1860 CENSUS

```
COLEMAN, Jas P, wood meusurer 2K/312   40 m VA    Mary T                        5/12 f
    Caroline                           45 f       Robert, shoemaker             21 m
    Joseph, clerk                      26 m       Thomas, barber                17 m
    Julia                              23 f       Adalaide                      13 f
    James, house carpenter             22 m    51-366
    Saml, moulder                      21 m
    Laura                              15 f    COLMIN, Francis, laborer         40 m
    Katie                              13 f       Ellen                         26 f
    Ethelbert                          11 m       Timothy                        4 m
214-1645                                        71-497

COLLANS, Charles H, moulder 1600/150   34 m MA   COLMIS, Joseph, cabinet maker   46 m BV
    Catharine                          34 f       Phillepena                    48 f
    Ada                                10 f       Fannie                        14 f VA
    Emily                              56 f       Phillipana                    13 f
197-1502                                        62-439

COLLEHORN, Ellen                       70 f    COLTON, Joseph, shoemaker        38 m MD
    Mary                               31 f       Harriet                       35 f VA
    Margaret                            2 f       William                       14 m
    Garret                            9/12 m      Mary                           9 f
183-1395                                          Sarah                          7 f
                                                  Josephine                      1 f
COLLINS, Ann (M)                       56 f    KING, Sally (B), domestic        20 f
    Richard, (M), laborer              32 m    59-415
    Ann E (M), seamstress              30 f
    Armistead (M), blacksmith          23 m    COMPTON, Silas                   37 m
    Margaret (M)                       18 f       Sarah                         40 f
    Victoria (M)                       16 f       Mary                          11 f
30-261                                            Laura                          8 f
                                                150-1108

COLLINS, Charles H, moulder 1600/150   34 m MA
    Catharine                          34 f VA  CONDEN, Joseph, laborer         35 m IR
    Ada                                10 f       Mary                          35 f
    Emily                              56 f    87-627
197-1502
                                                CONGER, Alice, seamstress       43 f
COLLINS, Elijah, RR engineer -/150     39 m MD    Luther, laborer               22 m
    Martha                             38 f       Chas, cotton spinner          15 m
    Reuben, appren machinist           17 m MD    Louisa                        12 f
    Joseph                             14 m    36-228
    Ewinia                             11 f
    Clara J                             7 f MD CONGHMAN, Jere, laborer          27 m
    Albert                              2 m       Catharine                     27 f
133-976                                           John                           1 m VA
                                                56-392
COLLINS, James (M), baker              24 m
    Julia (B)                          21 f    CONLIN, John, laborer            26 m
    Eliza (M)                           2 f       Catharine                     25 f
    Carrol (M)                        7/12 f      John                           5 m VA
GRIS, Louis (B)                         7 m       Bridgett                       2 f
26-157                                          27-403

COLLINS, Samuel C, gardner 4500/250    40 m NY  CONNIFF, John, laborer          40 m
    Rachael                            35 f       Catharine                     35 f
    Virginia                           12 f VA    Mike                           3 m VA
POSEY, Martha, domestic                16 f    55-386
FRAZIER, Wm, house carpenter           36 m ST
280-2138                                        CONWAY, Johanna (B), wash & iron 55 f
                                                WILLIAMS, Emily (B), semstrs    24 f
COLLINSWORTH, Wm, shoemaker 1K/50      35 m    WILLIAMS, Jas (B), wood sawyer   25 m
    Mary F                             22 f       Eliza (B)                      2 f
```

ALEXANDRIA VIRGINIA 1860 CENSUS

Sarah (M)	23 f	COOKSON, J C, distiller 5K/-	37 m MD	
136-994		Emily	24 f	
		Anna Mary	3 f	
CONWAY, Michael	28 m IR	SEYMOR, Lucinda (B)	10 f	
Rose	25 f	Charlotte (B)	41 f	
John	4 m VA	159-1181		
James	1 m			
138-1016		COOPER, George, clerk -/150	36 m DC	
		Angie	22 f MD	
CONWAY, Terrence	27 m	George	2 m	
Patrick	65 m	13-72		
Bridgett	65 f			
Ann	25 f	CORBETT, S B	41 m PA	
96-704		Jane	39 f	
		Emma	21 f	
COOK, Elemul, huckster -/50	30 m MD	Char	18 m	
Annie	29 f VA	George	12 m	
Emma	11 f	Bertha	10 f	
Annie	8 f	Frederick	5 m	
Mary	6 f	H Clay	2 m	
Amanda	f	KLINE, Geo, laborer	25 m	
OGDEN, Sarah	60 f	269-2082		
OGDEN, Elijah, house painter	26 m			
64-455		CORNWELL, Harrison, laborer -/30	46 m	
		Ann	29 f	
COOK, Henry, druggist 6K	54 m EG	Samuel, house carpenter	22 m	
Hortensia	60 f VA	Edward, laborer	21 m	
Mary	12 f	247-1922		
Kensy	10 m			
Charlotte	8 f	CORSE, John D, banker 20K/3000	39 m VA	
Llewellen	5 m	Lucy	28 f	
Douglas	2 m	Mary	4 f	
QUAID, Elizabeth, domestic	25 f	Montgomery, banker	42 m	
12-56		12-59		
		COSTIGAN, Edward -/20	30 m	
COOK, John T, shoemaker 650/50	35 m MD	Catharine	29 f	
Mary, house of prostitution	36 f	Catharine	9 f NJ	
John	20 m	Mary	7 f VA	
ROBINS, Elizabeth, prostitute	25 f	Laurence	4 m	
MILLS, Frances, prostitute	19 f	Annie	7/12 f WA	
HALL, Rachael, prostitute	21 f	ROACH, James	28 m IR	
James	11/12 m	Johanna	26 f	
229-1765		97-708		
COOK, Jos F, huckster -/100	26 m	COWLING, John, blacksmith	33 m EG	
Amelia	21 f	Sarah	31 f	
Theodore	6 m	Alice	5 f	
Francis	3 m	12-63		
TURLEY, Sarah	55 f			
2-9		COWOOD, Elizabeth	32 f NC	
		Mary	3 f	
COOK, Rebecca 700/20	81 f MD	161-1195		
GRIDLEY, Ellen	21 f VA			
Thomas	2 m	COX, Charles, gambler -/50	36 m	
143-1053		Cecilia	30 f	
		Franklin	12 m	
COOKE, John T, clerk	26 m DC	Alice	10 f	
Emma R	26 f VA	Charles	6 m VA	
Robt R	9/12 m	William	4 m	
Samuel R	4 m DC	Ella	3 f	
16-85		Ida	2 f	

ALEXANDRIA VIRGINIA 1860 CENSUS

Libby	5/12 m	Jno	13 m	
141-1031		WARD, Geo C, clerk hrdwr	15 m MD	
		HARRISON, C, clerk dry goods	17 m	
CRABBS, Joshua, miller -/1K	32 m MD	116-859		
Therza	26 f			
Mary	10 f PA	CROCKFORT, John, RR contractor -/10K	44 m EG	
Mifrom	8 f	Ellen	43 f	
Robert	6 m	Rosa Ellen	18 F	
Walter	4 m	Hamilton	17 m	
Emily	2 f	Lamb	16 m	
Infant	5/12 f	Frank	7 m	
Benjamin, miller	53 m	McCAULY, Mary	35 f NY	
Emily	50 f			
Emily	18 f	CRONK, Charles D, laborer -/30	43 m NY	
268-2075		Ann	27 f VA	
		Armistead M	13 m	
CRAIG, Eliza (M), seamstress	56 f	Chas F	8 m	
168-1259		Greenboy	7 m	
		BEACH, Levi, laborer	28 m	
CRAVEN, John, machinist -/150	52 m EG	77-550		
Sarah R	40 f VA			
George, cabinet maker	27 m	CROOCA, Chris, mechanisit -/150	52 m EG	
Virginia	12 f VA	..... R	40 f VA	
QUEEN, Rebecca	65 f	George, cabinet maker	27 m EG	
179-1338		Roberta	4 f	
		QUEEN, Rebecca	65 f	
		179-1338		
CRAWFORD, James, restaurant -/2K	40 m PA			
Mary	35 f MD	CROOK, Bernard, house carpenter 800/50	40 m	
John	12 m	Susan	48 f	
James	8 VA	Robert, house carpenter	18 m	
Parke	5 m	Hines, machinist	16 m	
McMULLEN, Sarah	68 f MD	Agnes	13 f	
62-442		Crawford	11 m	
		Roberta	9 f	
CRAWFORD, John, hotel keeper -/200	35 m PA	Josephene	1 f	
Elizabeth	34 f	Bernard	2 m	
Mary E	11 f	159-1185		
John	9 m NJ			
BUCKANAN, James, bar keeper	56 m MD	CROCK, Wm Smith, shoemaker -/75	75 m	
4-30		Eliza	25 f	
		171-1282		
CRAWFORD, Lucy, seamstress -/50	34 f			
Annie	10 f	CROSS, Jas, huckster -/400	65 m	
Helen, seamstress	38 f	Susan	55 f	
Harret	35 f	85-612		
Elizabeth	32 f VA			
		CROSS, Neuman, cabinet maker -/50	46 m	
CREDIT, John (M), laborer -/50	35 m VA	Martha	40 f	
Margaret (M)	21 f	John	23 m	
TALBOT, Frank (B)	50 m	Henrietta	19 f	
239-1855		Chas, printer	16 m	
		Sarah	11 f	
		Alice	10 f	
CREGAN, John, laborer -/20	30 m IR	JEFFERSON, Wm, cabinet maker	21 m	
Catharine	26 f	132-965		
Martha	3 f VA			
Mary Ann	11/12 f	CROSS, Richard, shoemaker 15K/5K	30 m	
96-701		Elizabeth	47 f	
		LUGANBEEL, Mary	42 f	
CREIGHTON, Jno T, hrdwr merch 4500/3K	46 m	Prince	11 m	
Mary	46 f	James	9 m	
Wm F, clerk drugstore	20 m			

ALEXANDRIA VIRGINIA 1860 CENSUS

Bettie	7 f	CURREN, John, stone mason	49 m IR	
Lillie	6 f	Biddie	40 f	
SIMPSON, Ann	70 f PA	Edward	16 m VA	
194-1477		Thomas	12 m	
		Billy	11 m	
CROWSON, Robert, shoemaker -/20	46 m	John	5 f	
Julia	24 f	Mollie	3 f	
Charles	18 m	234-1804		
Sarah	8 f			
221-1703		CURREN, William, laborer	28 m	
		Muna	30 f	
CRUMP, J T, butter maker	38 m	Margaret	3/12 f VA	
Ann E	32 f	DAILY, William	31 m	
Jas H	14 m	CONNERS, John	30 m	
RAMSAY, Sarah, domestic	14 f	CANLY, Thomas	25 m	
188-1425		95-690		
CRUMP, Kerion H, seamstress	36 f			
Carlyn	7 m	CURRIE, Abram, gardner -/30	40 m IJ	
William	3 m	Mary	45 f	
HAGAN, Eliza	9 f	Mary Ann, waitress	18 f	
46-320		Abram, laborer	16 m	
		Louisa, spinner	14 f	
CRUPPER, Robert, clerk -/350	61 m	John	10 m	
Sarah	61 f	Selena	7 f	
Florida	18 f	Edward	5 m	
51-360		INDLE, Wm, gardner	23 m	
		93-670		
CRYSS, James, boarding -/100	69 f			
Julia	19 f	CURRIE, Rowel, house carpenter 500/1K	32 m MD	
ROSS, John	35 m IR	Symphonia	32 f	
WINDEL, Jas, miller	27 m VA	Florida	9 f	
HAUVER, William	25 m MD	Joseph	4 m	
STERLING, Wm, carpenter	24 m DC	Robert	2 m	
CHEW, Francis	24 m	Sally	2/12 f	
EDMONDSON, Gruel	22 m	208-1596		
119-876				
		CURRIN, John, laborer	40 m IR	
CUBET, Robert (B), laborer	37 m	Ann	30 f	
Edith (B)	27 f	Ann	12 f NY	
Robert (B)	7 m	Mary	11 f	
George (B)	5 m	John	4 m VA	
Nancy (B)	1 f	29-182		
240-1863				
		CURTIS, Charles (B)	88 m	
CUBIT, Minnie (M), wash & iron	25 f	Ann M (B), wash & iron	26 f	
Kitty (M), domestic	20 f	Aldaline (B), domestic	26 f	
Henry (B)	7 m	30-262		
Nancy (B)	4 f			
William (B)	29 m	CURTIS, William (B), laborer	56 m	
Edward (B)	18 m	Lydia (B)	31 f	
22-127		RONE, Latita (B)	27 f	
		155-1150		
CUGAN, John, gas fitter -/100	33 m EG			
Jane	26 f	CURTIS, Wm H, negro trader -/3K	33 m NY	
218-1676		Mary	25 f	
		Mary	7 f	
CULLEN, Thomas, laborer	35 m	David	5 m	
Mary	33 f	Willie	3 m	
Daniel	7 m VA	Norman	5/12 m	
Mary	5 f	148-1094		
56-396				

ALEXANDRIA VIRGINIA 1860 CENSUS

CUZON, John, gas fitter -/100	33 m EG		Robt	2 m DC	
Jane	24 f		CAVIL, Margaret (M), domestic	15 DC	
218-1676			QUANDER, Gracie (M)	45 f	
			128-939		
DACEY, Johanna, boarding house -/50	33 f				
Bridgett	5 f VA		DANGERFIELD, Ed 20K/3K	53 m	
Roger	2 m		Margaret	41 f	
KEITH, David, laborer	40 m IR		282-2154		
McGRAW, John	39 m				
GALLIGAN, David	30 m		DANGERFIELD, Henry, farmer ? 130K/50K	59 m MD	
RILEY, Miron	45 m		Eliza	3? f	
MURPHY, John	30 m		Susan	33 f	
SULLIVAN, John	35 m		Ellen	28 f	
BRADLEY, Mark	50 m		Harry	12 m	
95-691			Kennedy	10 m	
			Lewis	5 m	
DAHONEY, Ed, laborer	45 m IR		250-1945		
Catharine	67 f				
Patrick	21 m		DANGERFIELD, J B, genrl merch 24K/30K	43 m	
Bridget	13 f		Rebecca H	65 f	
James	7 m		Mary	18 f	
244-1897			William	16 m	
			Edwin	12 m	
DAILY, Elenor, domestic	16 f EG		169-1266		
181-1374					
			DANIEL, Cornelia, house painter	23 m	
DAILY, Joseph, laborer	40 m IR		Melvina	18 f	
Catharine	43 f		Alando	1 m	
Patrick	17 m		43-295		
Anna	15 f				
May	12 f		DARBY, Sarah	56 f	
Elizzie	10 f NY		George, appren bricklayer	27 m	
Catharine	6 f CT		Henry, spinner	15 m	
Joseph	4 m VA		153-1131		
248-1928					
			DARLING, Wm, shoemaker -/50	37 m	
DALTON, Margaret, dressmaker -/30	56 f IR		Mary	35 f	
EWING, Michie, engineer RR	30 m VA		George	12 m	
Johanna	30 f IR		William	10 m	
116-853			John	8 m	
			Helen	16 f	
DAN, Fred, shoemaker -/50	44 m		Lonzo	2 f	
Mary	33 f		Eliza	5 f	
Robt	9 m		175-1312		
Samuel L	6 m				
Fred	2 m		DARNELL, Jas, machinist	40 m	
Wm W, appren	18 m		Mary	31 f	
Precilla	16 f		Mary	11 f	
81-579			William	8 m	
			Annenia	7 f	
DANA, C B, Epis minister	50 m NH		Virginia	5 f	
ARMSTRONG, Eliza, housekeeper	65 f VA		John	2 m	
THOMPSON, Elyabeth (M), domestic	20 f		220-1696		
KEITH, Mary A	27 f				
90-654			DARNELL, Robert (B)	23 m	
			Martha (B)	28 f	
DANAHAN, John, Meth minister -/6K	41 m VA		Henry (B)	8/12 m	
Mary	30 f MD		151-1117		
John	11 m VA				
Mary	11 f		DARNES, John F, farmer -100	35 m	
Timothy	9 m GT		Jane	35 f	
Helen	6 f MD		260-2021		

29

ALEXANDRIA VIRGINIA 1860 CENSUS

DAURAND, Phillapena, shirtmaker -/130 56 f FR
   Fanny 7 f NJ
130-950

DAVIDSON, Francis K, cab mkr 1800/100 50 m MD
   June 48 f EG
   Francis J, book keeper 21 m VA
   Anna 18 f
   William 9 m
   Harriet 13 f
174-1304

DAVIS, Ann (M), wash & iron 30 f
EVANS, Billy (B) 74 m
WIGGS, Ryner (M), wash & iron 51 f
244-1895

DAVIS, Aurelia (B) 32 f
   William (B) 15 m
   Jane (B) 12 f
   Ella (B) 7 f
167-1254

DAVID, Edward, laborer 29 m
   La..issa 28 f VA
   Daniel 6 m
   Josaphena 1 f
182-1380

DAVIS, Edward, constable -/100 48 m
   Susana
   Fannie 20 f
   Arthur 19 m
   Henry, rope maker 16 m
   Zachary 12 m
   Alberta 9 f
   Mary 3 f
41-272

DAVIS, Elizabeth 54 f
GETTS, Johanna, dress maker 25 f
   Mary 4 f
   Lotta 2 f
171-1285

DAVIS, Ferdinand, wheelwright -/30 29 m
   Julia 27 f
   Georgia 8 f
   Clara 6 f
   Amanda 5 f
   Indiana 1 f
KING, Sally 16 f
44-298

DAVIS, George, superv police -/200 63 m
   Sarah 60 f
   George W, carpenter 26 m
RUDD, John A, house painter 35 m
   Harriet M 28 f
DAVIS, Ruth (B), domestic 14 f
44-302

DAVIS, Henry (B) 75 f
28-177

DAVIS, John (B), laborer 400/40 45 m
   Rebecca (B) 14 f
   William (B) 11 m
   John (B) 9 m
238-1842

DAVIS, John F, farmer 36 m
   Jane 35 f
260-2021

DAVIS, John T, blacksmith -/200 25 m
   Elizabeth 22 f
   Charles 6 m
   Ada 1 f
39-254

DAVIS, Josiah H, plstr grindr 15K/300 76 m ??
   Sarah 45 f
   Josiah H, mail agent 35 m
   Thomas, plstr grinder 33 m
215-1658

DAVIS, Leanna (M), nurse 39 f
   Annabel (M) 10 f
28-175

DAVIS, Margaret 48 f
   Elizabeth, seamstress 27 f
   James, sailor -/220 23 m
   Isaiah, sailor -/225 21 m
   John 20 m
   Enoch 18 m
   Wesley, sailor 17 m
   Howard 14
   Edward 11 m
   Carry 6 f
111-822

DAVIS, Mary, prostitute 23 f
   Ann 11/12 f
187-1418

DAVIS, Melvina (M), domestic 40 f
234-1806

DAVIS, Peter, blacksmith -/63 58 m
   Jane 54 f
   Peter, blacksmith 23 m
   Roberta 17 f
   Harmonia 13 f
   Wm 1 m
74-522

DAVIS, Robert, church sexton -/100 51 m
   Henrietta 19 f
   John 17 m
   Ellen 15 f MD
WOOD, Ella 49 f
136-999

ALEXANDRIA VIRGINIA 1860 CENSUS

DAVIS, Thomas, harness maker -/20	21 m	DEACON, Michael, laborer	35 m IR	
Mary	29 f	Margaret	31 f	
WHITE, Nuttin	13 f	136-992		
195-1487				
		DEARBORN, Geo, grocer 900/1K	55 m ME	
DAVIS, Wesley	36 m	May	47 f	
Sarah	31 f	Marion	20 f	
Georgiana	14 f	Charles	12	
May	8 f	George	8 m	
Samuel	2 m	Mary	4 f	
268-2071		MAITLEY, Johanna	75 f ST	
		216-1667		
DAVIS, Wm, RR engineer -/75	30 m			
Louisa	20	DEEDLE, Adolphus, coppersmith -/75	30 m HC	
Alice	3 f	Caroline	21 f BD	
Susan	5 f	Adolphus	8/12 m VA	
245-1907		81-575		
		DEEDLE, Ed K, farmer 800/300	52 m	
DAVIS, William, carpenter 1200/100	53 m VA	Elizabeth	46 f	
Martenia	53 f	Indiana	21 f	
Mary	24 f	Martha	19 f	
Amanda	19 f	Virginia	17 f	
Morgan, carpenter	18 m	Esther	16 f	
Americas, dry food clerk	15 m	Alice	16 f	
Andrew, newsboy	14 m	Ames...	12 f	
139-1017		Silus	11 m	
		Mildred	9 f	
DAVIS, Wm L, sailor	35	Fanny	7 f	
Elizabeth	27 f	Ellison	3 m	
Alice	1 f	TAYLOR, Moses (B), laborer	16 m	
214-1653		257-1993		
		DEETON, Christopher, shoemaker	26 m	
DAVY, Thomas, grocer 16K/10K	70 m EG	Sarah	25 f	
Susan	64 f VA	George R	6 m	
LUGANBELL, Martha	36 f	Frances	3 m	
Emma	13 f	Ann	2 f	
118-875		BAGNE, Agnes, nurse	12 f	
		DEETON, George A, shoemaker	56 m	
DAW, Fred, shoemaker -/50	44 m EG	49-346		
Mary	33 f VA			
Robt	9 m	DEITZ, Doritha 3K/220	37 f	
Samuel L	6 m	155-1148		
Fred	2 m			
Wm W, appren	18 m	DELANEY, Henry (B), laborer 800/50	51 m	
81-579		Catharine (B)	33 f	
		John (B)	8 m	
DAWSON, Thomas B, farmer 5K/4700	44 m MD	Job (B)	4 m	
Elizabeth	37 f GT	Edgar (B)	1 m	
George	40 m	BUTLER, Mary (B)	63 f	
Annie	35 f	238-1843		
261-2028				
		DELEKAU, John	30 m IR	
DAY, Jane (B)	40 f	Biddy	34 f	
John (B)	16 m	90-649		
Lewis (B)	14 m			
Fran... (B)	8 m	DELPHI, Bart, huckster 1200/100	63 m DC	
Joseph (B)	6 m	Sarah	55 f	
Susan (B)	4 f	FIELD, George, house carpenter	24 m	
Robert (B)	2 m	Sarah	22 f	
266-2062		Ida	1 f	

ALEXANDRIA VIRGINIA 1860 CENSUS

```
    Esser                           17 f     DENTY, Edward, house painter -/30   28 m VA
176-1320                                       Mary                              25 f
                                               Emma                               5 f
DEMAIN, Wm, cabinet maker 1500/75   40 m       Ida                                1 f
  Elizabeth                         38         Mary, seamstress                  48 f
  Chas, dry good clerk              19 m       Anna                               7 f
  Elizabeth                         16 f   92-667
  Louise                            16 f
  Grace                              6 f   DENTY, Joseph, sailor -/50           25 m
  Mike                               9 m     Sarah                              27 f NJ
  Oscar                             12 m     Joseph                              3 m
  Letti                              3 f   233-1797
  Virginia                         4/12 f
134-979
                                            DERRICK, Robt (B), laborer           26 m
DEMPSEY, Jas, bank clerk 3K/510     50 m      Sophia (M)                         23 f
  Esther                            18 f     Betcy (M)                            5 f
  Amsa                              17 f     Jane (M)                             3 f
  Charles, clerk grocery            15 m   162-1207
  Sally                             13 f
  Plea...                           10 m   DESMOND, Morris, laborer              30 m IR
WASHINGTON, Mary                    22 f     Alice                               28 f
177-1321                                     William                              2 m VA
                                          56-391

DENCON, Michael, laborer            35 m IR DEVAUGHN, Jas H, cabinet mfg 8K/5K   44 m VA
  Margaret                          31 f     Emily                               36 f MD
136-992                                      Mary                                19 f VA
                                             Emma                                14 f
DENMEAD, Isaac, master machinist -/1K 45 m MD  Alice                              4 f
  Augusta                           47 f     Effie                                2 f
  Mary                              19 f MD 126-919
JOHNSTON, Anna, domestic            24 f VA
25-147                                      DEVAUGHN, John, shoemaker -/100      65 m VA
                                              Catharine                         63 f
DENNINGTON, Stephen, pilot          28 m MD   Samuel, tinner                    21 m
  Matilda                           25 f      Josephine                         18 f
  Stephen                            3 m      Emma                               6 f
ROBY, Uphennia, domestic            16 f   162-1204
230-1779
                                            DEVAUGHN, John T, shoemaker -/500   36 m
                                              Josephine                         37 f
DENNIS, Lewis, laborer              50 m      Isabella                          13 f
  May                               44 f      Ada                               11 f
  Charles                           15 m      Franklin                           5 m
  Agnes                              2 f      Thomas                             3 m
209-1605                                      Samuel                          3/12 m
                                              Ann                               62 f
DENNISON, Henry, laborer 200/20     27 m   BUTLER, James, appren                14 m IR
  Cornelia                          24 f   4-27
  Ronnie                             8 m
  Sarah                              6 f   DEVAUGHN, Samuel H, carter 2700/500  44 m
  Alice                              2 f     Harriet                            42 f
DIX, Corrie                         13 m     Anna H                             21 f
262-2034                                     Harvy                              20 f
                                             Isabella                           14 f
DENNISON, Jas, farmer 500/300       41 m     Mary                               10 f
  James, laborer                    16 m   195-1481
  John                              16 m
  Emma                               8 f   DEVAUGHN, William 9K/200             68 m
  Janet                              6 m     Susanah                            45 f
254-1977                                   51-356
```

ALEXANDRIA VIRGINIA 1860 CENSUS

DEVAUGHN, Wm H, cooper	43 m	DIGUS, Elizabeth (M)	55 f MD
Sarah	43 f	George (M)	22 m
Henry	18 m	212-1624	
William	16 m		
Jas R	12 m	DILLON, John, laborer	45 m
Jasson M	7 m	Catharine	38 f
Sarah	5 f	Patrick	14 m
20-114		Anne	12 f
		John	5 m VA
DEVIANE, Elizabeth, 1200/75	66 f	98-725	
Jane	18 f		
John, appren machinist	15 m	DILLY, Andrew, brickmaker	32 m
Jane	16 f	Elizabeth	25 f
Helen	10 f	Andrew	6 m
Eddie	8 m	Henry	4 m
Henry	4 m	May	1 f
GREGORY, Hamilton, journer -/1500	22 m NY	225-1730	
Marion	20 f		
FISHER, Thomas, machinist	30 m	DIRKSON, Sally (M), wash & iron	35 f
SPOTTS, Wm, blacksmith	35 m PA	Otho (B)	13 m
WALKER, Ann (B), domestic	14 f	Betsy (B)	11 f
139-1018		Henrietta (B)	9 f
		Catharine (B)	6 f
DEVINE, Michael, laborer -/50	60 m IR	John (B)	4 m
Betsy	40 f	George (B)	1 m
Patrick	13 m	PARKE, Kity (B)	67 f
Jackson	11 m	145-1067	
Daniel	9 m		
Michael	7 m	DISCALL, G M, shoemaker	25 f
Ellen	4 f	Annie	22 f
Katy	10/12 f	Mary E	4 f
89-639		Margaret	2 f
		17-95	
DEWEY, John, moulder 1500/150	70 m EG		
Elizabeth	59 f		
George	22 m	DISHMAN, Henry, house carpenter -/20	28 m
Anne	18 f EG	Lucinda	20 f
80-574		228-1753	
		DISHMAN, James, laborer	28 m
DEWEY, Jno R, laborer -/75	28 m EG	Sally	26 f
Anna	23 f VA	Fanny	2 f
Alton	1 m	211-1615	
80-573			
		DIX, Sarah, seamstress -/100	30 f
DICKSON, Francis, sailor	26 m	John	14 m
Lucy	25 f	Thomas	12 m
John	2/12 m	Geo W	9 m
213-1644		Sarah R	6 f
		Noble	3 m
DIENELT, Julius, dentist -/1K	30 m BR	BERRY, Thos, cooper	29 m
Fredericka	27 f PR	68-477	
Mary L	7 f PA		
Ida	5 f VA		
Alice	3 f	DIXION, Catharine (B), wash & iron	34 f
RILL, Mary, domestic	20 f HD	Rebecca (B)	4 f
18-102		James (B)	2 m
		Laura (B), 1800/20	4/12 f
DIGGS, Richard (M)	30 m	237-1832	
Rebecca (B)	29 f		
Eliza (B)	2/12 f	DIXION, Henry 800/30	52 m BV
200-1529		Ursula	47 f BV

ALEXANDRIA VIRGINIA 1860 CENSUS

```
    Mary ....                              16 f DC      Thomas (M)                        9 m
    Peter                                  10 m         Breiner (M)                       8 m
263-2043                                              217-1672

DIXION, Jno A 20K/1K                       40 m      DOGAN, Robt (M)                     35 m
    Fanney                                 30 f         Rebecca (B)                      25 f
    Ella                                   14 f         Leonard Gibbs (B)                16 m
    Arthur                                  1 m         Mary (B)                         16 f
76-537                                                  Edward (B)                       12 m
                                                        William (B)                       7 m
                                                        Harriet (B)                       6 f
DIXON, Turner, magistrate 3300/10K         50 m      111-825
    Mary                                   36 f
19-106                                               DOGLE, R, laborer                   25 m IR
                                                        Rose                             24 f
DOBS, Betsy (B)                            65 f      235-1814
    Benjamin (B)                           30 m
    Ignatius ()                             6 m
    Margaret (B)                            4 f      DONALDSON, John                     28 m
    Carter (B)                              2 m         Jenny                            30 f
    Margaret (B)                           21 f      159-1178
246-1917
                                                     DONALDSON, R R, Farmer 3K/300       60 m VA
DOBY, Ann, boarding house -/100            61 f         Ellen                            50 f
    Thomas W, house carpenter              26 m         Eliza                            30 f
    William, machinist                     17 m         Maria                            27 f
GIBEN, Eliza                               23 f         George                           26 m
    Robert                                  8 m         Hyman                            13 m
    Sarah                                  11 f         Webster                          10 m
JEFFRIES, James, baggage master RR         26 m      259-2008
    Cecila                                 26 f
    Annie                                 9/12 f     DONALLY, John T, hotel keeper -/100 23 m MD
DUNMEAD, Henry, machinist                  30 m MD      Mary F                           16 f MA
BALDWIN, Henry, machinist                  50 m      LOVEJOY, Isaac B, collector         50 m ME
RICHMOND, Daniel, machinist                26 m VA      Mary                             49 f MA
EDMONDS, Ephaim                            30 m MD      Francis H, laborer               24 m MA
KIDWELL, John T, fireman RR                24 m      110-816
JOHNSON, Jno, tanner                       26 m
MOONE, Clarence, dress maker               27 f      DONALDSON, Robert, farmer -/300     68 m
WOOD, Andrew, bridge builder               22 m MD      Elizabeth                        62 f
KELLY, Jack                                26 m         Nancy                            26 f
WELLS, Joe                                 30 m         Elmira                           21 f
221-1706                                                Martha                           24 f
                                                     260-2016

DOGAN, Anthony, laborer 400/50             38 m IR
    Margaret                               30 f      DONGAS, Eliza                       66 f IR
    Margaret                               16 f         Stewart, bookkeeper              40 m VA
    James                                  12 m         Virginia                         33 f
    Mary                                    6 m      KINKAID, Isabella                   36 f
    Charlotte                               5 f      MASON, Helen (B), domestic          34 f
    Rachael                                 3 f      CHASE, Maria (B)                    14 f
    William                                 1 m      44-299
36-234
                                                     DONNELL, Jas, machinist -/75        40 m
DOGAN, Anthony (M), laborer                69 m         Mary                             31 f
    Mirin (M)                              67 f         Mary                             11 f
    John (M), carter                       32 m         William                           8 m
    Lynn (M), ship carpenter               30 m         Annesia                           7 f
    Isabella (M)                           28 f         Virginia                          5 f
    Wm Henry (M)                           13 m         John                              2 m
    Luther (M)                             11 m      220-1696
```

ALEXANDRIA VIRGINIA 1860 CENSUS

```
DONNELL, Wesley (M), oyster saloon   31 m         DOWELL, Thomas, blacksmith -/50    34 m
   Louise (M)                        35 f            Jane                             31 f
   Eugene (M)                         3 f            Saml                            4/12 m
   Benjamin (M)                      15 m            Sarah                            52 f
157-1165                                           KIDWELL, Agnes                     16 f
                                                   89-636
DORSEY, Enoch (M), hack driver       62 m
   Mona (M)                          60 f         DOWNEY, John, laborer -/50          36 m IR
   Emily (M)                         15 f            Johana                           34 f
65-458                                                David                            9 m VA
                                                      Rachael                          8 f
DORSEY, H Carter, grocer 6700/1K     37 m             Joseph                           5 m
   Kate                              27 f             John                             4 m
   Florence                           5 f             Patrick                        9/12 m
   Kate                               3 f         137-1001
JONES, Bertha, domestic              75 f
54-377                                             DOWNEY, John                       63 m
                                                      Margaret, spinner               16 f
DOSSEY, Frances, coachman            38 m MD          William, card grinder           18 m
   Christina                         30 f         90-650
   William                           10 m VA
   Thomas                             8 m DC
   Ida                                5 f         DOWNEY, Michael, laborer            25 m IR
42-283                                                Julia                           20 f
                                                      Ella                          3/12 f VA
DOUGLAS, J E, grocer -/6K            32 m         90-643
   Annie                             30 f
   John                               6 m         DOWNEY, Michie, laborer             37 m IR
   Margaret                           5 f            Alice                            38 f
   James E                            3 m            Kate                             13 f
57-405                                                Lawrence                        10 m
                                                      Hannah                        6/12 f VA
DOUGLAS, Mel, farmer 7K/500          36 m DC      87-626
   Elizabeth                         30 f
   Mary                               5 f         DOWNEY, Patrick                     50 m
   Laura                              3 f            Mary                             35 f
   Clay                               1 m            Johanna                           6 f MD
263-2038                                              Ellen                            8 f
                                                   CREIGH, Michael                    25 m IR
DOUGLAS, W J, house painter          43 m DC      MURPHY, John                        20 m
   Sarah                             32 f         VINE, Danl                          25 m
   Annie                             12 f         BRICK, Martin                       50 m
   William                            6 m            Mary                             30 f
252-1965                                           95-692

DOUGLASS, George (B), blacksmith -/10 39 m        DOWNEY, Thos, grocer 600/300        32 m IR
   Harriet (B)                       28 f            Mary                             28 f
   Ruberta (B)                        9 f            John                              8 m
   Harriet (B)                        7 f            Mary                              3 f
   George (B)                         6 m            Thomas                            3 m
   Frances (B)                        4 f            Michie                         6/12 m
   Samuel (B)                         3 m         87-625
   Thomas (B)                         2 m
   Fairfax (B)                      4/12 m        DOYLE, Charles, house painter       30 m
43-293                                                Sarah                           28 f
                                                      Franklin                         9 m
DOWELL, Thom, blacksmith             26 m             Catharine                        7 f
   Jane                              21 f             Chas                             5 m
   Paul                             5/12 m            Mary                             1 f
KIDWELL, Sarah                       55 F         COOK, Wm, laborer                   50 m
   Agnes                             16 F         245-1900
50-347
```

ALEXANDRIA VIRGINIA 1860 CENSUS

DOYLE, P, laborer	25 m IR		Julia (M)	5 f	
Rose	24 f		Maggie (M)	3 f	
235-1814			DUDLEY, Jno (M)	7 m	
			211-1616		
DOZIER, Chas (B), laborer	57 m				
Mina (B)	54 f		DUFFEY, Francis, laborer	29 m IR	
Dennis (M)	9 m		Bridget	30 f	
Mary (B)	3 f		Margaret	5 f	
Elizabeth (B)	25 f		James	10/12 m PA	
164-1226			138-1007		
DRISCALL, Elizabeth	64 f		DUFFEY, Geo, silver smith -/200	40 m	
Margaret, seamstress	30 f		Sarah	30 f	
Frances	27 f		Benjamin	16 m	
Lucy	20 f		Rosalie	13 f	
17-96			George	11 m	
			Kate	7 f	
DROWN, Dilda, -/20	46 f VA		Charles	6 m	
William, plasterer	25 m		Bettie	4 f	
John, plasterer	20 m		Sarah	3 f	
Geo, house painter	18 m		Lucian	6/12 m VA	
Alice	10 f		Samuel	19 m	
Richard	7 m		61-434		
147-1087					
DRUMMOND, Noah, toll keeper	58 m		DUGANE, Edward, laborer	27 m IR	
251-1953			Mary	22 f	
			Philip	2 m VA	
DRYFUS, Simpson, rag merch	58 m WT		96-698		
Caroline	48 f				
Bettie	24 f		DUNCAN, Jas, laborer 600/50	35 m IR	
Julius	18 m		Ann	31 f	
Everhart	16 m		Elizabeth	5 f	
Rachael	10 f		William	3 m	
Joseph	7 m		James	10/12 m	
147-1086			WILKINS, Elizabeth	70 f IR	
			DUNCAN, William	38 m	
DUDLEY, Benj F, master carptr -/500	35 m		94-685		
Mary	31 f				
Julia	6/12 f		DUNCAN, John, laborer -/25	29 m IR	
VERNON, Susana	63 f		Martha	23 f	
144-1058			Harriet	2/12 f	
			93-675		
DUDLEY, Jas, gardner -/30	57 m VA				
Margaret	52 f		DUNN, Henry, hackster	50 m MA	
Mary	17 f		Sarah	30 f VA	
John	14 m		CANNON, Catharine	93 f	
283-2164			31-200		
DUDLEY, Joseph, carpenter -/50	29 m				
Mirnva	24 f MD		DUNNAWAY, Jas	38 m IR	
Washington	3 m VA		Bridget	20 f	
Wm R	1 m		Mary	2 f VA	
162-1208			144-1063		
DUDLEY, Wm (M), cook	45 m		DURAND, Bernard, laborer	40 m	
Nancy (M)	67 f		Mary	40 f	
John (M)	14 m		Bernard	13 m	
Sophia (M)	17 f		Patrick	11 m	
John Cubet (M)	13 m		Owen	7 m	
Sarah (M)	11 f		Elizabeth	5 f VA	
Ada Heurt (M)	7 f		244-1899		

ALEXANDRIA VIRGINIA 1860 CENSUS

DUVAL, John, laborer	30 m	
Nancy, seamstress	33 f	
WALKER, John	13 m	
MONTJOY, Cloa, domestic	58 f	
87-629		
DWYER, Thomas, civil engineer -/300	37 m IR	
Susan	30 f VA	
Philip	11/12 m	
MURPHY, Susan, domestic	27 f IR	
ROTCHFORD, Philip -12K	37 m VA	
171-1283		
DYAN, John, ship smith -/50	29 m	
Eliza	28 f	
Mary	5 f	
Annie	3 f	
189-1450		
DYAR, Debra -/1K	70 f	
Elisha	10 m	
Walter, sailor	16 m	
Thomas, laborer	44 m	
234-1805		
DYER, John H, RR office clerk 3K/500	43 m VA	
Rosalie	41 f	
Maggie	- f	
Virginia	13 f	
Lucy	9 f	
Margaret 4K/3K	65 f	
166-1242		
DYER, Michael, laborer -/15	35 m IR	
Kate	20 f	
KINCAMM, Kate	50 f	
210-1607		
DYER, Robert, house carpenter	32 m VA	
Rebecca	27 f	
Elizabeth	8 f	
Alice	6 f	
William	3 m	
Virginia	3/12 f	
270-2088		
DYSON, James L, clerk 500/5K	42 m MD	
Mary A	52 f	
MANKIN, Ann D	22 f	
DYSON, Adie	17 f	
Franklin	11 m	
John	16 m	
1-2		
EATON, Ed H, bar keeper	32 m DC	
Georgana	22 f VA	
107-788		
ECTIN, Jane, tailoress	37 f	
Robert, tailor	21 m	
Richard, jeweller	19 m	
132-963		

EDD, John, baggage master -/100	38 m	
Mary	28 f	
Alice	5 f	
Kate	3 f	
George	8/12 m	
Chas	14 m	
72-506		
EDELIN, Robert J, clock maker	62 m MD	
Marion	35 f	
Elizabeth	68 f	
John R	15 m	
Elizabeth	11 f	
Maria	7 f	
Mary	2 f	
LEE, Henry, appren	19 m MD	
HENDRICK, Frank	20 m	
MURRAY, Charles, appren	18 m	
George	17 m	
PITMAN, Vincent	17 m	
FIFER, Wm, journeyman coachmaker	23 m	
SPEDENS, Wm	23 m DC	
15/16-83		
EDELIN, Thos, shoemaker 800/100	22 m VA	
Jane	22 m DC	
Esther	9 f VA	
87-624		
EDEN (?), Edwin (B) 800/30	75 m VA	
Lucy (B)	64 f	
82-593		
EDWARDS, Wm, house carpenter -/20	24 m	
Margaret	19 f MD	
207-1588		
EDWARDS, Wilson, carpenter -/100	32 m	
Julia	32 f	
William	7 m	
HENRY, Robt	40 m	
Amanda	23 f VA	
Euman	3 f	
John Letcher	1 m	
CHAC, Rosana, seamstress	50 f	
Rubertan	14 f	
James	12 m	
DIREMUS, Susan, domestic	15 f	
65-461		
ELDRIDGE, M, shipping merchant -/450	38 m MA	
Sybel	28 f ME	
Chestena	9 f MA	
Edward	2 m VA	
Rebecca	8 f MA	
AVERY, Francis, shipping merchant	26 m	
Maranda	26 f	
WOOD, Willia	16 m ME	
22-124		
ELLIOT, Jefferson, coachman	45 m	
Jane	38 f	

ALEXANDRIA VIRGINIA 1860 CENSUS

William, shoemaker	25 m	EMERSON, Louise, teacher -/50	30 f
Franklin, house painter	23 m	Ada	11 f
Betty, spinner	18 f	Mary	7 f
Mary, waitress	16 f	Bryson	4 m
Robt	11 m	179-1339	
Alice, spinner	12 f		
Helen	10 f	EMMERSON, J S, auctioner 12K/75	63 m
Ewina	4 f	Ann C	53 f
THOMPSON, Bridgett, spinner	16 f PA	Benjamin, tin & coppersmith	23 m
92-668		Henry, reporter	26 m
		Charles	11 m
ELLIOTE, Ellit, farmer	37 m	Eveline	8 f
Casina	35 f	221-1705	
Edward	12 m		
William	10 m	ENGLAND, Jas M, carpenter -/100	32 m
Thomas	2 m	Sarah	27 f
264-2048		William	9 m
		Elizabeth	6 f
		Rosa	1 f
ELLIOTT, John, gardner & florist	45 m	Rob, house painter	21 m
Julia	40 f	COOK, Martin, house carpenter	23 m
May	18 f	152-1127	
Frank, gardner	17 m		
Virginia	13 f	ENGLISH, Jas, restaurant 5K/200	70 m NJ
John	11 f	Anna	59 f VA
Anna	7 f	60-426	
Ida	5 f		
Sally	1 f	ENGLISH, James A 11K/2K	43 m
ROBINSON, John, laborer	60 m	Bitti	23 f
Robert	2 m	Emily H	21 f
236-1818		Janette	19 f
		Alberta	17 f
ELLIS, Samuel, steamboat fireman	33 m MD	Mary J	13 f
Laura	33 f	Horace	12 m
John	5 m	Charles	11 m
Matilda	10 f	Edmund	8 m
DANIELS, Lucretia	20 f	175-1315	
Walter, laborer	17 m		
219-1693		ENGLISH, Zeph, comm merchant 2500/15K	30 M
		Helen A	20 f MD
		ENER?, Jno, clerk	20 M VA
ELWOOD, Richard, house painter 2K/200	35 m	103-762	
May J	33 f		
James	12 m	ENNISS, William, wheelwright -/100	27 m
William	10 m	Martha	23 f
George	5 m	Mary	5 f
Catharine	2 f	Thomas	3 f
ATWELL, John, machinist	32 m MD	65-312	
GATFIELD, Martha, blacksmith	48 f NY		
BEACHAM, Joseph, house carpenter	23 m VA	ENTWISLE, Jas, bank teller 2500/400	65 m EG
ATWELL, Pamelia	40 f	Eliza	54 f
Benjamin	3 m	Amanda	25 f
SHAY, Robert, house painter	22 m	Nanie	17 f
SHAY, Eliza	26 f	Flirken	5 m
MILLER, William, machinist	28 m NY	60-427	
215-1660			
		ENTWISLE, Jas Jr, druggist 4K/1000	36 m
EMERSON, John P, butcher	52 m VA	Emily	29 f NY
Prudence	48 f MA	Mur..h	3 m
Isabel	18 f	William	9/12 m
Annie	15 f	FLUIR, Eugene, appren druggist	16 m
202-1539		120-886	

ALEXANDRIA VIRGINIA 1860 CENSUS

ENTWISLE, Mary -/800	68 f EG	EVANS, Paul, bridge builder -/1500	35 m	
May	40 f	Emma	25 f	
Edwin	15 m VA	Thomas	4/12 m	
129-945		ZIMMERMAN, Martha	19 f	
		247-1921		
ENTWISLE, May -/60	34 f DC			
William	12 m VA	EVANS, Revel R, sailor -/50	37 m VA	
Mary	4 f	Christina	41 f	
Emma	5/12 f	Laura	10 f	
BECK, Wm, bridge builder	36 m PA	William	6 m	
Sarah	27 f	Hester	5 f	
215-1661		John	9/12 m	
		107-792		
ENTWISLE, Wm J, book store -/500	31 m			
Mary	27 f	EVILITH, John, miller -/150	58 m	
William	2 m	Julia	45 f	
Norton Sprigg	6/12 m	Sally	20 f	
134-980		Kate	14 f	
		James, clerk comm merchant	16 m	
EPOLT, Henry, shoemaker -/150	35 m DC	SMITH, C (B)	16 m	
Anna H	33 f MD	216-1666		
Frances	13 f VA			
Saml	7 m	FADELY, C W, house carpenter -/30	25 m	
Ida W	3 f	Catharine	22 f	
78-553		Willie	4 m	
		Henry	2 m	
EVANS, Edward (M), baker	45 m	219-1685		
Latilda (M)	46 f			
Orlando (M), house carpenter	25 m	FADELY, Jas, master carpenter 1K/150	45 m	
211-1619		Virginia	26 f	
		Nutton, irish mecht	18 m	
EVANS, Elizabeth	40 f	JOHNSTON, Bill (M)	11 m	
Charles, laborer	18 m	218-1680		
James	12 m			
John	14 m			
Robert	7 m	FAGAN, Patrick	40 m IR	
227-1745		Elizabeth	28 f	
		Margaret	2 f DC	
EVANS, J Lewis, engineer RR 1K/100	35 m PA	101-745		
Ida	3 f			
Evan	73 m	FAHANNERY, John, florist -/200	31 m	
May	75 f	Mary	29 f	
Mary	37 f	James	8 m	
247-1926		Charles	30 m	
		281-2152		
EVANS, Jas, RR agent	45 m			
Anna	41 f	FAIRFAX, Orlando, physician 6K/18200	51 m VA	
Virginia	14 f	Mary R	44 f	
Jane	11 f	Corey O, printer	26 m	
Mary	9 f	Mohinia	21 f	
Libby	6 f	Jance C	19 f	
Ella	1 f	Randolph	18 m	
146-1076		Ethelbert	17 m	
		Edith M	13 f	
EVANS, John (B), brickmaker -/30	31 m	Thomas	11 m	
Mary (B)	30 f	Albert, medical student -/3K	26 m	
LUCAS, Monica (B)	83 f	53-374		
198-1512				
EVANS, Jno T, hat & bonnet 500/1K	66 m VA	FALLS, Wm, farmer	38 m EG	
ROACH, Wm, clerk	18 m VA	Jane	29 f	
117-867		263-2036		

ALEXANDRIA VIRGINIA 1860 CENSUS

FANLER, William, RR conductor	48 m FK		FEEBRY, Nicholas, farmer	60 m	
Imogene	42 f		Amanda	42 f	
Mary	19 f		BALL, Elizabeth	69 f	
Benjamin, brakeman	17 m		PAYNE, Matilda (M), domestic	32 f	
Maria	10 f		Alpine (B)	4 m	
HOLLINGER, William (B), domestic	13 m		253-1971		
MELVIN, Jennie (M)	10 f				
45-313			FELES, Anna	77 f	
			Marion, seamstress	35 f	
FANNON, Michael, grocer 1K/200	35 m IR		Sarah, dress maker	32 f	
Mary	28 f		143-1049		
Richard	7 m				
Mary	4 f		FENDALL, Townsend, bank clerk -/1K	43 m MD	
Elizabeth	2 f		Eliza	30 f	
RICE, James, laborer	35 m		Benja	9 m	
O'HEARA, John	36 m		Nannie	7	
CINGHLAND, Thos	21 m		Willie	6 m	
COX, John	23 m		EACHES, Connie	22 f	
71-498			DADE, Mary	65 f	
* see page 116 for FASSETT			215-1657		
FAULKNER, Henry, mail carrier	24 m				
Mary A	23 f		FENNICKS, Ann (B), domestic	50 f	
39-260			Robert (B), domestic	15 m	
			206-1575		
FAWNES, James, laborer	44 m				
Elizabeth	46 f		FERGUSON, Martha, dressmaker	35 f	
Thomas, laborer	19 m		Sarah E	10 f	
Frances	15 f		Mary	8 f	
William	13 m		Harriet	6 f	
Emily	10 f		Smith	4 m	
46-326			33-212		
FEARSON, Columbus, sailor -/50	29 m GT				
Mary E	22 f		FERGUSON, Robert, laborer	46 m	
Char	8/12 m		Anna	30 f	
252-1962			Min..	11	
			William	9 m	
FEDDON, Jno F, sailor -/50	38 m		Robert	7 m	
Sarah	36 f		Moncuy	3 m	
111-821			144-1060		
FEEBRY, Henry, farmer 6K/-	33 m		FEWELL, Wm F, trans agent 100/500	46 m	
Margaret	30 f		Elizabeth	46 f	
William	9 m		Sarah	18 f	
James	7 m		Bittie	16 f VA	
Ida	5 f		Lucian	15 m	
Kate	6 f		William	15 m	
Sally	2 f		Margaret	9 f	
ENNIS, Michel, laborer	17 f		Fanny	5 f	
254-1977			156-1161		
FEEBRY, Lewis E, farmer 10K/500	29 m				
Mary	24 f		FIELD, John A, city collector 2K/500	34 m	
Ellen	4 f		Mary	30 f	
Anna	1 f		114-842		
253-1972					
			FIELD, Stephen, printer -/150	30 m	
FEEBRY, Moses, farmer 8K/1500	30 m		Isabella	26 f	
Caroline	28 f		Corebel	3 f	
Virginia	6 f		Henry	3/12 m	
Alice	3 f		HAUSBY, Lucinda (M), domestic	26 f	
253-1973			13-68		

ALEXANDRIA VIRGINIA 1860 CENSUS

FIELD, Stephen, shoemaker -/2K	73 m ME	Martha	19 f		
Catharine	49 f VA	Rebecca	11 f		
Edgar, watchmaker	26 m	51-355			
Franklin, blacksmith	19 m				
Margaret	16 f	FISHER, Sally, house of prostition	25 f NJ		
....ub	14 m	62-437			
24-138					
		FITZCHARLES, Jere, laborer	30 m IR		
FIELD, Wm (B), blacksmith	29 m	Catharine	30 f		
Moran (B)	23 m	Catharine	9 f		
McHenry (B)	2 m	56-391			
Infant (B)	3/12 m				
Cecilia (B), wash & iron	42 f	FITZHUGH, Anna Maria 6K/1K	55 f MD		
203-1550		BANKS, Wm H (B), domestic	45 m VA		
		51-358			
FIELDS, Wm H, farmer	56 m				
Mary	39 f	FITZJOHN, Sarah, wash & iron	30 f IR		
Jas, laborer	18 m	Ellen	12 f		
William	15 m	Sarah	10 f		
Catharine	13 f	James	5 m		
Joseph	10 m	96-699			
255-1980					
		FITZPATRICK, Jas, mat maker 600/300	35 m IR		
FIGITT, Augustus, shoemaker -/100	68 m	Mary	26 f NB		
Ann, boarding house	47 f	Thos	56 m IR		
JOURDAN, Susan	44 f	Mary Ellen, domestic	25 f VA		
ALLEN, Sarah	60 f	77-545			
David, laborer	60 m				
AUDLEY, T	35 m	FLEICK, Wm, laborer	40 m GR		
BAILY, Peter	29 m	102-752			
ERUPT, Henry, wheelwright	48 m PA				
Rebecca	31 f				
McHENRY, Wm, carpenter	62 m MD	FLEMING, A J, 27K/3K	49 m		
JENKINS, Geo, blacksmith	25 m VA	Mary	57 f		
ALLISON, Robert, appren carpenter	18 m MD	Eliza	47 f		
60-428		DOUGLAS, Kate	27 f		
		Sarah	27 f		
FINCH, William, laborer	48 m	HARPER, Kate	10 f		
Catharine	38 f	169-1265			
George	10 m				
Nancy	8 f				
William	6 m	FLEMING, Archibald, stmb stw 3K/150	50 m		
84-601		Mary	43 f		
		Henry, clerk	25 m		
FINESTRY, Jas, farmer -/75	65 m	Edgar, watchmaker	23 m		
Nancy	50 f	Eurma	19 f		
Eliza	18 f	GIBSON, Albert, grocer	28 m		
Jimmy	16 f	Susan	26 f		
Marcunda	16 f	25-149			
Row	12 f				
William	6 m	FLEMING, Mary	38 f VA		
268-2072		Mary	20 f		
		William, machinist	18 m		
FISHER, F W, grocer -/150	47 m HN	NICHOLLS, Thos, super RR cars	45 m PA		
Elizabeth	61 f	26-155			
Frederick, grocery clerk	19 m				
110-819		FLETCHER, Edward C, bank clerk 5K/3K	60 m		
		Ann C	50 f		
		Edward W	21 m		
FISHER, Jonas, RR clerk -/200	67 m PA	WILSON, Eliza	62 f		
Harriet	47 f	Mary (B), domestic	12 f		
Anna	22 f	123-903			

ALEXANDRIA VIRGINIA 1860 CENSUS

FLETCHER, Matilda 2K/5K	57 f	Andrew (B)	16 m
172-1289		Jimmy (B)	5 m
		George (B)	2 m
FLOOD, John, laborer 1K/150	45 m IR	144-1061	
Margaret	35 f		
Mary	6 f	FOOTE, Mary L 6K/3K	45 f MA
Michael	16 m IR	WHITING, Mrs, teacher	50 f VA
LATCHFORD, Cath, domestic	23 f	21-118	
MURTOUGH, Peter, laborer	30 m		
240-1865		FORD, Chas E, wheelwright	33 m MD
		Susanna	27 f
FLUCK, Wm, laborer	40 m GR	Susan	6 f
Ellen	35 f	Willie	5 m
102-752		Annie	3 f
		154-1142	
FOGG, Samuel, boss cotton mill	38 m MA		
Alice	30 f MD	FORD, Daniel (M), laborer	35 m
George	9 m VA	Louisa (M)	26 f
Virginia	7 f	Biley (M)	16 m
SULLIVAN, Mary, weaver	20 f	Julia (M)	11 f
Catharine, weaver	22 f	Robt (M)	3 m
BURGIE, Ann, weaver	36 f	Louisa (M)	1 f
76-540		203-1557	
FOLEY, Jere, laborer	30 m IR		
Eliza	30 f	FORD, J W, shoemaker	50 m MD
202-1548		Jane	46 f
		Clarence, painter	17 m
FOLEY, Patrick, farmer	30 m IR	Alice	8 f
Julia	30 f	45-308	
Philip	7 m		
Martha	5 f	FORD, John (B)	33 m
Dennis	3 m	Cecilia (B)	28 f
Martass, laborer	32 m IR	Rosalie (B)	3 f
273-2106		238-1837	
FOLINER, Mary, confectionary 2K/300	37 f GR	FORD, Ignatious, laborer -/20	28 m
Mary	11 f VA	Charlotte	23 f
Betty	7 f	John	2 m
Louis	5 m	SIMPSON, Margaret, seamstress	25 f
Christina	3 f	91-659	
21-122			
FOLLY, Patrick	35 m	FORD, Josiah, wheelwright -/700	36 m MD
Johanna	30 f	Mary	34 f
91-661		Mary	14 f
		Frances	12 f
FONSHILL, John, gunsmith -/1K	38 m MD	Stephen	9 m
Ruth	20 f	Landon	6 m VA
Ruth	4 f VA	Peter Simon, wheelwright	29 m MD
Julia	2 f	DAVIS, Benjamin, blacksmith	26 m
5-33		147-1089	
FOOD, George, comm clerk -/200	39 m EG	FORES, John, laborer	29 m
Amanda	25 f	Winney	22 f
Henry	5 m VA	Ann	5 f
Edwin	2 m	Lucy	2 f
HARE, Bridgett, domestic	13 f IR	Saml	63 m
235-1810		Nancy	60 f
		Washington, laborer	21 m
FOOTE, Anna (B), wash & iron	50 f	Fanny	36 f
Sarah (B)	30 f	24-136	

ALEXANDRIA VIRGINIA 1860 CENSUS

FOSSETT, Jas, livery keeper 3700/300	56 m	
Catharine	40 f	
Henry	22 m	
Emma	20 f	
Mary	18 f	
Marion	15	
John	13 m	
Kate	9 f	
Louse	8 f	
Ida	2 f	
MULLIGAN, Mary, domestic	12 f	
131-957		

FOSTER. John, laborer 45 m IR
  Susan 43 f
  Susan, spinner 18 f
  Jane 15 f
  Elizabeth 13 f VA
  Patrick, laborer 17 m IR
88-633

FOSTER, Louise, washer 70 f
198-1513

FOTHERSON, James, ... maker 39 m
  Ella 40 f IR
  Emma 12 f VA
  William, appren printer 17 m VA
158-1173

FOWLE, Geo D, comm merchant 100K/55K 38 m
  Sarah E 35 f
  Anna H 13 f
  Ellen B 7 f
  Bernard 5 m
  Geo D 1 m
183-1386

FOWLE, Wm H, comm merchant 35K 51 m
  Elegin J 51 f
  William H, comm merchant 20 m
  Jas H, clerk 18 m
  Annie 16 f
BAILOR, Harriet (B), domestic 33 f
106-782

FOX, Kitty -/500 76 f VA
155-1153

FRAGANS, Angeline (M), wa & ir 300/30 24 f
237-1830

FRANCES, Aron (M) 67 f
165-1237

FRANCES, Emanuel, brickmason 10K/1500 61 m
  Julia 30 f
MANSFIELD, Robert, appren 11 m
FRANCES, Lucy 12 f
  Ida 7 f
  Carne 5 f
WHITE, May (B), domestic 77 f

MUDT..., David (B), labour 22 m
196-1497

FRANCES, Peter, sailor 700/600 27 m SD
  Amanda 31 f VA
  Sarah 14 f MD
  Peter 7 m
  James 1 m VA
223-1717

FRANKLIN, Benjamin 30 m
  Sally 23 f
116-855

FRANKLIN, Benjamin (B) -/40 44 m
  Cornelia (M) 30 f
  Margaret (M) 2 f
240-1858

FRANKLIN, Lucinda, wash & iron 30 f VA
  Catharine, wash & iron 30 f
  Mary L 13 f
  Agnes 12 f
  Geo Washington 17 m
  Ann 3 f
66-468

FRANKS, Jere, sailor -/50 40 m
  May 36 f
  Caroline 16 f
  May 16 f
  Otis 4 m
  Evaline 1 f
224-1727

FRANTIN, Samuel 2K/200 40 m MD
  Barbara 15 f
  John 13 m
  Samuel 9 m
  George 7 m
  Elizabeth 5 f
  Andrew 2 m
MORCIS, Wm, laborer 23 m
  Bashful 17 f
GORAM, Wm, laborer 24 m
273-2097

FRAZIER, Jere (B), laborer 500/60 40 m
  Sarah (B) 35 f
  Sarah (B) 15 f
  Wm H (B) 4 m
  Mary (B) 3 f
  Alice (B) 10/12 f
239-1856

FRAZINS, Anthony, farmer 40K/20K 65 m
  William, physician 33 m
  Cornelia 30 f
  Frances 25 f
  Maranda 21 f
  Antonia 19 f
276-2122

ALEXANDRIA VIRGINIA 1860 CENSUS

FRENCH, Chas E, farmer 5K/500	32 m CT	FURSTON, David, lawyer 4400/2K	41 m
Josephene	25 f NY	Susan	36 f
Estella	4 f VA	Mary C	14 f
BIRCH, John F, laborer	18 m DC	David M	10 m
COLE, Phebe, domestic	50 f NY	Robert	9 m
255-1985		Ea...	8 f
		William	6 m
FRENCH, D M, physician 1K/-	37 m VA	James J	4 m
Mary E	29 f	Lizzie L	3 f
George	10 m	George M	5/12 m
Mac	7 m	BLACK, Libby, nurse	28 f
May	3 f	168-1264	
HAMILTON, Sally (B)	13 f		
249-1939		GAINES, Mary 2200/100	32 f BA
		Ann	12 f
FRENCH, Geo E, book store 30K/6K	37 m CT	Mary	10 f
Virginia	37 f VA	Walter, house carpenter	43 m
Clarance	6 m	245-1901	
Robert	3 m		
Infant	5/12 m		
McBLOOD, Biddie, cook	21 f IR	GALES, James, machinist -/100	35 m NY
WHITE, Mary H	30 f VA	Anna	22 f
Maria	23 f	Edgar	3 m
121-888		SPINKS, Alice	13 f
		236-1824	
FRENCH, James S, groc clerk 5K/5K	45 m		
Susan J	29 f	GALLAHEN, Ann (M), wash & iron	45 f
Sallie	9 f	THOMPSON, Amos (M), waiter	23 m
Laura	7 f	Massachusetts (M)	5 m
James L	2 m	43-296	
61-433			
		GALLIGAN, James	50 m IR
FRENCH, Louise, seamstress	44 f	Elizabeth	33 f
Charles, appren printer	17 m	James	12 m
Sarah	16 f	Edward	4 m VA
PARKS, Sarah	74 f	84-602	
159-1176			
		GALLIGAN, Pat, laborer	25 m
FRYE, Thomas B B, physician 9250/1500	40 m DC	Mary	19 f
Ann	40 f EG	55-389	
Laura	16 f		
Walker	13 m		
259-2006		GALLIM, John, cooper -/50	45 m MD
		Ellen	30 f IR
FUETCHOEL, A H, jeweller -/5K	31 m BR	John	13 m MD
COMELY, Alfred, journey jeweller	33 m	Josephene	11 f PA
QUENZEL, C, watchmaker	50 m SW	Greenbury	9 m MD
116-560		Mary	2 f VA
		Geo W	1 m
FUGET, Benjamin, printer -/250	34 m	116-854	
Harriet	26 f		
Lewis	2 m	GAMBRILL, Benjamin, machinist -/150	30 m MD
CLARK, Alexander, carpenter	29 m	Hannah	20 f
Caroline	52 f	Mary	7 f
Bettie	16 f	Juliet	5 f
33-211		BOW, Georgiana (B)	17 f
		159-1184	
FULLIN, Julia (M), prostitute -/30	24 f		
Sally (B)	6 f	GARDNER, James, Meth minister -/6500	30 m MD
Ida (M)	3 f	Monia	48 f
SILLS, John (B), laborer	63 m	Anna	16 f VA
206-1573		Fanny	18 m

ALEXANDRIA VIRGINIA 1860 CENSUS

Cafron	16 m	MATHERS, Hannah	20 f	
Orlando	12 m	Norman	3 m	
194-1479		210-1613		
GATTAN, James R, laborer	23 m	GIBSON, Caleb (M)	55 f	
Ann	21 f	BADEN, Amanda (M) -/600	26 f	
James	1 m	Alexander (M)	33 m	
231-1788		Reverdny ? (M)	29 m	
		BROOKS, Virginia (M)	17 f	
GEDNEY, Samuel, Capt steamer 900/150	40 m NY	Rebecca (M)	15 f	
Susan	32 f	212-1626		
Edward	8 f			
Susan	2 f	GIBSON, Joshua	41 m	
WHITE, Mary (B), domestic	12 f	Elizabeth	27 f	
180-1347		James	19 m	
		John	16 m	
GELLAN, John	50 m IR	Margaret	12 f	
Margaret	40 f	Susan	10 f	
282-2155		Robert	7	
		Rosa	5 f	
		Virginia	3 f	
GENTZBERGER, Leopold, clother 800/2K	39 m BV	CARTER, Martha (B), domestic	19 f	
Bettie	39 f HN	272-2095		
Mayer	8 m MD			
Soloma	4 f VA	GIBSON, Mary (B), wash & iron	30 f	
Isaac	2 m	Frances (B)	3 f	
Sigmont	1 m	James (B)	3/12 m	
GALLAKER, Margaret, seamstress	26 f IR	42-282		
COOK, Margaret, domestic	33 f NY			
10-50		GILLAN, John	50 m IR	
		Margaret	40 f	
GENTZBERGER, Leyman, rag merch -/20	36 m BD	282-2155		
Susan	29 f			
Janice	3 f	GIMMELS, Calvin D, i & b fdr 1500/2K	25 m NY	
Caroline	1 f VA	Elizabeth	28 f EG	
222-1711		Allen	1 m VA	
		31-198		
GEORGE, Colin, laborer 600/200	53 m			
Jane	50 f	GLASCOCK, George, huckster	56 m	
Cornelia	23 f	Amelia	44 f	
Joseph	7 m	Henry, bricklayer	20 m	
282-2158		Florida	14 f	
		49-344		
GEORGE, Isaac, retired merch -/1200	70 m	GLASCOE, Lenins, laborer	38 m	
Elizabeth	27 f VA	Emily	28 f	
19-109		Henry	2 m	
		Daniel	7 m	
GERMANN, Michael, baker 2500/250	45 m BV	220-1694		
Catharine	36 f			
Catharine	15 f VA	GLASCOW, Milton, RR conductor -/100	31 m MD	
George	12 m	Emily	30 f	
Daniel	6 m	Infant	2/12 m	
Henry	3 m	ATWELL, Susan	50 f	
HEBBNER, Henry, baker	32 m HP	Milton Michelle	12 m	
Louise	23 f MD	75-525		
BAKER, Phebe	12 f			
SWOPE, John, laborer	25 m HD	GOINS, Calvin, laborer 600/200	53 m	
126-922		Jane	50 f	
		Cornelia	23 f	
GIBBS, Mary -/100	54 f	Joseph	7 m	
Mary	23 f	282-2158		

ALEXANDRIA VIRGINIA 1860 CENSUS

GOINS, Henry, laborer	27 m	
Sarah	26 f	
Susan	4 f	
Emma	3 f	
George	2 m	
Thomas	3/12 m	
282-2160		
GOINS, John	50 m	
Susan	49 f	
282-2159		
GOLDING, Henry B, farmer -/150	53 m NY	
Jane	52 f	
Harrison, laborer	21 m	
Nathaniel	18 m	
Perceval	10 m	
Frank	8 m	
255-1984		
GODDARD, Amos, RR engineer -/150	35 m PA	
Maria	22 f NY	
Ellenora	10/12 f VA	
Lewis, bridge builder	24 m	
141-1035		
GOODHAND, Nathan(M),ms sh cp 1500/300	57 m MD	
Caroline	39 f	
George, ship carpenter	26 m	
Elmira	20 f	
Virginia	18 f	
William	12 m	
BERRY, Patsey (B)	24 f	
232-1793		
GOODRICH, Francis, laborer -/30	40 m	
Martha	30 f	
Josephene	13 f	
George	3 m	
BOTEMORE, Elizabeth	13 f VA	
184-1400		
GOODRIDGE, Wm W, farmer -/80	46 m MA	
Irene	38 f	
Charles, carter	18 m	
William	16	
Edmund	12 m	
Vim.na	10 f	
Willes	7 m	
Kitty	4 f	
Alice	2 f	
164-1223		
GOODS, Jas C, council messenger	56 m VA	
Elizabeth	57 f	
Mary E	26 f	
Benjamin, machinist	22 m	
Geo A	20 m	
DAVIS, Rosene (M), domestic	16 f	
GOODS, Elizabeth	12 f	
102-754		

GOODWIN, Mary F, seamstress -/25	37 f	
SHERWOOD, John A, appren printer	15 m	
Mary	13 f	
Joshua	10 m	
Thomas	6 m	
78-555		
GORDON, Elizabeth H	75 f	
Caroline	35 f	
84-606		
GORDON, John T, lawyer -/1K	30 m	
75-534		
GORMON, Edward, laborer	38 m IR	
Bridgett	30 f	
Patrick, appren cabinet maker	18 m	
Margaret	7 f VA	
Michael, laborer	28 m IR	
82-583		
GORSAGE, Reason, carpenter -/50	41 m VA	
Catharine	24 f	
David	19 m	
128-937		
GOSLIN, Lewis, sailor	33 m	
Sarah	23 f	
Ada	5 f	
Infant	5/12 m	
231-1783		
GOVER, Anthony P, pres fire co 3K/10K	73 m	
Mary	35 f	
Cornelia	30 f	
BLACK, Lucy (B)	50 f	
Mary (M)	10 f	
171-1280		
GOWOOD, Saml M, mail contr 10K/1K	39 m NJ	
Elizabeth	37 f	
Emma	14 f	
Mary	12 f	
Frank	8 m	
Eliza	5 f	
Sally	2 f	
140-1029		
GRAHAM, Chas, grocer 10K/1K	70 m IR	
Elizabeth	50 f	
George	23 m VA	
Mary	21 f IR	
WELSH, Annie	16 f VA	
50-351		
GRAHAM, Jas W, carpenter 800/100	38 m	
Margaret	38 f	
Mary	40 f	
James	5 m	
Edgar	2 m	
45-307		

ALEXANDRIA VIRGINIA 1860 CENSUS

GRAHAM, John, kerosene Man 5k/1K	52 m PR	Virginia	25 f	
Mary	40 f	Indiana	23 f	
Henry	12 m	Stephen	21 m	
Charles	9 m	Aline	19 f	
Mary	12 f	Emma	13 f	
251-1950		Minnie	4 f	
		Sally	2 f	
GRATTAN, James R, laborer	23 m	STALLY, Andrew, machinist	32 m DC	
Ann	21 f	Louise	32 f	
James	1 m	WHEATLY, Wm	23 m	
231-1788		223-1719		
GRATY, Sarah, gardner -/1K	30 f VA	GRAY, Jenny (B)	26 f	
William	13 m	Jimmy (M)	5 m	
Hester	11 f	Ella (B)	2 f	
Jane	9 f	13-71		
Grigsby	7 m			
Eliza	5 f	GRAY, John, laborer	49 m	
247-1924		Susan	53	
		Rebecca	17 f	
GRAVES, Jas W, toll keeper 500/200	29 m	276-2125		
Emily	20 f			
Alice	6 f	GRAY, John	50 m MD	
Emily	3 f	Jane	50 f	
MILLS, Clarence	14 m	Becca	16 f	
273-2098		270-2086		
GRAY, Albert W, gr & comm merch -/18K	29 m VA	GRAY, John, sailor -/250	58 m	
Matilda	29 f	Ann	35 f	
Charles D	6 m	Loudonia	21 f	
Henrietta	5 f	179-1340		
James T	4 m			
TAYLOR, Susan	17 f	GRAY, John R, watchman -/50	29 m VA	
105-777		Julia	30 f	
		Laura	2 f	
GRAY, Alfred (M), laborer	27 m	Bushrod, waiter	14 m	
Marion (B)	22 f	Lucian	10 m	
Jane (B)	4 f	Chas	8 m	
Cornelia (B)	2 f	BROADUS, Saml, boss cotton mill	30 m EG	
Hillman (B)	10/12 m	BETTELL, Jenny	73 f VA	
WEEKS, Ellen (B)	60 f	91-656		
THORNTON, Frances (B), domestic	15 f			
239-1850		GRAY, Martin (B)	30 f	
		Alice (M)	9 f	
GRAY, Asher W, whsale grocer -/30K	42 m	Jane (M)	7 m	
Martha	37 f	George (M)	1 m	
John	16 m	239-1851		
Newton	12 m			
Lallah	10 f	GRAY, Martha (B)	30 f	
Robt A	7 m	Alice (M)	9 f	
Bettie S	4 f	Jane (M)	7 m	
ROACH, Adalaie, domestic	18 f	George (M)	1 m	
DAVIS, Ann (M), domestic	35 f	239-1851		
105-775				
		GRAY, Mary (M), pie baker -/50	60 f	
GRAY, Charles, fisherman -/75	34 m	John (M), dining room st	16 m VA	
Henrietta	26 f	Franklin (M)	11 m	
Laura	6 f	Matilda (M)	8 f	
73-512		Martha (M)	2 f	
		Mary (M)	2 f	
GRAY, James, fisherman -/100	63 m	Wesley (M), brickmaker	24 m	
Susan	42 f	150-1113		

ALEXANDRIA VIRGINIA 1860 CENSUS

GRAY, Nelly (B)	45 f	Maggie	27 f	
Ann (B)	30 f	Major	5/12 m	
28-176		Jas E	22 m	
		Annie	19 f	
GRAY, Wm (M), butcher 1700/250	28 m	Lydia	18 f	
Laura (M)	27 f	Emma	16 f	
Sarah (M)	13 f	GREEN, C W, druggist	23 m	
DOZAN, George (M), appren	14 m	GILBERT, E L, clerk RR office	23 m	
153-1133		JANNEY, I J	25 m	
		CLAGGETT, P A, bookkeeper	24 m	
GRAYSON, Thos (M), laborer -/200	27 m	WITHERS, Littleton, clerk	23 m	
Sarah (M)	25 f	GRADY, F J, clerk	19 m	
John F (M)	8 m	HILL, G P, merchant	22 m	
Susan (M)	4 f	BARLEY, Wm H, hardware merch	28 m	
Thomas (M)	2 m	WARD, H C, comm merch	27 m	
40-266		WITHERS, John, banker	84 m	
		STEUART, Mrs	25 f	
		Frank	7	
GREEN, Cathy, seamstress	44 f	WHARTON, ..., RR engineer	48 m	
136-998		HILL, H J, lawyer	33 m	
		AGNEW, . J, coal agent	35 m	
GREEN, Ed, RR 3K/400	75 m EG	ENGLEBRIGHT, J C, music teacher	43 m GR	
Ann	50 f	Carrie	8 f	
Louis, RR clerk	31 m	FLOTTINGHAM, Geo, clerk	30 m	
Ursula	19 f	WILLYTON, Mrs	25 f	
Jane	17 f	FOWLE, Susan	70 F MA	
Eliza D	15 f	SMITH, John C, RR construction	25 m	
Sarah A	13 f	FULLER, Martin, stuart	30 m IR	
203-1559		EVANS, John, bookkeeper	20 m EG	
		GRACE, George, telegraph appren	21 m NY	
GREEN, Elizabeth, var store 2500/2K	52 f MD	PERRY, Thomas, comm merch	30 m MD	
James F, clerk comm	21 m VA	BARBER, J, pres of O & A RR	39 m VA	
Elizabeth	17 f	ROGERS, William, bookkeeper	65 m	
HASLIP, Mary E	51 f MD	Jane	40 f	
113-838		Pendleton	17 m	
		Monie	13 f	
GREEN, George, laborer	36 m	FELL, C W, clerk	25 m	
Biddy	28 f IR	HUMPHEYS, A, bookkeeper	32 m	
May	4 f VA	PRITCHARD, A P, mail agent	24 m	
George	2 m	PLACIDE, M P, RR construction	24 m MD	
230-1777		McCLAIN, R A, clerk court	27 m VA	
		BREWIS, T A, comm merch 500/5K	32 m EG	
		NOVALL, J B, RR engineer	28 m VA	
GREEN, George Henry, shoemaker -/400	30 m	COLLINS, Sarah, pastry cook	28 f	
Martha	27 f	THEUWELL, Mrs	30 f EG	
Laura	8 f	CAWOOD, Samuel, porter	21 m VA	
James	6 m	FALLES, R W, express agent	27 m MD	
Ada	2 f	Jane	25 f	
192-1462		Bessie	6 f VA	
		POTHAM, Mary E	57 f	
GREEN, Hannah	68 f	STEWART, Geo L, bookkeeper	33 m	
FERRELL, Ellen	54 f	Susan	18 f	
74-517		BARRES, Kate	21 f	
		DAVIS, John Anna, washerwoman	25 f	
GREEN, James, hotel keeper 200K/20K	58 m EG	Bordgett	40 f	
Jane	56 f	Ellen	25 f	
John M, cabinet maker	36 m	JENY, Mary M	40 f	
Fanny	26 f	NEVELL, Bridgett, chambermaid	20 f	
William	6 m	SUFTWICH, J, vestry minister	28 m	
Katie	4 f	Julia	21 f	
James J	8/12 m	FOERTCH, J C, music teacher	28 m	
Stephen A	29 m	GOLDSBOROUGH, J M, civil engineer	39 m MD	

ALEXANDRIA VIRGINIA 1860 CENSUS

HOPKINS, Daniel (M)	19 m		Alice	12 f
COLLINS, Rosa, chambermaid	21 f IR		CANNON, Cassen	60 f
7/8/9-46			GAHAGAN, Mary	67 f IR
			134-981	
GREEN, John, shoemaker	53 m			
Mary J	47 f		GREGG, Jas, laborer	25 m IR
Sarah E	26 f		283-2168	
John, shoemaker	22 m			
Anne	18 f		GREGG, Joseph, grocer -/11K	67 m EG
Mary	14 f		Mary	37 f
Kate	10 f		Jane	33 f
Maranda	8 f		Samuel, grocer	31 m
Richard	6 m		32-205	
35-225				
GREEN, John W, cabinet ftry 12K/6500	33 m		GREGORY, Douglas, dry goods merch	34 m
Fanny	27 f CN		133-975	
James	5 m			
Kate	4 f		GREGORY, E H, turner -/500	34 m NY
Willie	4/12 m		Esther	30 f
179-1341			Chas	7 m
			Fred	5 m
GREEN, Mary 1200/150	50 f		Walter	3 m
Sarah	60 f MD		JETTET, Maria	50 f NY
GA.NT, Agnes (B), domestic	62 f VA		125-916	
225-1737				
			GREGORY, Samuel F, clerk	43 m MA
GREENWAY, Nevill, Meth Prot minister	36 m EG		Isabella	27 f VA
Ann	34 f		Arthur	5 m
Annie	10 f PA		HAMILTON, Maria	45 f
Emma	7 f MD		62-438	
Nevill	4/12 m VA			
DAVIS, Eugen (B), domestic	15 f			
115-847			GREGORY, Wm, bank pres 100K/10K	70 m ST
			Mary D	48 f MD
GREENWOOD, A J, carpenter -/50	32 m		Wm B, physician	80 m VA
Catharine	63 f		Isabella	20 f
Edward	32 m		Julia	18 f
Rescote, laborer	36 m		Mary	13 f
Rebecca	24 f		Jesse	8 f
MYERS, May	85 f		84-605	
187-1420				
			GRIER, Geo, laborer	36 m
GREENWOOD, John, laborer	32 VA		Biddy	28 f IR
Ellen	29 f		May	6 f
William	6 m		Gerr	2 m
SAVAGE, Julia, seamstress	19 f		230-1777	
231-1782				
			GRIFFIN, James, lime burner -/40	39 m MD
GREENWOOD, John B, carpenter 1500/10	56 m		Elizabeth	38 f
Mary	52 f		William	29 m
OGDEN, George, shoemaker	35 m		Emma	10 f
Mary	27 f		James	4 m
Sarah	1 f		John	2 m
GREENWOOD, Chas, carter	23 m		194-1475	
72-502				
			GRIFFIN, John, printer -/50	24 m
GREGG, Ann	48 f		Alvira?	24 f
Henry, printer -/300	21 m		Mary	5 f
Joseph, tailor	18 m		John	3 m
John, clerk bookstore	16 m		Charles	2 m
Curson	16 m		220-1700	

ALEXANDRIA VIRGINIA 1860 CENSUS

GRIFFIN, Pat, laborer	36 m		GRIMES, Susan	50 f
Nancy	45 f		Rose, cotton mill	18 f
94-680			Michael	11 m
			Nancy	7 f
GRIFFIN, Robert, sailor -/30	39 m VA		90-651	
Jane	39 f			
Charles	73 m		GRIMES, Wm, shoemaker 2K/300	60 m
Louise	11 f		Jane	36 f
James	7 m		Isaac	10 m
THURSTON, Sarah J	21 f		Jane	7 f
181-1377			Bettie	
			Johnston	2 m
GRIFFITH, Kinzey, gun smith 900/200	37 m		213-1637	
Phebe	35 f			
William	11 m		GRIMSLY, Albert, omnibus agent -/100	40 m
108-799			Juliana	33 f
			IVEN, James, omnibus driver	25 m
			HUTCHISON, Mary	8 f
GRIFFITH, Mary A -/3300	55 f		81-580	
Greenberry, machinist	22 m			
108-798			GRUBB, Jas H, clerk comm merch -/1K	37 m
			GIVENS, George (M), domestic	45 m
GRIFFITH, Sally 5K/600	70 f		Caroline (M)	45 f
Mary Hoxton	13 f		104-767	
Winslow	12 m			
GRIFFITH, Elizabeth	53 f		GUNNELS, Calvin D, i & b fdr 1500/100	25 m NY
Eleanor	17 f		Elizabeth	23 f EG
25-145			Allen	1 m VA
			31-198	
GRIGSBY, Robert -/50	62 m			
Margaret	37 f		GURLOCK, John, shoemaker	25 m GR
Sarah	12 f		Mary	30 f
Virginia	11 f		Annie	3 f
William	8 m		Charles	1 m
Mary	6 f		191-1453	
252-1958				
GRIMES, Chas, ms carpenter 1400/112	46 m		GUY, Chas, fisherman -/75	36 m VA
Sarah	35 f		Hennietta	24 f
William	17 m		Laura	6 f
74-524			73-512	
GRIMES, James G, huckster -/50	48 m		GUY, Jas, fisherman -/100	63 m
Ann	50 f		Susan	42 f
James	17 m		Virginia	25 f
John	14 m		Indiana	23 f
Lucretia	11 f		Stephen	21 m
HERNDON, Mary, domestic	20 f		Alice	19 f
44-297			Emma	13 f
			Minnie	6 f
			Sally	2 f
GRIMES, Joseph, comm merch 1500/3K	52 m		STALLY, Andrew, machinist	32 m DC
Margaret	57 f		Louise	32 f VA
Aura E	25 f		WHEATLY, Wm	23 m
James, machinist	23 m		223-1719	
Catharine	19 f			
PLAINE, John	11 m			
ANTHONY, James, miller	25 m MD		GWINN, David, comm merch -/20K	51 m VA
ANTHONY, Mrs	25 f		Frances F	45 f
Willec	9/12 m		Thomas, comm merch	23 m
O'NEAL, John, drayman	29 m MA		Fanny D	19 f
Mary	26 f		Mary	16 f
182-1383			Oreble?	14 f

ALEXANDRIA VIRGINIA 1860 CENSUS

```
    Lavice                        13 f    HALL, Geo, RR foreman -/100    22 m
    George                         2 m        Martha                    21 f
66-464                                         Diana                     2 f
                                           40-264
HACKETT, Dennis (M)              76 m
    Amy (B)                      50 f    HALL, Joshua, shoemaker -/100   60 m MD
237-1835                                      Thomas, house carpenter    30 m
                                              Harriet                    4 f
HAGHY, Samuel (B)                45 m         William, appren apothecary 19 m
196-1494                                      Augustus, ambrotype appren 17 m
                                           219-1690
HALBUT, Ed W, shoemaker -/200    43 m MD
    Elizabeth                    42 f MD  HALL, Littleton S, cartman -/150  40 m
    Laura                        23 f         Caroline                  37 f
    Emma                         16 f         George                    16 m
    Aurnba                       12 f         Charles                   12 m
    James                        10 m         Joseph                    10 m
    Sarah                         7 f         Frank                      8 m
    John                          5 m         Virgin..                   3 f
    Chas R                        3 m         Edward                     1 m
130-946                                    243-1887

HALL, Alfred, blacksmith         28 m    HALL, Maria, wash & iron        30 f
    Ann                          28 f        Densley                     2 m
45-309                                     48-332

HALL, Andrew, cartman 800/100    30 m    HALL, Mary                      58 f MD
    Nancy                        31 f        John, cooper                25 m VA
    Mallan                        9 f        Margaret                    21 f
    James                         6 m        James, clerk                18 m
    Geo                           3 m     48-333
40-265
                                         HALL, Rachael (B)                8 f
HALL, Basil, farmer 10K/1500     48 m DC BLACK, Clara (B)                60 f
    Frances                      23 f    173-1294
    Ignatius                     12 m
    Elvira                        7 f    HALL, Rhoda                     63 f
    Lau...                        2 f        Mary, weaver                16 f
    MERCHANT, Thomas             65 m    214-1649
253-1968
                                         HALLOWELL, Benjamin 22800/1100  63 m
HALL, Chafers, fisherman         49 m        Margaret                    60 f
    Susana                       56 f        Mary                        19 f
245-1904                                     DUMAS, Margaret, domestic   30 f IR
                                         51-357
HALL, Eliza (M)                  37 f
    Mary (B)                     20 f    HALLOWELL, Caleb, teacher 12K/2K  42 m PA
    Emma (B)                     16 f        Ainice                     43 f
    Jane (B)                    8/12 f        Mary                       19 f VA
    Margaret (M)                6/12 f        Charles                    17 m
127-929                                       Emma                       12 f
                                              STEVENS, Harriet, housekeeper 30 f
HALL, Elizabeth                  30 f    198-1517
    John                         12 m
    James                         3 m    HALLOWELL, Jas, teacher 11K/1500  39 m PA
234-1803                                      Margaret                   35 f MD
                                              Edward S                   12 m VA
HALL, Fanny (M), midwife         38 f         Annie                      10 f
    John (B), laborer            19 m         Alice                       7 f
    Caroline (M)                 12 f         James                       5 m
    Sarah (B)                     8 f         Julia                       1 f
118-868                                       LEE, Elizabeth, tailoress  40 f PA
```

ALEXANDRIA VIRGINIA 1860 CENSUS

SHIPLY, Ensley J, tailoress	22	f	NY	HAMPSON, Joseph, clk comm merch -/200	60	m
RHOAN, Sally, domestic	20	f	IR	Julia	57	f
GILPIN, Rachael	55	f	VA	SAMPSON, Julia	18	f
Fanny M	18	f	MD	McDOYAL, Sarah	70	f
65-463				GREEN, Geo King, shoemaker	30	m
				Martha	27	f
HALST, Garret, grocer -/4K	49	m	NY	Laura	8	f
16-90				James	6	m
				Ada	2	f
HAMILTON, Philip (B)	77	m		192-1462		
Catharine (B)	77	f				
Catharine (B)	18	f		HANCOCK, John B, constable 1100/150	62	m VA
Benjamin (B)	10	m		Mary	59	f
237-1833				209-1601		
HAMMEL, Henry, shoemaker 250/50	45	m		HANDELLY, Betty	47	f IR
Bridgett	35	f		Michael	19	m
CONARY, Henry, laborer	18	m		Peter, teamster	16	m
CUNNINGHAM, Martin	50			Ellen	13	f
HASKIN, Dennis	45	m		98-717		
70-492						
				HANEY, Heji, laborer	49	m
HAMMEL, Patrick, shoemaker	35	m IR		Lenora	45	f
Bridgett	29	f		Mary	17	f
John	9	m VA		William	11	m
Kate	8	f		Vincent	8	m
George M	9/12	m		Eliza	4	f
RYAN, Kate, domestic	40	f IR		221-1704		
MITCHELL, Geo, shoemaker	25	m				
ROHAN, John	40	m		HANNOCK, Benjamin, shoemaker -/75	42	m MA
WANTON, William, shoemaker	37	m IR		Mary	36	f VA
64-456				William	3	m
				John F	2/12	m
HAMMER, Benj, farmer	45	m		107-793		
Emily	42	f				
Martha	19	f				
May	17	f		HARLIN, Michael, laborer -/30	50	m IR
Rachael	15	f		Ann	34	f
.arr	14	m		Michael	13	m
Kithston	10	f		Margaret	9	f
John	8	m		Maria	3	f
Joseph	6	m		72-503		
Benjamin	3	m				
Emily	2	f		HARMAN, Allen C, grocer -/210	40	m ME
BROWN, Henry (M), laborer	23	m		Margaret	40	f
267-2064				Mary	16	f
				Virginia	14	f
HAMMERSLY, Jas, carter 1K/300	60	m		Annie	12	f
Eliza	27	f		Thomas	10	m VA
Mary A	8	f		Maggie	8	f
William	5	m		Jane	5	m
John	3	m		Loucie	2	f
40-268				73-515		
HAMMOND, James, pilot -/50	52	m EG		HARMAN, Daniel, whsale shoe 2K/300	33	m
Eliza	37	f		Mary E	28	f
James	18	m		Chas	6	m
Annie	15	f		Mary	4	f
Savinia	14	f		Eliza	2	f
Mary	10	f		Daniel	10/12	m
John	7	m		DAVIS, Mary (B), domestic	10	f
230-1780				1120-828		

52

ALEXANDRIA VIRGINIA 1860 CENSUS

HARPER, Ann E 1K/400	55 f MD		William	18 m
Edgar, farmer 800/-	23 m VA		BOYER, Susan	61 f
Jno W	6		231-1787	
Mary A	32 f			
OWENINGS, Jesse	24 m MD		HARRIS, Jas, laborer	31 m MD
Carrie	26 f		Ann	30 f
130-948			257-1991	
HARPER, Geo G, tailor -/500	45 m		HARRIS, Louise	31 f
Elizabeth	43 f		HARRIS, James, blacksmith	41 m
George W	23 m		GRANALE, Emma	12 f
Washington	21 m		WILSON, Frances	12 f
Hiram	13 m		185-1407	
Anthony	8 m			
Henry	6 m		HARRIS, R W, clerk hardware -/150	32 m VA
116-856			Mary	30 f PA
			JANNY, A D	57 f
HARPER, Newton, grocer 10K/3K	37 m		Eliza	23 f
Sarah F	35 f		Sallie	21 f MD
Mary	13 f		HOPKINS, John, clerk hardware	20 m VA
Ruberta	3 f		MEHT, Frances	17 f
106-781			170-1271	
HARPER, Rachael (B), huckster	40 f VA		HARRIS, Thomas, blacksmith	32 m IR
Clara (B), wash & rion	21 f		Bridgett	25 f
Catharine (B), domestic	21 f		Francis	6 m
Mary (B), domestic	15 f		John	4 m
Thomas (B)	11 m		Thommy	2 m
Eva (B)	6 f		38-244	
Ella (B)	8 f			
Mark (M)	6 m		HARRIS, Walter, grocer 4K/1700	63 m
David (B)	4 m		Julia Ann	50 f
Laura (B)	1 f		VIRSON, Mary	21 f VA
137-1004			ATKINS (M), laborer	19 m
			147-1082	
HARPER, Samuel, cigar maker	39 m			
Martha	33 f		HARRISON, Joshua, carpenter 1400/50	38 m MD
John, appren broom maker	15 m		Mary	33 f
Washington, cotton spinner	11 m		John T	15 m
Ida	5 f		George	12 m
37-238			Rosina	10 f
			Sarah	5 f VA
HARPER, Sarah 1500/2K	75 f		MILLER, Lucretia	65 f MD
Ellen	33 f		79-562	
Samuel, dry good merch -/3K	31 m			
GARNETT, Sally	26 f		HARTLEY, Samuel, comm merch	65 m BR
Muscoe	3 m		Rachel	60 f MD
Samuel	1 m		Ephraim, clerk	22 m
120-883			...ig	16 f
			JOHNSTON, Maria (B)	60 f
			18-101	
HARPER, W W, dry good store 5K/2K	50 m			
Isabella	30 f			
John	12 m		HARTLEY, Thomas -/30	54 m
Frank	7 m		Catharine	45 f
Margaret	5 f		James	19 m
E.ier	3 f		Ann, carter	16 f
120-882			Margaret	8 f
			DUNN, Anthony, laborer	31 m
HARRIS, Geo W, bookkeeper 800/100	52 m		Mary	22 f
Eliza	50 f		97-709	
Elizabeth	18 f			

ALEXANDRIA VIRGINIA 1860 CENSUS

HARTLY, Mark	50 m EG		Georgiana (B)	10 f	
Elizabeth	49 f		Silena (B)	? f	
James	12 m		Mary (B)	5 f	
Mark	9 m		Robert (B)	4 m	
264-2050			208-1595		
HARVEY, Henry, tailer -/400	33 m		HAYS, Jere, laborer	25 m IR	
Margaret	32 f		Johanna	26 f	
Susan	9 f		Patrick	1 m VA	
Jane	8 f		BRYAN, Jas	23 m VA	
Mollie	5 f		139-1022		
Infant	1 m				
187-1422			HAYS, Julia	36 f	
			Thomas, clerk	16 m	
HARVEY, Lydia (B), wash & iron	50 f		William, folder c...	14 m	
David (B)	5 m		Julia	6 f	
141-1037			GORDON, John T, lawyer -/1K	30 m	
			75-534		
HARVEY, Rachael (B), wash & iron	29 f				
Elizabeth (B)	11 f		HAYS, Meliena	48 f	
Joshuia (B)	10 m		Anna	16 f	
Lewis (B)	7 m		Money	14 f	
Henry (B)	4 m		Alonzo	11 m	
208-1593			Douglas	7 m	
			263-2037		
HARYDEN, John -/250	36 m				
Elizabeth	21 f VA		HAYS, Patrick, grocer -/50	50 m IR	
John	4 m		Margaret	50 f	
Samuel	1 m		Thomas, drayman	22 m	
233-1801			Margaret	10 f	
			89-642		
HAUMNERDWIGER, John, baker -/600	52 m HD				
Maria	45 f VA		HAYSON, Lou... (M)	40 f	
William, plasterer	23 m		John (B), laborer	26 m	
Fannie	21 f		Isaac (B)	23 m	
Julia	16 f		Samuel (B)	22 m	
Emma	13 f		Li (B)	20 f	
PASCAL, Rebecca	68 f		Martha (B)	12 f	
29-179			Chas (B)	7 m	
			Eliza (B)	5 f	
HAUTZMAN, Henry, gas house -/75	69 m MD		Jonah (M)	3 m	
Elizabeth	60 f		Infant (B)	9/12 f	
Robert, fireman RR	29 m		254-1979		
Joseph, carpenter	22 m				
Elizabeth	26 f		HAYWOOD, M J	50 f	
George, shoemaker	22 m		Jas W, laborer	20 m	
Hannah	19 f		John W	16 m	
RICHARD, George, carter	29 m		George Henry	8 m	
JOHNSTON, Wm H	15 m		207-1585		
Caroline	13 f				
Mary	25 f		HAZZARD, Sarah -/30	55 f VA	
71-499			Eliza, seamstress	24 f	
			BEAIHAN, Susan	16 f	
HAUTZMAN, William H, gas fitter -/10	38 m		189-1449		
Mary	27 f MD				
Chas	4 m VA		HEARSE, Nancy, wash & iron	35 f	
Virginia	2 f		180-1349		
TODD, Emma	18 f				
71-500			HEART, Jno, pump maker 4K/1K	33 m EG	
			Betsy	60 f VA	
HAWKINS, Robert (B), ostler -/30	38 m		WOOD, Jno, appren	17 m	
Henson (B)	37 f		MITCHELL, Dolly (M), domestic	21 f	

ALEXANDRIA VIRGINIA 1860 CENSUS

Joseph (M)	5 m	MADDOX, Elizabeth	16 f
HEART, Jno, clerk -/1K	22 m	HOFFMAN, P E, bank cashier	55 m VA
180-1348		TALIFERO, H D, clerk	26 m
		ROBINSON, R H P	26 m
HEART, John, laborer	36 m IR	WISE, C J, grocer 800/1K	25 m
Mary	34 f	HUNT, D, shoemaker	25 m ME
168-1258		PARKERSON, J	23 m
		ALT, S, die sinker germ	25 m
HEART, Wm A, druggist	36 m	9/10-47	
Julia	68 f		
Sarah	35 f	HELLMUTH, Jacob, butcher -/600	29 m BD
Jane	34 f	Catharine	27 f
Henry, grocery clerk	30 m	Willie	3 m
JOURDAN, J P, drug clerk	16 m	Charles	7/12 m
122-893		BAUBACK, Ann	18 f BD
		HELLMUTH, Peter	13 m
HEATH, John, cabinet maker -/50	33 m	212-1628	
Ann	29 f		
John	9 m	HEMIK, Geo R, genl? agent 1500/500	46 m VT
Millie	7 f	Harriet	41 f PA
Edward	5 m	Augusta	21 f NY
Mary	3 f	Lewis C	12 m DC
George	2 m	SMITH, Joseph (B), domestic	20 m
189-1445		261-2023	
HEATH, Leona (M)	76 m	HEMMERSLY, William, farmer 800/630	39 m
141-1036		James, livery keeper	18 m
		SIMPSON, Adaline, house keeper	35 f
HEFLEBOWER, Samuel, hotelkpr 12K/10K	50 m PA	30-194	
Elizabeth	48 f		
Bettie	16 f	HENDERSON, Chas, laborer	31 m
Willela	14 f	Alberta	25 f
TAYLOR, J C, RR construc	30 m	Evaline	7 f
CROSS, James	50 m	Stephen	4 m
LYNN, M D, RR construc	28 m	Jane R	2 f
LUCY, Henry, bridge builder	33 m NY	109-808	
BORFFEY, John E, clerk	35 m		
MANN, W H, mail agent	?? m	HENDERSON, John E, grocer 12K/7K	49 m
AVERETT, Wm H, mail agent	25 m	Emily	45 f
ROSE, W F, mail agent	22 m	Sarah E	24 f
WORTHLIFFE, A J, clerk	73 m	John T, grocer clerk	23 m
BRENT, A M	21 m	Annie	20 f
BLEURO, James, clerk	27 m	William	19 m
Sally F	22 f	Harriet	17 f
Ross	2 m	James	15 m
Infant	2/12 m	Jenny	13 f
BLYTHE, W, super RR	50 m	Ada	11 f
Mary	45 f	Julia M	? m
Susan	18 f	Cora	7 f
MARSHALL, John, lawyer	28 m VA	BARKER, H S W, grocer 4K/4K	39 m VA
DOGLE, Kate	18 f	136-995	
HENTON, R H, liquor dealter	38 m VA		
ICHBECK, J, clothier	30 m GR	HENDERSON, Julia	42 f
ROSENTHAL, J, shoe dealer	29 m	George, bricklayer	25 m
ROSENTHAL, E	20 m	Frances	13 f
AVERY, J Q, clerk	28 m MD	George	10 m
GURTLE, J L, clerk	26 m VA	49-341	
ADAMS, J H, clerk	26 m VA		
McGUIRE, M G, physician	25 m	HENDERSON, Peter, ms brickmason -/113	52 m
POWER, G F, clerk	23 m NY	Elizabeth	52 f
Julia	17 f	Alanda, brickmason	21 m
MADDOX, Jane	45 f KY	Amelia Kams	13 f

ALEXANDRIA VIRGINIA 1860 CENSUS

Ida	10 f	Mary	19 f IR
Jane	27 f	Bridgett, domestic	16 f
LEONARD, Maggie, domestic	17 f	Mathew	6 m VA
McNEAR, Jane (M), domestic	10 m	29-181	
73-513			
		HEPBURN, Anderson (M), cook	50 m
HENING, Geo W, carpenter -/100	21 m MD	John (M), laborer	24 m
Martha	25 f	Elizabeth (M)	18 f
Ida	4 f	68-475	
Willie	2 m		
GREENWOOD, Eliza	18 f	HERNDON, Jacob, carpenter -/150	32 m
GREENWOOD, Jay	13 m MD	Elizabeth	31 f
27-164		Rebecca	5 f
		2-10	
HENRY, A, laborer	34 m IR		
Ann	46 m	HERRICK, George R, genrl agt 1500/500	44 m VT
Bryan	16 m	Harriet	41 f PA
Larry	16 m MD	Augusta	21 f NY
James	11 m VA	Lewis C	12 m DC
Alexander	9 m	SMITH, Joseph (B), domestic	20 m
William	6 m	261-2023	
93-676			
		HERRISH, Wm T, harness maker -/600	34 m
HENRY, Gerry (B), blacksmith	54 m	145-1066	
Sarah (M)	46 f		
Albert (B), brickmaker	24 m		
Sarah (M)	18 f	HERRSING, Lewis, broom factory -/500	33 m
Margaret (B)	14 f	Magdelene	30 f
Laura (B)	19 f	WHITFIELD, Thos, broom maker	18 m
Lizzie (B)	12 f	HERRSING, Awdrey	63 f
Gertrude (B)	10 f	WHITFIELD, Sarah	16 f
Garey (B)	8 m	125-913	
Clara (B)	6 f		
... (B)	2 f	HEUSON, Evaline (B)	33 f
WEST, Chas (B), laborer	35 m	Ellen (B)	1 f
274-2110		131-955	
HENRY, George W, carpenter -/100	28 m MD	HEUSON, Henry (B)	26 m
Martha	25 f VA	Ellen (B)	24 f
Ida	4 f	Henry (B)	3 m
Willie	2 m	Infant (B)	3/12 m
GREENWOOD, Eliza	18 f	Charles (B)	8 m
GREENWOOD, Jay	13 m MD	48-328	
27-164			
		HEWBERRY, Wm, blacksmith	28 m IR
HENRY, Maria (B)	42 m	Jane	25 f
196-1491		98-724	
HENRY, Robert, house carpenter	45 m	HICKS, John F, laborer	45 m
224-1729		Sally	35 f
		Thomas	16 m
HENRY, Sophia (M), wash & iron -/20	60 f VA	Benjamin	12 m
Rebecca	25 f	Thorton	6 m
136-993		Reuben	3 m
		266-2058	
HENRY, William, laborer	30 m IR		
Isabella	30 f ST		
Martha	5 f VA	HICKS, Nehemiah, grocer	60 m MD
91-657		Elizabeth	58 f VA
		George, grocer clerk	21 m
HEOCH, Ann	40 f IR	Elizabeth	19 f
COXTON, Henry, butcher	25 m VA	188-1427	

ALEXANDRIA VIRGINIA 1860 CENSUS

HIGDON, Mary A -/100	30 f VA	HODKIN, T D, wheelwright 500/600	29 m VA
Julian	7 m	Mary E	23 f
Sarah	5 f	Chas E	2 m
Kate	3 f	Ida S	6/12 f
FRANKLIN, Sarah	71 f	SMITH, Sarah	25 f
89-641		PARSONS, Franklin, appren	15 m DC
		53-373	
HIGDON, Wm J, house painter -/50	43 m		
Eliza	17 f	HOEINSTEIN, Fred, farmer 1K/150	55 m FK
Bernard	14 m	Rachael	56 f BD
Wm Posey	10 m	Fred, farmer	23 m VA
Rebeca	70 f	Mary	13 f
156-1155		281-2150	
		HOGAN, Richard, carpenter -/50	59 m MD
HILL, J P, ambrotypist 2K/100	33 m	Jerianna	59 f
Elvira	33 f MD	James T, blacksmith	28 m
May	8 f VA	Sarah	27 f
John	7 m	Josaphene	25 f
Francis	5 m	Richard, cotton spinner	20 m
Hugh	1 m	Margarett	19 f
WHITE, Frances (B)	12 f	Mary Ann	15 f
MONROE, John, shoemaker	30 m MD	COURTWELL, Enoch, laborer	26 m
(MARRIOT, John?)		46-317	
219-1688			
		HOGE, Henry, machinist	27 m HN
HIPKINS, Lewis, cabinet maker -/75	39 m	Susan	28 f
Jane	37 f	Clara	2 f
Lewis	17 m	SHANK, Susan	58 f
Mary	10 f	Mat...	15 f
Emma	8 f	245-1905	
Jane	6 f		
Margaret	4 f	HOGE, Michael	36 m IR
Mildred	1 f	Ellen	36 f
83-599		Thomas	10 m
		Peter	5 m VA
HOBSON, Elizabeth, weaver	33 f EG	Mary Ann	4 f
Sarah	16 f MD	Catharine	1 f
Mary	14 f	138-1013	
Caroline	12 f		
John	10 m	HOLBROOK, John, laborer	24 m
Emma	6 f	Alice	24 f
William	8 m	97-712	
88-631			
		HOLBROOK, Michael	29 m
HODGKINS, John, carpenter -/50	40 m	Ann	26 f IR
Mary	39 f	96-705	
Wm H, appren soap maker	16 m DC		
Mary	10 f VA	HOLLENBURG, Jno N, brickmkr 2500/100	54 m
Martha	8 f DC	Julia	45 f
Alice J	4 f	Charlotte	43 f
Susan	2 f	Harriet	40 f
38-251		Frances	38 f
		SHERWOOD, Joseph, blacksmith	39 m
HODKIN, Robert 8K/150	64 m	74-516	
Elizabeth	63 f		
HAMEL, Sarah	60 f	HOLLET, Joseph, machinist -/50	27 m MD
Annie	41 f	Virginia	18 f
Robt	25 f	146-1074	
Roberta	23 f		
Bemone, blacksmith -/450	22 m	HOLLEYHEAD, John, laborer	46 m
53-371		Catharine	41 f

ALEXANDRIA VIRGINIA 1860 CENSUS

```
    Johana                          7 f DC    Julian                           30 f
138-1015                                        WOOD, Nancy (B)                22 f
                                            179-1342
HOLT, Henry E, shoemaker -/50      35 m DC
    Anna H                         33 f MD   HOOFF, Philip H, comm merch 50K/5K  60 m
    Frances                        13 f VA       Elizabeth                    35 f
    Samuel                          7 m           Lucian                       13 m
    Ida W                           3 f           Norman                       10 m
78-553                                            Bettie R                      6 f
                                            182-1382
HOLT, Israel, printer              31 m SC
    Jane                           37 f      HOOK, W W, bridge builder -/100   29 m MD
FISHER, Sally, domestic            12 f VA       Sarah                         29 f
201-1537                                          Richard                       7 m
                                              SANDS, Thomas, blacksmith        20 m
                                              GRANT, Catharine                 86 F VA
HOLTZER, Fred, distiller -/15      31 m BD   152-1122
    Emma                           23 f
    Lewis                          2/12 m
219-1692                                     HOOKER, Levin, shoemaker          28 m
                                                 Virginia                     24 f
HOLLY, Jesse (M), laborer          26 m          Acadenia                      6 f
    Rebecca (M)                    28 f          Eunia                         5 f
46-325                                            Isadora                      4 f
                                                 Andrew                        2 m
HONESTY, Allen (B), farmer         75 m      48-334
    George (B), laborer            18 m
    Daniel (B)                     15 m      HOOPER, John, clerk -/30          29 m
    Frank (B)                      13 m          Kate                         23 m
    Margaret (B)                    9 f      PADGETT, Harriet                  50 f
258-2000                                     30-190

HONESTON, Henry (B), laborer       38 m      HOPKINS, John D
    Martha (B)                     35 f          Sarah                        28 f
    Sally (B)                       7 f          Sarah                        12 f
253-1968                                         Mary C                        9 f
                                                 Ada                           5 f VA
HOOE, Dan T, comm merch 5500/40K   61 m          Lucy                          2 f
    Mary                           61 f      186-1414
    Sarah                          50 f
108-795                                      HOPKINS, Peter (M), laborer       32 m
                                                 Martha (M)                   41 f
                                             WHITING, John (M), waiter         22 m
HOOFF, Charles, cashier bank 3K/700  33 m VA HOPKINS, Dana (M)                 18 m VA
    Rebeca                         31 f          Albert (B)                   17 m
    Lewis                           7 m          Emma (M)                      7 f
    Collien                         5 f          Martha (M)                    8 f
POSEY, Ann, domestic               18 f IR       Alice (M)                     3 f
178-1330                                         Ida (M)                      33 f
                                            164-1221

HOOFF, J W, clerk comm store 1K/300  35 m
    Jannet                         35 f      HORSEMAN, Elijah, watchman -/50   53 m
    Mary                            7 f          Elizabeth                    50 f
    Douglas                         2 m          Joseph                       28 m
127-930                                          Mary E                       24 f
                                                 Ann                          16 f
HOOFF, Mrs John 10K/25K            49 f          Susannah                     14 f
    Mattie                         14 f          Elijah                       12 m
170-1272                                     VERMILLION, Nelson, carpenter     22 m MD
                                             MUNKINS, Edgar, soapmaker         16 m
HOOFF, Lewis, bank teller -/500    60 m      PILES, Kitty, domestic            38 f
    Eliza                          45 f NY       Benjamin                      2 m
```

ALEXANDRIA VIRGINIA 1860 CENSUS

Infant	4/12 f	HOUSE, Richard, carter -/80	57 m VA
VERMILLION, Alice	5 f	Nancy	57 f
41-273		Ann	30 f
		Jno, carpenter	25 m
HORSEMAN, Jas E, farmer 3500/2500	57 m	Charles H, printer	22 m
Ellen	45 f	Caroline	15 f
Robert	20 m	Margaret	3 f
Raymond	16 m	148-1090	
Andrew	14 m		
Amos	5 m	HOWARD, Wm R, ms carpenter 1K/200	43 m VA
Julia	9 f	Martha	38 f
Mary	16 f	Mary	17 f
Ellen	13 f	Ella	11 f
Victoria	8 f	Ida	9 f
273-2103		Chas	5 m
		Alice	2 f
HORTENBURGH, Tobias, grocer 2500/-	67 m NY	WOK, May (B)	10 f
Urselia	32 f	216-1662	
Caramine	22 f		
Cornelia	17 f	HOWDESKELL, Wal, grocer -/100	24 m
32-203		Margaret	19 f
		William	2 m
HOSKINS, George, carter	16 m	NALLS, John, house carpenter	24 m
276-2123		246-1915	
HOUDSHEAR, Bridget	43 f	HOWELL, John, hatter	43 m MD
Patrick, mechanist	19 m	Elizabeth	43 f
May	17 f	John, hatter	21 m
Michael	12 m	Emory, hatter	20 m
John	3 m IR	Mary C	17 f
Patrick Mark	13 m	Francis	15 m
May	14 f MD	Joseph	13 m
178-1328		Purcelia	12 f
		Samuel	8 m
HOUGH, Ed S, coll custm house 2200/2K	45 m	Chas W	5 m
Susan	45 f	Edward	4 m
George	22 f	Elizabeth	9/12 f MD
Harrie	18 m	Pamelia	67 f
Alice	6 f	108-797	
Annie	4 f		
DOGAN, Rose, domestic	18 f IR	HOWELL, Samuel, clerk	29 m
Kate	16 f	Adie	21 f
HOUGH, Susan	82 f VA	LAFETTE, Fanny	20 f
250-1944		6-41	
HOUGH, Mary S, printer	51 m MD	HOYLE, Geo A, carpenter -/50	32 m MD
Ann	47 f	Eliza	27 f PA
Lewis	25 m	Geo	8 m
Erma	21 f	Isabella	3/12 f
Julia	16 f	Wm, house painter	18 m
Charles	14 m	HOYLE, Christine	6 f
Alice	12 f	37-241	
George	10 m		
Lizzie	8 f	HOZE, Henry, machinist -/50	27 m HN
193-1470		Susan	28 f VA
		Clara	2 f
HOUSIN, Alfred, laborer	32 m	SHANK, Susan	38 f
Ada	30 f	Mahallock	15 f
Alice	7 f	245-1905	
Ada	9/12 f		
REAVES, Robt, carter	24 m	HUBERING, H	46 m
148-1095		Maria	48 f

ALEXANDRIA VIRGINIA 1860 CENSUS

George	16 m		HUGHS, Mora (B)	60 f	
LUTHER, John, laborer	40 m		MADISON, Rosana (B), wash & iron	22 f	
256-1988			James (B)	1 m	
			203-1551		
HUDDLESTONE, Mark, slater -/50	30 m				
Jane	27 f		HUGHS, Thomas, farmer 3K/500	56 m	
John	5 m		Julia	56 f	MD
George	3 m		Julia	26 f	
Jane	9/12 f		Mary	25 f	
Elizabeth	67 f		Semple	20 m	
258-2005			273-2107		
HUDSON, A G, tanner -/2K	50 m		HULL, Mary J, seamstress	28 f	
Georgiana	47 f		Martha	21 f	
Mary	19 f		37-236		
....	17 f				
Jenny	15 f		HUMMER, James W, farmer -/100	43 m	VA
Mary	13 f		Frances	43 f	
Willie	9 m		Martha	15 f	
Lucy	7 f		Annie	13 f	
WREN, Robt, house carpenter	30 m		Willie	12 m	
Martha	29 f		Catharine	10 f	
Harmon	3 m		Elizabeth	27 f	
Infant	2 f		269-2076		
199-1521					
			HUMPHREYS, John A, tbco & cgrs -/500	26 m	
HUGHES, Benjamin, huckster 1500/100	37 m		Mary V 1500/-	26 f	MD
Elizabeth	36 f		Edwin	1 m	
Georgiana	15 f		WADE, Susan, nurse	12 f	
Elizabeth	11 f		130-953		
Sarah	8 f				
Benjamin	7 m		HUMPHREYS, William, tobacnist -/300	49 m	
John	7 m		Susan	45 f	
Julia	4 f		Margaret	21 f	
Infant	4/12 m		Adaline	18 f	
128-933			Eliza	15 f	
			William	12 m	
HUGHES, George, hatter 800/-	45 m NY		17-94		
Mary	44 f				
219-1686			HUNT, William L, brickmaker	34 m	MD
			Helen	32 f	
HUGHES, John O, gardner -/3K	45 m WL		Caleb	9 m	
Sophia	30 f EG		Franklin	7 m	
Elizabeth	14 f		Catharine	5 f	
87-623			94-687		
HUGHES, Saml	42 m EG		HUNTER, B W, US Navy 30K/40K	57 m	
Ann	41 f		Mary	40 f	
270-2085			Fanny	20 f	
			Eliza	18 f	
HUGHES, Edward, chandler -/900	48 m		Alice	17	
Mary	57 f		Anna	16 f	
James	6 m		Mary	11 f	
Thomas	2 m		Jane	7 f	
John	7/12 m		Isabel	5 f	
HENNESSAY, Jas, laborer	33 m IR		Jane	62 f	
DOGLE, Garnet	32 m		GARNETT, E	55 f	
70-490			BLOW, Wm	9 m	
			271-2091		
HUGHS, Glen, hatter -/800	45 m NY				
May	44 f		HUNTER, Elizabeth 25K/35K	60 f	
219-1686			Wilkinson	32 m	

ALEXANDRIA VIRGINIA 1860 CENSUS

Anna	25 f	HURDLE, Albion, house painter -/100	42 m GT
William	7 m	Louisa	36 f
Robt	2 m	Chas	12 m
Sophia	25 f	Julian	8 m
Edith	19 f	Cora	10/12 m
233-1795		Thos, house painter	52 m MD
		SATERFIELD, Fanny, domestic	17 f MD
HUNTER, Joseph H, ship carpenter	42 m	143-1055	
May	35 f MD		
William	15 m	HURDLE, Armstead, rope maker -/150	25 m VA
Alton	13 m MD	Elizabeth	25 f NY
Ida	9 f	Estelle	3 f
Edward	6 m	Infant	3/12 m VA
Frank	3 m	143-1056	
Chas	2 m		
WHITE, Amy (M), cook	25 f	HURDLE, Levi, house painter 4500/100	57 m MD
232-1794		Lydia	47 f NY
		Levi, sailor	23 m VA
		Allen, surveyor	10 m
HUNTER, Julia, seamstress	68 f	Tommy	
WORTH, Wm H	11 m	Mary	13 f
76-539		Annie	9 f
		132-966	
HUNTER, Lourza, farmer 30K/5K	65 m		
TOMS, Clement, sailor	28 m MD	HUSSEY, Andrew J, sea captain -/300	54 m MA
Moran	24 f DC	Maria	48 f
Clement	7 m	Indiana	23 f
Joseph	3 m	James, sailor	22 m
Louise	2 f	Andrew, clerk	18 m
271-2092		Frank, clerk	15 m
		Mary	10 f
HUNTER, M C 1500/200	67 f VA	Fontleroy	7 m
Mary A	40 f	31-197	
Ann	32 f		
Geo W, dealer --	30 m VA		
Jas R, dry goods clerk	28 m	HUSSEY, Saul B, sailor -/8K	48 m ME
134-982		Sybel -/5K	44 f
		WOOD, Robt L, dry goods merch -/5K	28 m VA
HUNTER, Margaret 4K/50	45 f VA	Malissa	23 f ME
Martha	17 f	Juda	3 f VA
Albert	15 m	JEFFERSON, Tom	11 m CH
Emma	13 f	JACKSON, Julia (B), cook	45 f VA
Lee	10 m	THORTON, Mary (B), nurse	12 f VA
Mary J	8 f	129-943	
Margaret	6 f		
16-86		HUTCHINS, B F, printer	30 m
		Sarah	25 f
		William	6 m
HUNTINGTON, Thomas, hotel keeper -/1K	45 m VA	Mary	10 f
Elizabeth	41 m	Hector	7 m VA
EVANS, Jas, butcher	22 m	Chas, huckster	33 m
Abner, drayman	21 m	Tacy, domestic	8 m
Sarah	21 f	205-1570	
Martha	19 f		
Mary	16 f	HUTCHINS, George W, chr painter -/30	33 m
HUNTINGTON, Joseph	12 m	De..	39 f
Jane	8 f	Austin	9 m
Lilly	3 f	Fulton	8 m
Sanford, bankkeeper	22 m	Roper	5 m
James, coachman	21 m	Charles	3 m
George, coachman	17 m	Fanny	3/12 f
154-1141		193-1472	

61

ALEXANDRIA VIRGINIA 1860 CENSUS

HUTCHINS, Wm, carter -/75	62 m	IVY, E, farmer	39 m MD	
Sarah	56 f	Rachael	38 f	
HENRY, Polly, laborer	30 m	Sarah	16 f	
Jane	21 f	Wm	15 m	
195-1482		Benj	12 m	
		James	9 m	
HUTCHISON, Edward, dr gd merch -/5550	30 m	Joseph	6 m	
Elizabeth	28 f	Emma	4 f	
Harvey	5 m	Edward	2 m	
Loue	3 f	282-2162		
Kate	1 f			
Cynthia	35 f	JACKSON, Arthur, pump maker	25 m	
57-407		Ann	22 f DC	
		Samuel	9 m VA	
		Obediah	7 m	
HUTCHISON, Joseph (M), laborer	58 m	Eliza	6 f	
Ann (M)	59 f	Robert	3 m	
BERRY, Catharine (M)	25 f	Lorenzo	7/12 m	
John (M)	23 m	186-1412		
SYPHAX, David (M)	26 m			
Margaret (M)	23 f	JACKSON, Betsy (M), domestic	50 f	
Adalaide (M)	5 f	Edward (M)	17 m	
Edith (M)	3 f	Annie (M)	15 f	
David (M)	6/12 m	156-1157		
HUTCHISON, Jane (M)	17 f			
Maria (M)	20 f	JACKSON, Geo, gov messenger 2500/300	38 m	
137-1005		Sally	17 f	
		Monica	4 f	
HYDE, Christopher, gardner -/300	40 m HD	Sarah	59 f	
Margaret	40 f	Samuel	86 m	
Christopher	17 m VA	Alice	16 f	
George	14 m	JACKSON, Mary	32 f DC	
Jimmy	12 f	262-2033		
99-731				
		JACKSON, Henry (B)	50 m	
HYMES, Aura, lynacu? 4K/200	37 f IR	Jane (B)	33 f	
John	16 m	Amelia (B)	3 f	
Frances	12 m	George (B)	5/12 m	
Matilda	6 f	258-1999		
Mary	6 f			
223-1721		JACKSON, John (B), laborer	30 m	
		Adaline (B)	29 f	
HYSON, Mary (B)	30 f	John (B)	4 m	
John (B)	28 m	Louise (B)	2 f	
Leanora (B)	14 f	STUCKLEY, Fanny (B)	50 f	
Mary (B)	20 f	239-1849		
256-1989				
IDEN, James, omnibus driver 800/100	25 m	JACKSON, John (B), laborer	39 m	
81-580		Sallie (M)	40 f	
		Henry (M)	24 m	
		190-1444		
INGOLLS, Reuben 500/30	66 m NY			
Rebecca	56 f	JACKSON, John (M), farmer 3K ?	40 m	
Roxana	24 f	Delia (B)	32 f	
Mary	22 f	Rachael (B)	10 f	
Erastus	14 m VA	Ellen (B)	8 f	
99-733		Benjamin (B)	3 m	
		Octavia (B)	3/12 f	
IRVING, Chas J, blacksmith -/25	26 m MD	258-2003		
Lettia	23 f			
George	9/12 m	JACKSON, Nace (B), drayman -/25	38 m	
247-1923		Lucy (B)	30 f	

ALEXANDRIA VIRGINIA 1860 CENSUS

Mary (B)	12 f	SHERDEN, Patrick, asslt & bty	30 m IR	
Nace (B)	3 m	HALL, Jane, infanticide	30 f VA	
Rosa (B)	6/12 f	84/85-613		
CHASE, Geo (B), laborer	40 m			
BROOKS, Sarah (B)	38 f	JAMIESON, Maria 1500/600	40 f	
237-1828		76-533		
		JAMIESON, Robt, biscuit baker 17K/4K	54 m VA	
JACKSON, Robert A, pump maker 3K/100	60 m VA	Elizabeth J	50 f	
Mary	54 f VA	Robt, bookkeeper	27 m	
May	18 f VA	George W, bookkeeper	25 m	
187-1417		Mary	28 f	
		Cathanie P	17 f	
JACKSON, Wm, laborer	30 m	SMITH, Sarah K	42 f	
Charlotte	20 f	65-462		
Caroline	2 f			
Annie E	5/12 f	JAMIESON, Samuel, restaurant	46 m MD	
229-1768		Margaret	37 f	
		Charles	18 m	
JACKSON, William	95 m	Charlotte	14 f	
Elizabeth	47 f	Paul	7 m	
Amelia	17 f	David	2 m	
Sally	12 f	Cathrine	13 f	
180-1370		TATSAPAUGH, Richard, machinist	32 m	
		62-440		
JACOBS, Alfred, shoe maker 400/-	38 m VA			
Elizabeth	31 f	JAMIESON, Thos S, ms machinist -/7K	31 m	
Ann	17 f	Julia	31 m	
Sarah	14 f	Joseph	8 m	
LINDSAY, Emma	14 f	Catharine	4 f	
163-1216		Sandford	4/12 m	
		DAVIS, Melvina (M), domestic	40 f	
		NEUKINS ?, Jane (M)	15 f	
JACOBS, Charlot 800/1K	65 f	234-1806		
34-217				
		JAMIESON, Wm, US Navy 1500/200	65 m	
JACOBS, Harrison, barber 4K/100	36 m	Catharine	50 f	
Susan	34 f	Willie	14 f	
Emma	12 f	250-1946		
ROGERS, Julia	17 f			
Henry	11 m	JANNEY, Richard H, clerk cm mc 2K/300	34 m VA	
Mary	6 f	Margaret	34 f MD	
KELLY, Lawrence, appren	18	John	10 m VA	
SIMMS, Sarah (M), domestic	35 f	Nannie	8 f	
177-1325		Willie	6 m	
		Infant	5/12 m	
JAIL		183-1388		
COLE, Jas, jailor -/100	40 m			
Mary	35 f	JANNEY, Samuel H, clk treasury 500/5K	55 m	
Martha	18 f	Elizabeth	40 f	
William	13 m	Mayland	17 m	
John	12 m	O'SULLIVAN, Kate, cook	30 f IR	
Edgar	8 m	113-837		
Louis	6 m			
Bella	4 f	JARBOE, Rachael (B)	60 f	
Charles	2 m	Andrew (B), laborer	19 m	
PRISONERS:		Jomple (B)	17 m	
SCEDMORE, John, carptr-stabbing	40 m	Hainsa (B)	26 f	
DAUGHTNY, Daniel, laborer-asslt & bty	25 m IR	Mary (B)	8 f	
BALL, David, sailor-asslt & bty	21 m MA	Edw (B)	3 f	
PETTITE, Robt, theft	20 m VA	200-1527		
DUNN, Henry, laborer-nonpay of fine	50 m MA			

ALEXANDRIA VIRGINIA 1860 CENSUS

JARVIS, Harrison, ms brklyr 1500/200	40	m
Elizabeth	30	f
Richard	16	m
Harry	9	m
Andrew	6	m
Rebecca	11	f
Ann	4	f
Missouri	1	f
William	13	m
William	16	m
John, bricklayer	18	m
78-556		
JARVIS, Jas A, bricklayer -/100	39	m
Sarah	29	f
KIDWELL, Harriet, monthly nurse	46	f
Jane	23	f
William, printer	21	m
Robert	19	m
James	16	m
135-984		
JARVIS, Jno D, bank runner -/200	49	m
Victoria	44	f
Hattie	9	f
123-904		
JARVIS, Nancy, seamstress -/30	46	f
Emily	23	f
Thomas, laborer	18	m
Gertrude	15	f
George	12	m
Charles	8	m
Ella	3	f
BOWMAE, Edwin	15	m
155-1145		
JARVIS, Randolph, bricklayer	23	m
Georgiana	20	f
249-1935		
JEFFERS, Mary E, shoe binder	25	f
John	2	m
JEFFERS, John, house carpenter	32	m
185-1406		
JEFFERSON, Henry, tanner	52	m
Minerva	48	f
Joseph	27	m
Charles	10	m
MELBOURNE, Charlotte, domestic	18	f
JEFFERSON, Benjamin, house carpenter	29	m
199-1522		
JEFFERSON, Reuben R, shoemaker -/75	24	m
Lucy	22	f
Margaret	1	f
ATKINS, Margaret	40	f
BURKE, Josephine, nurse	10	f
WRIGHT, Francis, domestic	21	f
59-414		

JEFFERSON, Robert, laborer	48	m VA
Jane	42	f
William	16	m
Samuel	14	m
James	12	m
Alice	10	f
Geneva	7	f
Charles	1	m
230-1773		
JEFFERSON, Samuel, house carptr -/50	35	m
Rebecca	30	f
Julia	8	f
Adaline	5	f
Ida	2	f
ANDERSON, Mary, domestic	20	f
245-1909		
JEFFERSON, Wm, tanner	50	m
Columus, omnibus driver	19	m
Bower	17	m
Emma	12	f
Ella	10	f
Clara	8	f
BOSEY, James, cabinet maker	31	m MD
Mary	21	f
Wm	1	m
241-1869		
JENKINS, Arthur, pump maker	25	m
Ann	22	f DC
Samuel	9	m VA
Obediah	7	m
Elizzie	6	f
Robert	3	m
Lorenzo	7/12	m
186-1412		
JENKINS, Henry, ms carptr 17K/8K	36	m MD
Lenona	13	f
Fannie	10	f
Bettie	8	f
Minnie	4	f
Hannah	3	f
BROWN, Elizabeth, housekeeper	26	f
Thomas	3	m
61-431		
JENKINS, Mary, grocer	50	f
Arthur, huckster	22	m
Sarah	20	f
Samuel	2/12	m
William	12	m
Norman	8	m
Cornelia	21	f
Laura	19	f
Monroe	15	f
Emma	10	f
205-1569		
JENKINS, William, crpenter	35	m
Martha	31	f VA

ALEXANDRIA VIRGINIA 1860 CENSUS

```
  Hemmatta Michel                   11 f      DONELL, Geo (B)                      41 m
63-449                                         JOHNSTON, Wm (B)                     5 m
                                                 Emma C (B)                      4/12 f
JENKS, Elizabeth T, farmer -/6K     57 f MA      Mary L (M)                        14 f
  Winfield                          18 m         Georgana (B)                      11 f
270-2087                                         Richard (B)                        8 m
                                                 Vicoria (B)                        5 f
JENOUGH, John, shoemaker -/30       26 m         John T (B)                         2 m
  Julia                             31 f     151-1114
  George                            16 m
  Harriet (M)                       69 f     JOHNSTON, J B, physician 100/1300    29 m VA
166-1246                                       Mary                               29 f
                                               Mabel                               2 f
JERWARD, Jacob, machinist -/60      51 m NY  WHISKEY, Georgana (M), domestic      47 f
  Susannah                          48 f EG  132-967
  James                             19 m NY
  Mary                              17 f WA  JOHNSTON, James T, Epis mn 7500/26K  50 m GA
  Lewis                             12 m       Jane                               50 f NY
203-1553                                     DOGINS, Caroline, domestic           25 f
                                             166-1244
JESSE, Spencer, shoemaker           64 m CT
VERNION, James, carpenter -/60      25 m VA  JOHNSTON, John, house painter        36 m
  Mary                              24 f       Lizzie                             31 f
  William                            8 m       Mary                                9 f
  Sarah, seamstress                 20 f       Emma                                7 f
149-1097                                       Laura                               4 f
                                               Maggie                              2 f
JETT, Cyrus, carpenter -/20         40 m     230-1778
  Jane                              35 f
  Emily                              8 f
PENN, Joseph, moulder               23 m MD  JOHNSTON, John, day scavenger -/30   75 m
  Mary                              17 f VA    Ann                                67 f
  Ada                             5/12 f       Virginia                           15 f
149-1098                                     242-1874

JETT, John, pilot                   39 m     JOHNSTON, John M 70K/500             61 m
  Jane E                            35 f       Rebecca J                          50 f
  Sarah                             18 f       Marjoretta                         22 f
  Georgiana                         16 f       Virginia                           20 f
  Mary                              12 f       Robt                               17 m
  Jane                              10 f       Mary E                             14 f
  Edward                             2 m       John M                             12 f
KING, Albert                         8 m       Gertrude H                         10 f
14-74                                        117-865

JEWELL, H C, farmer 10K/350         36 m GT  JOHNSTON, John R, farmer 10K/6K      33 m
  Elizabeth                         37 f NY    Sarah                              31 f
  Elizabeth                         71 f GT    Richard                             3 m
  George                            40 m       William                         10/12 m
  Annie                             35 f     RIGGS, Townsby 800/1K                65 m
  Kate                               6 f     275-2114
261-2027
                                             JOHNSTON, John R, farmer -/80        45 m VA
JOHNSTON, Ann C, hat store -/200    48 f VA    Elizabeth                          26 f
  Agnes                             16 f       Elizabeth                          19 f
  Caroline                          16 f       Laura                              27 f
  Paulena                           11 f       Anne                               17 f
109-804                                        Jennie                             15 f
                                               George                             14 m
JOHNSTON, Ellen (B), wash & iron    33 f       Sally                              10 f
  Lucy (B)                          29 f       Ada                                 2 f
  Lavinnia (B)                      80 f     205-1566
```

ALEXANDRIA VIRGINIA 1860 CENSUS

JOHNSTON, John T, grocer 12K/2K	42 m		Eliza (M)	40 f
Caroline M	32 f		2076-1576	
Virginia	5 f			
PLANEL, Benjaimin K, clerk	18 m		JOHNSTON, Thomas, house carptr 5K/-	43 m
WEADEN, Geo W, clerk	20 m		Martha	28 f
104-769			John, appren chair painter	15 m
			Edward	12 f
JOHNSTON, Joseph, farmer -/80	30 m		Josepatto	9 f
Elizabeth	28 f		Sarah	8/12 f
Joseph	6 m		166-1240	
Charles	4 m			
Sarah	2 f		JOHNSTON, Wm, cabinet maker -/25	32 m
Henry	1 m		May	22 f
205-1567			Wm H	5 m
			John J	3 m
JOHNSTON, Martha, seamstress	43 f		Enock	4/12 m
LEE, Willia	18 f		210-1609	
Maretta	10 f			
146-1079				
			JOHNSTON, Wm, shoemaker	48 m
JOHNSTON, Mary (B)	47 f		Mary	19 f
Mary (B)	22 f		William	17 m
Catharine (B)	21 f		Samuel	11 m
John (B), laborer	15 m		210-1610	
William (B)	9 m			
Julia (B)	7 f		JOICE, Charles, machinist -/100	33 m MD
Frank (B)	4 m		Altia	29 f
Emma (B)	2/12 f		Edwin	9 m VA
James (M)	7/12 m		Chaarles	2 m
206-1574			77-542	
JOHNSTON, Nancy (B), domestic	70 f		JONES, Benj (B), laborer -/20	60 m
KING, Sarah (B), wash & iron	30 f		Susan (B)	51 f
Fred (B)	7 m		209-1604	
Mary (B)	5 f			
157-1167			JONES, Edward, bricklayer 1K/100	50 m MD
			Jane	40 f
			Edward	21 m
JOHNSTON, Reuben (B), laborer	26 m		Emma	16 f
Sarah (B)	50 f		Madona	12 f
POTTS, Martha (B), domestic	19 f		143-1047	
Mary (B)	17 f			
131-956			JONES, Eliza M	38 f
			Catharine	11 f
JOHNSTON, Reuben, treas RR Co 2500/1K	50 m		Alice	8 f
Mary C	40 f NJ		William	2 m
Anna	19 f VA		COOMBS, Elizabeth, wash & iron	59 f
Reuben	8 m		91-658	
Mary	6 f			
Philip	5 m		JONES, Henry (M)	28 m
Charles	9/12 m		Jinny (B)	22 f
CLEW, Maria	70 f MD		Lila (B)	11 f
102-753			James (B)	4/12 m
			256-1982	
JOHNSTON, Richard, sailor 750/500	34 m			
John, sailor	33 m			
William, sailor	25 m		JONES, Jas, laborer	27 m IR
Noble	18 m		Margaret	15 f VA
Harriett	22 f		BRADY, Jas, tailor	30 m IR
69-482			Kate	30 f
			Ann	7/12 f VA
JOHNSTON, Robert (M), wood sawyer	31 m		92-664	

ALEXANDRIA VIRGINIA 1860 CENSUS

JONES, John, laborer -/75	29 m VA	William	15 m	
Winney	22 f	Benj	12 m	
Ann	5 f	James	9 m	
Lucy	2 f	282-2162		
Samuel	63 m			
Nancy	60 f	JOYCE, Dennis, laborer	50 m IR	
Washington, laborer	21 m	Catharine	40 f	
Fanny	36 f	Hannah	11 f	
23-136		Eliza	6 f	
		BLAND, Nora, domestic	55 f	
JONES, John, tailor 5500/132 EG	45 m	McCARTY, Jere, laborer	26 m	
Mary	30 f VA	209-1600		
Mary E	16 f			
Caroline	14 f.	JULIUS, Elthelbert (B), wsh & irn -/2	36 f	
John	13 m	GRAYSON, Julia (B), nurse	18 f	
115-849		CHICK, David (B), laborer	40 f	
		135-990		
JONES, John A, brakeman -/1K	29 m VA			
Margaret	29 f	KAILON, Michael, laborer -/30	50 m IR	
Floeida	6 m	Ann	50 f	
Absolam	3 m	Michael	13 m	
38-252		Margaret	9 f VA	
		Maria	3 f	
JONES, Joseph (B), gardner -/300	60 m	72-503		
Mollie (B)	60 f			
Ada (B)	10 f	KAMS, Adam (B), laborer	25 m	
Albert (B)	17 m	40-267		
251-1951				
		KANE, Charles, laborer	28 m	
JONES, Sarah	57 f	Elinor	17 f	
EVANS, Adaline	31 f	Mary C	12 f	
THAS?, WILLIAM	6 M	Timothy M	11 m	
15-81		35-227		
JONES, Stephen B, farrier	50 m VA	KANE, Levi, laborer	45 m	
Susan	65 f	Mary	47 f	
Mary	28 f	Levi	12 m	
Rosalie, dress maker	27 f	Annie	9 f	
Stephen B, machinist	23 m	35-226		
COARSON, Joseph, carpenter	25 m			
63-444		KATIN, Patrick, laborer	37 m IR	
		Sarah	19 f NJ	
JONES, Wm, laborer 300/75	35 m	Caroline	1 f VA	
Sarah	30 f	144-1062		
Ellen	8 f			
Sarah	6 f	KAY, Joseph W, farmer 4K/100	48 m NJ	
Asberry	3 m	Amelia	34 f MD	
277-2126		266-2059		
JONES, William (B), laborer	38 m	KEATIN, Kate	39 f	
JONES, Levi (B)	18 m	John	12 m	
251-1952		Ned	5 m	
		Johann	7 f	
JONES, Wm H, clerk RR	35 m IR	O'BRIEN, Thos, laborer	45 m IR	
Harriett	22 f MD	162-1210		
Jack	2 m			
James	4/12 m VA			
201-1538		KEINER, Elizabeth, taileress -/300	50 f	
		Adeline, taileress	32 f	
JOY, Edward, farmer	39 m MD	Lucy, taileress	17 f	
Rachael	38 f	KINNER, John M	10 m	
Sarah	16 f	109-811		

ALEXANDRIA VIRGINIA 1860 CENSUS

KELL, Isaac, coppersmith 3500/2500	46 m	HOLLOWAY, Mary, domestic	60 f IR	
Mary	41 f	LAFERTY, Chas, laborer	35 m	
Harrison	18 m	KANE, Patrick	35 m	
Martha	16 f	101-749		
Mary	11 f			
Thomas	6 m	KENT, John, hotel keeper	26 m MD	
Milton	4 m	Louise	23 f	
KELL, Thomas, tin smith 2500/?	52 m	Millard	3 m	
2-13		Sarah	68 f	
		ANUALINE, Henry	16 m	
		186-1409		
KELLER, Benjamin, tanner	38 m MD			
Kate	32 f	KERPER, Jacob, barber	28 m	
Augustus	12 m	Elizabeth	27 f	
Eugenia	9 f	William	6 m	
Albert	6 m	Frances	5 m	
Margret	6 f	Eliza	1 f	
239-1854		217-1673		
KELLY, Ann, grocer 500/50	47 f IR	KESTERSON, Amanda, seamstress	50 f	
Bridgett	17 f	Laura	17 f	
Mary	15 f	Thomas	11 m	
99-728		George, turner	21 m	
		229-1769		
KELLY, Ann, grocer	49 f IR			
Bridgete	18 f	KEYGENDAPPER, G, light house kpr -/50	60 m GR	
May	17 f	Catharine	59 f	
277-2131		ELKINS, Mary, domestic	22 f	
		BLACK, Fanny (B)	8 f	
KELLY, Ann E	60 f IR	229-1770		
245-1902				
		KEYS, Elizabeth, boarding house	40 f	
KELLY, John -/800	75 m CT	Sarah	16 f	
Ellen	49 f MD	Mary	14 f	
Thomas, bricklayer	21 m VA	Josaphene	11 f	
Chas	18 m	Misson	10 f	
John	14 m	John	7 m	
Hannah	11 f	Melissa	2 f	
214-1648		WOOD, Samuel, sailor	40 m	
		KEYS, Francis, pilot	47 m	
KEMP, Thomas E, ms carptr 1K/300	28 m MD	LEE, Rose (B), domestic	22 f	
Ann	22 f VA	Infant (B)	7/12 f	
188-1426		110-815		
KEMPER, Delaware, teacher	27 m	KEYS, John T, machinist -/100	32 m	
Kosciuska	25 f	Margaret	30 f	
Iraetta	26 f	May	10 f	
McGRAW, Mary, domestic	17 f IR	William	7 m	
LYLES, Wm (M), domestic	65 m	Eddie	2 m	
Jane (B)	55 f	72-517		
William (M), waiter	13 m			
50-350		KEYS, Nathan, RR engineer -/100	30 m NY	
		Winnie	25 f VA	
KENNEDAY, Jno, weaver -/1350	70 m IR	Annie	4 f	
Mary	64 f	Lon	2 m	
BAKER, Susana	64 f EG	BLACK, Laura, domestic	14 f	
82-587		139-1019		
KENNEDY, Dennis, laborer	40 m IR			
Mary	27 f	KIDWELL, Alfred, boss ctn mill 400/77	32 m	
William	2 m VA	Sarah	19 f	
Dennis	7/12 m	Jacalin	11 f	

ALEXANDRIA VIRGINIA 1860 CENSUS

GRAY, William, boss ctn mill	25 m	KING, James, sailor	28 m	
Mary	18 f MD	Mary	26 f	
88-632		222-1709		
		KING, James W, steam engineer -/75	29 m VA	
KIDWELL, Geo T, boss ctn mill -/50	23 m MD	Jane	27 f	
Sarah	19 f VA	James	4 m	
DODSON, Catharine	60 f	May	1 f VA	
SEWELL, Edward	1/12 m	207-1589		
76-541				
		KING, Joane -/30	50 f	
KIDWELL, H, shoemaker -/100	31 m	Margaret, seamstress	35 f	
Martha	26 f	Jane	20 f	
78-557		189-1446		
KIDWELL, Joseph, shoemaker	22 m	KING, Jno W, shoemaker -/150	55 m VA	
Elizabeth	16 f	Ann	50 f MD	
BEACH, Docia	47 f	Edgar, clerk dry goods	21 m	
107-789		Arthur, appren tailor	19 m	
		Mary	16 f	
		Francis	10 m	
KIGGING, Jas, laborer	30 m IR	130-951		
Biddy	28 f			
John	4 m VA	KING, Mildred, boarding -/2250	45 f	
Mark	3 m	PLAIN, Catharine	35 f	
Alice	5/12 f	Beryman, grocery clerk	18 m	
85-610		Ann	15 f	
		Mildred	12 f	
		John	10 m	
KILLBRIGHT, Anna, shoe bonder	60 f	Catharine	8 f	
BALLINGER, Eliza	60 f DE	Caroline Amy	5 f	
HENDERSON, Louisa	50 f MD	SWAIN, Samuel, machinist	47 m MA	
123-905		188-1429		
KILPATRICK, Robert, tailor -/50	26 m	KING, Samuel, laborer	33 m	
Sarah	25 f	May	27 f	
75-528		Willie	12 m	
		Samuel	9 m	
KINCHELOE, Sally	50 f	Thomas	2 m	
James, laborer	22 m	TRACEY, Margaret	56 f	
114-841		223-1718		
KING, Betey (B)	37 f	KING, Shirley, overseer -/30	26 m	
Waller (B)	16 m	Margaret	25 f	
Sarah (B)	13 f	77-547		
Laura (M)	3 f			
196-1490		KING, William, shoemaker	39 m	
		Elizabeth	35 f	
KING, Daniel, laborer	33 m	James	18 m	
May	27 f	William	11 m	
William	12 m	Mary	4 f	
Samuel	9 m	Alexander	10 m	
Thomas	2 m	116-857		
MANING, Margaret	56 f			
223-1718		KING, William D, shoemaker -/100	52 m	
		Catherine	48 f	
		Catherine	22 f	
KING, J T, trader	28 m	Jas H, clerk wood yard	17 m	
Hanna	14 f	Lydia	15 f	
Wm, laborer	17 m	Martha	10 f	
Ann	41 f EG	Mary	4 f	
280-2144		127-924		

ALEXANDRIA VIRGINIA 1860 CENSUS

KING, William W, tailor	21 m	HAMILTON, Will	12 m	
Margaret	17 f	WATSON, John, carter	19 m	
15-80		HENRY, Robert, house carpenter	45 m	
		Amanda	23 f	
KINGSTON, Jeremiah, laborer	39 m	John	2 m	
Julia	10 f	Emma	4 f	
Margaret	5 f	224-1729		
Jeremiah	13 m			
150-1107		KNORR, Stephen S, machinist -/30	27 m PA	
		Margaret	23 m	
KINSLOW, Mary 500/-	58 f IR	Willie	9 m	
FORDHAM, Andrew	42 m	Margaret	5 f VA	
229-1767		Douglas	2 m	
		214-1647		
KINZER, J Louis, lawyer 5K/3K	36 m PA			
Maggie -/5K	36 f VA	KNOX, James, laborer	57 m IR	
Katie	8 f	Mary	50 f	
Maggie	6 f	Patrick, bricklayer	21 m	
Willie	5 m	Thomas, laborer	19 m	
Annie	3 f	John, clerk grocer	17 m	
Florence	2 f	May	16 f	
WISE, Margaret	64 f IR	Catharine	8 f VA	
Susan (B), domestic	33 f VA	KEATON, David, driver	14 m	
124-909		102-751		
KIPP, Ezra, farmer 6K/2K	52 m NY	KNOX, John H 10K/30K	68 m	
Margaret	48 f	Anne S	30 f	
James	19 m	Jennet	27 f	
Elizabeth	12 f	SUMMERVILLE, M C	33 f	
Eaton	6 m	Robt F, comm merch -/5K	25 m	
269-2077		SUMMERVILLE, Geo	4 m	
		105-773		
KIRK, Harrison, huckster 700/75	40 m VA			
Margaret	38 f	KNOX, Jno S, comm merch -/10K	32 m	
Virginia	16 f	Eleyne	25 f	
Margaret	12 f	Alice	4 f	
Marion	10 f	Jno S	2 m	
Harry	10 f	Joseph	2/12 m	
Anna	5 f	106-780		
Mary	2 f			
59-417		KOOTZ, Rosana, confectioner -/1K	26 f MD	
		Jefferson, carpenter	34 m NY	
KIRWIN, Merthe, tailor 800/100	30 f IR	Wm A	7 m	
Mary, tailor	25 f	Edward	5 m	
SHAY, David, tailor	25 m	Maranda	26 f NY	
75-527		GLEEN, Wellington, laborer	22 m NY	
		128-932		
KISPER, Jacob, barber -/100	28 m			
Elizabeth	27 f	KROES, Peter, Cath priest	62 m BV	
William	6 m	RAMBURGH, Henry	35 m BV	
Francis	5 m	193-1467		
Eliza	1 m VA			
217-1673		KURTZ, Rosanna, confectioner -/1K	24 f MD	
		Jefferson, confectioner	34 m NY	
KITCHIN, Andrew, machinist	70 m PA	Wm	7 m	
68-477		Edmund	5 m	
		Maranada	26 f	
KNIGHT, Ferdinand, cooper -/100	31 m	GLEEN, Wellington, laborer	22 m	
Ann	25 f	127-931		
John	8 m			
Amanda	4 f	LACY, Wm B, farmer 6K/4K	38 m NY	
Clinton	1 m	Mary	40 f	

ALEXANDRIA VIRGINIA 1860 CENSUS

Seven Weeden	16 m	Margaret	2 f	
Mary E	15 f	Corvosso	2/12 m	
Daniel	13 m	42-281		
John F	11 m			
Frances Lacy	7 f	LAMPHIN, John, grocer 15K/2K	50 m IR	
Emma	6 f	Mary	32 f	
William H	5 m	John B	2 m	
Genieve	9/12 f	Lewis P	2 m	
251-1954		LAVINE, Mary	60 f IR	
		LAVINE, Elizabeth	36 f VA	
LAFFERTY, Jeremiah, laborer	25 m	10-49		
Mary	26 f			
John	1/2 m	LANAHAN, John, Meth minister -4K	41 m VA	
98-718		Mary	30 f MD	
		John	11 m VA	
LAFLEE, Jesse, machinist -/75	29 m MD	Mary	11 f	
Elizabeth	24 f	Timothy	9 m GT	
Sarah	7 f	Helen	6 f MD	
David	5 m	Robt	2 m MD	
WALKER, John	60 m	CAVIL, Margaret (M), domestic	15 f DC	
190-1449		QUANDER, Gracie (B)	45 f VA	
		128-939		
LAIRCE, Mary, seamstress	43 f			
STEELL, Ann Spring, wash & iron	37 f	LANCASTER, R (B), carter	37 m	
Margaret	8 f	Sarah (B)	40 f	
Mary	6 f	Richard (B)	16 m	
48-330		Elizabeth (B)	13 f	
		HOOPER, Mary (B), domestic	30 f	
LAIRN, Ira, farmer 1800/200	57 m CT	167-1249		
Phebe	27 f			
Albert	32 m	LANDOGAN, Michael, laborer	55 m IR	
268-2073		May	45 f	
		John	18 m	
		Mary	19 f	
LALLY, John, laborer 250/20	32 m IR	PAYNE, William (B)	35 m	
Annie	27 f	COLLINS, Arrina (M), domestic	26 f	
Mary	2 f VA	CARTER, Lonaz (B), washer	26 f	
Jane	7/12 f	276-2119		
69-481				
LAMBERT, B H, conf act 25K/20K	55 m MD	LANE, Patrick, laborer	29 m	
Adelaide	50 f	Hannah	3 f	
Edgar L, civil engineer	21 m	Michael	8 m	
Benjamin	18 m	Thomas	6/12 m	
Louisa	17 f	150-1105		
Charles	14 m			
Ernest	12 m	LANE, William (M), ostler	46 m	
Jourden	10 m	Ann (M)	42 f	
SPOLDING, Elizabeth	32 m	John (M)	10 m	
EDWARDS, Sarah, housekeeper	22 f	CANDLISS, Zach (B)	45 m	
183-1391		147-1083		
LAMBERT Wm H	31 m	LANGLEY, Geo, shoemaker	40 m ME	
Louisa	28 f DC	Margaret	39 f	
183-1392		William	17 m MD	
		Martha	12 f	
LAMDEN, John R, ms carptr 400/150	34 m MD	Frances	10 f	
Elizabeth	35 f	George Ellen	7 f	
Milton	10 m	246-1910		
Sylvanus	9 m			
Samuel	7 m VA	LANGTON, Mary A, farmer 200/200	38 f	
William	5 m	Margaret	16 f	

ALEXANDRIA VIRGINIA 1860 CENSUS

Wm H	15 m	LAWSON, Drady 700/150	56 f MD	
Thos W	7 m	Nora	25 f VA	
257-1994		Josephus, carter -/100	23 m	
		153-1132		
LARKIN, Lucian, dry goods merch 150/-	26 m			
Sallie	25 f	LAYCOCK, Edward, laborer	65 m	
William, clerk	22 m	Nancy	45 f	
Thomas, clerk	18 m	Virginia	18 f	
NORMAN, Thomas, clerk	18 m	George	16 m	
29-185		Lucy	12 f	
		LOVELACE, Mary	45 f	
LARSON, Jas	23 m	WINDSOR, Wm	25 m	
Margaret	20 f	186-1413		
97-707				
		LAYCOCK, Wm, sailor -/600	38 m VA	
LATHAN, Hugh, omnibus prop 8K/7K	47 m DC	Elizabeth	30	
Eliza J	45 f MD	Joseph	11 m	
Alice	17 f VA	COLE, Jane E, seamstress	52 f	
William	12 m	222-1707		
STRIDER, Jas E, express messenger	40 m			
John	69 m MD	LEA, Luke (B), caulker -/40	70 m	
Phoebe	63 f	Sylvia (B)	60 f	
Alice	5 f VA	240-1860		
James	2 m			
Eveline	30 f MD	LEADBEATER, Mary P 18K/12K	52 f	
BANKHEAD, Louise	24 f	Edward L, druggist	24 m	
CROSON, Robt, omnibus driver	35 m VA	Lucy	22 f	
PRICE, Edgar, carpenter	21 m	Mary G	20 f	
Marrion	20 f MD	Annie	15 f	
COOK, Eli (B)	55 m VA	Thomas	12 m	
WARD, Chas (B), drover	35 m VA	FOSSETT, Henrietta	9 f	
James	14 m	ASAUS, Emily, domestic	30 f	
114/115-845		119-879		
LATHAN, Jno F, trans appren -/3K	55 m			
Catharine	55 f VA	LEAR, Michael, laborer	39 m	
Frances	30 f	Rosanna	39 f	
Jeannie	28 f	Francis	8 m WA	
John, clerk shoe store	22 m	Mary	6 f VA	
George	15 m	137-1003		
Rose	12 f			
CONSTABLE, Kate	8 f	LEATHERLAND, Jno, laborer -/30	35 m EG	
BAYNE, Paterson, whsale store 500/3K	35 m	Sarah	35 f	
Louisa	26 f	John	12 m	
Catharine	8/12 f	William	9 m	
111-827		101-743		
LATOUCHE, John, merch-taylor 700/2500	39 m EG	LEE, Ann H -/7K	60 f	
Fanny	30 f MD	Edward J	37 m	
Paul	2 m VA	Jane	25 f	
Johana	5 f MD	Mary	22 f	
117-866		Frederick	42 f	
		Lucy L	25 f	
LAWLER, Edward, machinist -/50	40 m IR	George T	30 m	
Mary	33 f	Mary P	25 f	
Ellen	15 f	H Nelson	1 m	
Mary	13 f	LEE, Sallie	45 f	
Margaret	12 f	50-349		
Robert	8 m			
SAULSBERY, Hugh, tanner	26 m	LEE, Anthony (B), laborer	38 m	
LAWLER, Martin, machinist	30 m	Cecelia (B)	33 f	
235-1809		Clegette (B)	6 m	

ALEXANDRIA VIRGINIA 1860 CENSUS

```
    Daniel (B)                      3 m      Ann (M)                          8 f
    Ephraim (B)                     1 m      William (M)                      1 m
311-1621                                   240-1861

LEE, Catharine E                   39 f MD  LEGG, Hains (M), laborer -/30    25 m
    William, news boy              15 m       Mary (M)                       25 f
COOK, John H, huckster             23 m    165-1235
    Susan                          18 f
40-426                                      LEGG, Wm, levery stable -/330    55 m
                                              Ann                            50 f
LEE, Elizabeth (M), domestic       33 f       Cecilia                        23 f
    Pauline (B)                     8 f       James, carpenter               22 m
    Harriet (B)                     3 f       Margaret                       21 f
CHASE, Betsey (B)                  80 f       Thadeus -/30                   16 m
212-1629                                   135-983

LEE, H (B), ship caulker -/20      42 m    LEGHMAN, Wm, sail rigger -/30    25 m
    Rebecca (M)                    29 f       Lycretia                       60 f MD
211-1617                                   186-1408

LEE, Michael, laborer              35 m GR LEONARD, Peter, soap & cndl mkr -/50  30 m DC
    Eizabeth                       36 f       Fawnea                         25 f
    Frank                          11 m       Mary Ann                       6/12 f
    May                             9 f    148-1093
    Annie                           5 f
    Augustus                        1 m    LESSLIE, Jesse, machinist -/75   29 m
278-2135                                      Elizabeth                      24 f
                                              Sarah                           7 f
LEE, Nancy (B), seamstress         26 f       David                           5 m
206-1579                                   WALKER, John                      60 m
                                           190-1449
LEE, R E, US Army 22K/-            53 m
    Mary C                         52       LEWIS, Ira, frmer 1K/-           57 m CT
    Custis, US Army                27 m       Phebe                          54 f
    Annie                          21 f       Albert                         33 m
    Agnes                          18 f    268-2073
    Robert                         17 m
    Mildred                        16 f    LEWIS, M M, physician 7K/3K      33 m
    Mary C                         26 f       Eveline                        23 f
264-2046                                   BRENT, Florence                   19 f
                                           18-100
LEE, Samuel (B), blacksmith        32 m
    Jane (B)                       40 f    LEWIS, Precilla (M), cook -/25   50 f
    Amanda (B)                     14 f    135-989
    Joseph (B)                     12 m
    Robert (B)                     10 m
    Lizzie (B)                      7 f    LEWIS, Wm B, RR clerk -/100      47 m
    Thadeus (B)                     4 m       Jane                           48 f
    Martha (B)                      2 f       Frances                        26 f
244-1894                                      Charles, machinist             21 m
                                              William, house carpenter       19 m
LEE, Sarah (B)                     67 f       Mary                           16 f
PETERS, Lucy (B)                   40 f       Margaret                       12 f
    Fanny (B)                      24 f       Sarah                          10 f
198-1515                                      Jimmy                           7 m
                                           248-1934
LEGETT, Wm (M), domestic           54 m
    Ann (M)                        40 f    LIGHTFOOT, John, bricklayer       47 m
    Eliza (M)                      15 f       Mary                           24 f MD
    Charles (M)                    13 m       William                        2/12 m VA
    Caroline (M)                   10 f    30-189
```

ALEXANDRIA VIRGINIA 1860 CENSUS

LILIENTHAL, Samuel, clother -/3K	29 m HC	LOVELACE, Elizabeth	35 f	
Johannah	32 f HD	49-345		
Moses	3 m MD			
Jacob	2 m VA	LOCKWOOD, Henry, w s clerk	25 m NY	
Louis A, grocer	27 m HD	Margaret	23 m NY	
Sprinnie?	54 f	EDWARDS, Henry	11 M WI	
11-53		256-1989		
LINDSAY, Jane W	65 f	LOKINS, Sally (B), domestic	50 f	
Mary E -/10K	23 f	William (B)	27 m	
127-925		Noble (B), laborer	20 m	
		Rudolph (B), brickmason	17 m	
LINDSAY, Jas, hotel keeper -/1K	38 f	JACKSON, Christena (B), wash & iron	30 f	
Julia	32 f	James (M)	13 m	
Thomas	15 m	Camp (M)	13 m	
Noble	12 m	Alice (B)	6 f	
Jimmy	9 m	Ada (B)	8 f	
Samuel	5 m	204-1564		
Sarah	69 f			
107-790				
		LOMAX, Ann (B), wash & iron	32 f	
LIPPETT, E R, Epis mn 20K/80K	62 m RI	Henry (B)	9 m	
Mary F	56 f	28-173		
Laura	20 f			
Armistead	18 m	LOMAX, Ellen (B), wash & iron	69 f	
280-2141		Elizabeth (B)	18 f	
		David (M)	20 m	
LLOYD, Ann H 7K/4K	60 f	48-329		
Edward J	37 m			
Jane W	25 f	LONDON, Fred (B), carpenter	55 m	
Mary	22 f	Nancy (B)	27 f	
Frederick	42 m	Frederick (B), laborer	24 m	
Lucy L	25 f	John (B)	21 m	
George T	30 m	Nancy (M)	20 f	
Mary P	25 f	Henry (B)	16 m	
H Nelson	1 m	Clinton (M)	3 m	
LEE, Sally	45 f	Ainnias (M)	1 m	
50-349		165-1230		
LLOYD, Henry 2500/50	19 m	LOUNCE, Henry, laborer	42 m	
100-739		Elizabeth	39 f	
		Emily	19 f	
LLOYD, John J, farmer 29K/10K	60 m	Harriet	15 f	
Eliza	40 f	Frances	11 f	
Mary	14 f	Edward	9 m	
Rebecca	11 f	James	2 m	
John	9 m	185-1402		
Helen	7 f			
Eliza	5 f	LOVEL, Jane	45 f	
Arthur	3 m	Charles, appren carpenter	18 m	
280-2141		Nancy, cotton mill	15 m	
		Albert, cotton mill	12 m	
LLOYD, John L, shoemaker	34 m VA	Missouri	9 f	
Mary A	33 f	Joseph	7 m	
Samuel	11 m	ROXBERRY, Mary	64 f	
John	9 m	77-548		
Sarah	7 f			
James	4 m	LOVELACE, Lewis	37 m	
238-1846		...	23 f	
		Charles	5 m	
LLOYD, William, well digger	56 m	162-1201		

ALEXANDRIA VIRGINIA 1860 CENSUS

LOVELACE, Maria -/50	35 f	LUTHERN, Richard, farmer 20K/6K	68 m EG
Robt, machinist	21 m	Frances	70 f
Arthur, news boy	17 m	DONALDSON, Sarah	15 f
Luther, appren printer	16 m	Atwalter	13 m
Minetta	13 f	SHREVE, Richard	21 m
Gerrainja	9 f	266-2063	
Ida	3 f		
171-1286		LYCER, Lewis, cooper -/1K	47 m VA
		Matilda	42 f
LOWE, D A, notary public 1500/450	49 m	Samuel, laborer	16 m
Jane	48 f	Wm H	13 m
Fanny	22 f	Lewis	11 m
Phoebe	16 f	Sarah	9 f
David A	15 m	Jas R	4 m
Fred	11 m	Alice	1 f
RAMSAY, Edgar	5 m	WARD, Frances, domestic	30 f
Christina -/17K	73 f	74-519	
183-1389			
		LYLES, Christopher, shoemaker -/100	28 m
		Margaret	35 f DC
LOWE, Jacob, coachman -/100	33 m MD	Emma	15 f VA
Caroline	26 f	Arthur	10 m
John Alfred	5 m	Thomas	8 m
Wm	3 m	Margaret	5 f
42-284		Francis	2 f
		46-316	
LOWE, Jno F M	60 m MD		
Sophia 10K/2K	60 f	LYLES, Enoch H, restaurant	28 m
Julia	21 f	Johannie	42 f IR
162-1205		Richard	16 m VA
		Rebecca	40 f
LOWER, Henry 800/30	52 m BV	McCLANY, Mich, sailor	35 m IR
Henrieta	47 f BV	SANDERSON, Samuel, machinist	44 m DC
Margaret	16 f DC	SAWLER, Johanna	32 f IR
Peter	10 m	Edward, blacksmith	17 m
263-2043		Joseph	14 m
		BULGER, Alice	9 f NY
LUCAS, Anne, wash & iron	45 f MD	182-1381	
WEIPHEG, Mary, prostitute	20 f MD		
86-618		LYLES, Geo H, shoemaker	24 m
		Elenor	21 f
LUCAS, Susan	44 f VA	George L	2 m
Joseph	18 m	Isabella	1/12 f
215-1655		46-323	
LUDGINS, Ann	60 f MD	LYLES, Isabella, seamstress	54 f
MARSTON, Frances	36 f	Anna	23 f
SIDES, Wm H	9 m	Edgar, shoemaker	21 m
Geo B	7 m VA	Lambert	19 m
188-1431		Mary, seamstress	17 f
		Rachael	14 f
		46-324	
LUNT, Martha, soap mfg 6600/650	46 f		
William, bookkeeper	19 m	LYLES, Matilda 900/50	62 f
Mary	16 f	Samuel, cooper	30 m
Samuel, appren apothecary	14 m	Alexander, carpenter	24 m
Hannah	11 f	145-1070	
John	8 m		
RANKIN, William, soap mfg	30 m MD	LYLES, Richard (B), ship carpenter	24 m
COE, Henry, clerk	30 m	Mary (B)	22 f
RANKIN, Margaret	27 f	William (B)	3 m
62-441		243-1885	

ALEXANDRIA VIRGINIA 1860 CENSUS

57 m John		6 m	
Hannah (B)	52 f	Jane	4 m
SMITH, Matilda (B)	28 f	Elizabeth	2 f
JOHNSTON, Louis (B)	7 m	Henry	13 m
1630-1217		235-1813	
LYNCH, Jere, laborer -/40	51 m IR	McCAIN, James, carpenter	50 m
Tracy	63 f MD	Robert, carpenter	35 m
Michael, RR fireman	22 m	Agnes	25 m
George	21 m	Robert	8 m
James, blacksmith	19 m	Lizzie	6 f
DUNN, Edward, machinist	65 m	Emma	1 f
Rosa	5 f MD	William, laborer	21 m
204-1565		235-1815	
LYNCH, John, laborer 400/1100	35 m IR	McCAIN, Robert, carter -/50	36 m
Mary	28 f	Mary	29 f
William	28 f	Martha	12 f
Mary	4 f VA	Bobby	9 m
John	2 m	Infant	4/12 f
Thomas	8/12 m	200-1530	
36-235			
		McCAINE, Edward, sailor 200/20	33 m
LYNCH, Maurice, laborer	30 m IR	Evaline	22 f
Mary	27 f	Mary	2 f
John	3 m	69-486	
Patsey	9/12 f	* see page 78 for McCANE	
191-1451		McCANN, Barney, laborer	33 m IR
		Aleixa	29 f
LYONS, Mary	38 f MD	Mertle	5 m VA
Alpha	8 f VA	Bridgett	3 f
Alice	7 f	Hugh	4/12 m
212-1630		96-702	
LYONS, Richard, sailor	31 m	McCANN, Jno, laborer	32 m IR
Mary	36 f	Sarah	28 f
Jamison	9 f	Hugh	6 m
Lucinda	6 f	Peter	4 m
221-1701		John	3 m
		101-744	
LYONS, Sarah	19 f MD		
John, tailor	20 m	McCANN, Peter, laborer	39 m IR
229-1762		Rose	26 f IR
		Patrick	11 m IR
McBURNEY, Geo, liquor dealer 3K/1K	45 m IR	Frank	7 m VA
Agnes	43 f	Anna	3 f
George	10 m	96-697	
Alexander	8 m		
Jane	16 f	McCARTY, Chas, laborer	40 m IR
Mary	14 f	Eliza	37 f
Agnes	6 f	Hannah	7 f VA
Alice	2 f	Joseph	4 m
161-1197		70-495	
McCAIN, Dennis	36 m IR	McCARTY, Florence, lock keeper -/30	31 m IR
Annie	25 f	Margaret	7 f VA
Joseph	4 m VA	MANSFIELD, Johana	50 f IR
Owen	2 m	95-688	
71-496			
		McCARTY, John, RR brakeman	40 m
McCAIN, Jas, house carptr 500/100	25 m IR	Agnes	35 f
Mary	24 f	244-1894	

ALEXANDRIA VIRGINIA 1860 CENSUS

McCARTY, Michael, laborer	38 m	McCLUSKEY, Jas, overseer	26 m VA	
Bridgett	26 f	Julia	21 f	
95-689		278-2134		
McCATH, Dongal, cooper -/50	60 m	McCONY, Celea (B), wash & iron	44 f	
Nancy	50 f	James (B), laborer	22 m	
CHURCH, Susan	54 f	William (B)	20 m	
64-454		156-1158		
McCHAY, Richard, laborer	38 m	McCORMACK, Ann M, teacher -/500	30 f	
Jane	35 f	Augustine	13 f	
Michael	14 m	Kate	9 f	
Sarah	10 f MD	WHITWALL, Anna	8 f WA	
Maggie	8 f VA	Mary	5 f NY	
James	5 m	NEWTON, Ann S	40 f EG	
Alice	2 f	Virginia	25 f VA	
Thos	2/12 m	WALLOCK, Maggie	13 f	
FOX, Martin	26 m IR	66-469		
BLAKE, Jas	30 f			
70-491		McCORMICK, John, bookkeeper	32 m MD	
		Jane M	60 f	
McCHERRY, Ann L -/600	48 f	CHEWS, Thom, super RR	38 m	
Charles, clerk	26 m	Martha	25 f	
Edwin, clerk	22 m	John, bookkeeper	18 m	
Joseph, clerk	20 m	Armes Ste..	16 m	
Saml, clerk	18 m	Ellen	10 f	
Alice	16 f	Hector	7 m	
Mary V	14 f	Frank	6 m	
75-531		Mary	9 f	
		THOMPSON, Caroline (B), domestic	20 f	
		DUVAL, Robt (B)	27 m	
McCHERRY, Michael, laborer	30 m IR	63-445		
Margaret	27 f			
Thomas	5 m	McCORMICK, Thomas -/1500	69 m	
Patrick	3/12 m	Latelea	67 f MD	
70-488		MERTIN, Mama	60 f	
		McCORMICK, Luther	31 m	
McCLESH, A, comm merch -/10K	25 m	135-985		
Margaret	22 f			
John	2 m			
Archie	10/12 m	McCORMICK, Thomas A, auditor -/500	38 m MD	
106-785		Jane B	35 f VA	
		Mary H	16 f	
McCLEURS, M, physician 7K/3000	33 m	Elizabeth	12 f	
Eveline	23 f	NEWTON, Joseph, comm merchant	45 m	
BRENT, Florence	19 f	Mary H	38 f	
18-100		HARRISON, Elias, Presby mn 6K/600	72 m NJ	
		DAVIS, Emma (B), domestic	23 f VA	
		60-422		
McCLISH, George, ms carptr 14K/3K	58 m VA			
Catharine	56 f	McCORMICK, William -/800	48 m IR	
George, comm clerk	19 m VA	Margaret	33 f	
Elizabeth	84 f	John	11 m	
WOOLS, William 2500/2200	70 m	McCARTY, John	32 m	
GOINS, Mary (M), cook	30 f	MULLIGAN, David	35 m	
193-1469		70-489		
McCLUSKEY, Barney, laborer	50 m	McCRACKEN, Jas, laborer 800/100	55 m	
Mary	30 f	Jane	40 f	
Mary	5 f	George, weaver	16 m	
Peter	2 m	Nancy	12 f	
36-231		Robt	8 m	

ALEXANDRIA VIRGINIA 1860 CENSUS

Maxen	6 m VA	McDOWELL, James, laborer		28 m IR
Mary	18 f IR	Mary		23 f MD
97-711		Robt		5 m VA
		James		3 m
McCRACKEN, John, grocer 100/2K	50 m MD	Mary		1/12 f
Mary	39 f	56-394		
Ella	11 f VA			
182-1384		McFARLANE, Bridgett		51 f
		Patrick		22 m
McCRACKEN, Tim	50 m	John, cotton mill		17 m
97-706		Michael		15 m
		Bridgett		8 f
McCANE, John	45 m	97-710		
Susanna	50 f			
William, sailor	21 m	McFARLANE, John, laborer		30 m IR
Albert	13 m	Catharine		22 f
Mary	11 f	James		4/12 m VA
102-757		95-694		
		MacFUNIS, Wm (M), laborer		56 m
McCUIN, Jas	50 m	Rebecca (M)		56 f
Robert, carpenter 2K/-	35 m	May (M)		18 f
Agnes	25 m	William (M)		16 m
Robert	8 m	Jane (M)		14 f
Lizzie	6 f	237-1836		
Emma	1 f			
William, laborer	21 m	McGINNIS, Hugh, grocer -/400		30 m IR
235-1815		Annie		28 f
		Mary		2/12 f VA
McCUNN, Robert, carter -/50	36 m	James, drugman		28 m IR
Mary	29 f	57-408		
Martha	12 f			
Bobby	9 m			
Infant	1/12 f	McGINNIS, John, laborer		35 m IR
200-1530		Eliza		30 f IR
		Jimmy		4 m VA
McDANIEL, Calvin, printer -/600	26 m NC	Mary		2 f
Sarah	35 f	91-663		
William B	11 m			
James C	9 m	McGRATH, Agathy, grocer -/100		78 f MD
Annie	3 f	Julia		40 f GT
Lewis	1 m	A serv maid, refused to give name		33 f f
Bettie (B), domestic	8 f	171-1279		
204-1561				
		McGRAW, Jas E, sumac mfg 2K/1558		38 m GT
McDONAGH, Michie, laborer	40 m IR	Ellen A		38 f
Biddie	35 f	Kate		16 f
Mary	9 f VA	Laura		16 f
Thos	7 m	Ada		12 f
Martin	3 m	Esther		10 f
Caroline	1 f	Julia		8 f
138-1010		Mary		7 f
		Edward		4 m
McDONALD, Patrick, laborer	69 m IR	HOLLY, Fanny (M), domestic		10 f
Bridgett	44 f IR	PHILIPS, Ann		40 f
97-715		19-108		
McDONNELL, Lawrence, carter	22 m IR	McGRAW, Margaret -/1200		54 f IR
Patrick, laborer	17 f	48-336		
Mary	10 f			
Hugh	7 m	McGRAW, Wm, laborer		27 m
98-716		Mary		23 f

ALEXANDRIA VIRGINIA 1860 CENSUS

Robt	3/12 m	McKINY, James, laborer	25 m MD
97-713		Georgiana	19 f
		William	5/12 m
McGRUDER, Peter (B), well digger	40 m	228-1755	
Harrit (B)	33 f		
WHITLEY, Eli (B), laborer	47 m	McKNIGHT, Wm H, ms carptr 4K/475	60 m
143-1051		Margaret	58 f
		Elizabeth	26 f
McGUIRE, Wm, laborer	30 m MA	William, carpenter	22 m
Mary	34 f IR	173-1292	
Mary	8 f		
81-584		McLAIN, Anthony, gov clerk 4500/500	46 m
		Sara	43 f
McHENRY, Michael, laborer	30 m IR	Malcolm	14 m
Margaret	27 f	Donald	10 m
Thomas	3 m VA	23-130	
Patrick	3/12 m		
70-488		McLEAN, Joseph, cooper 3500/200	67 m
		Elizbeth	63 f
		James	37 m
McINTOSCH, Catharine, seamstress -/20	24 m	Martha	2 f
Mary	3/12 f	RIARDON, Rachael	96 f
207-1587		61-429	
McINTOSH, Thomas, carpenter	25 m VA	McLINN, Owen, laborer	35 m
Lucy	26 f	Catharine	27 f
Charles	2 m	Mary	10 f MD
McHENRY, Virginia	9 f	Suzanna	7 f NY
27-166		Jemima	6 f VA
		70-493	
McKEE, Thomas, stm engine mech -/150	49 m IR		
Sarah	43 f PA		
Robt	13 m	McLISH, George, master cooper 14K/3K	55 m VA
John	10 m	Catharine	56 f MD
Ella	5 f	George, comm clerk	19 m VA
82-488		Elizabeth	86 f
		WOOLS, William -/25	70 m
		GOINS, Mary (M), cook	30 f
McKENSIE, Lewis, pres RR 5600/1100	48 m	193-1469	
Mary	35 f		
Esther	25 f	McMAHON, John, stone cutter -/50	40 m IR
114-844		Ann	30 f
		Edward	12 m PA
McKINEY, John W, laborer	30 m MD	Burnard	9 m
Jane	30 f	Frances	7 m
Lucinda	7 f	John	6 m
Noble	5 m	Peter	2 m
228-1756		TOTLE, Mary A	16 f IR
		23-135	
McKING, Jas, laborer	25 m MD		
Georgana	19 f	McMANN, Dennis, cartman	26 m
William	5/12 m VA	Mary	25 f
228-1755		Peter	7 m
		Richard	5 m
McKINIKER, A M, gardner 4K/600	29 m ST	Michael	4 m
Elizabeth	29 f	Dennis	2 m
Margaret	3 f	35-222	
Mary	2 f		
Elizabeth	8/12 f	McMAW, Augalette -/60	45 f IR
MALORY, John, laborer	20 m IR	Barney	16 m
STIMSON, Wm	26 m VA	Mary	11 f
281-2147		94-679	

ALEXANDRIA VIRGINIA 1860 CENSUS

McMULLEN, John, laborer	35 m MA	McVEIGH, Jas H, whsale grocer 15K/1200	57 m		
Martha	27 f EG	Job G, lawyer	24 m		
Martha	2 f MD	Louisa	26 f		
283-2167		James H, grocer	20 m		
		Louisa	17 f		
McNAMARA, Jas, blacksmith	46 m IR	Thomas E	15 m		
Margaret	45 f	Isabella	12 f		
John	22 m	Newton	10 m		
Mike, appren	14 m	Cynthia	8 f		
Margaret	13 f	GUEST, Elizabeth	70 f		
100-737		HENRY, Adalvie (M), domestic	16 f		
		57-406			
McNAMARA, Mark, laborer -/40	26 m IR	McVEIGH, Newton, bank pres 80K/13K	50 m		
Bridgett	25 f	Jane	50 f		
Samuel	3 m VA	Mollie	22 f		
Bridgett	1 f	Willie, clerk shoe store	21 m		
MARREY, James	55 m	-ewilliam	18 m		
BEACH, John	9 m	Harvey	15 m		
100-735		170-1277			
		MACY, Geo, farmer	26 m VA		
McQUAIN, James, overseer	26 m VA	Eloise	22 f		
Julia	21 f	252-1963			
278-2134					
		MACY, Wm 1500/150	45 m		
McQUEEN, John S, overseer 1K/-	29 m	Nancy	45 f		
Elizabeth	20 f	Elizabeth	26 f		
Caroline	8 f	Robert	30 m		
Georgiana	6 f	William	23 m		
Lucy	4 f	Rosier	18 m		
264-2045		252-1964			
MacRATH, Geo H, tanner & currer 9K/3K	49 m	MADELLA, R (B), cooper	64 m		
Mary	40 f EG	BUTLER, Peter (B), cooper	18 m		
Sarah E	20 f VA	SMITH, Wm (B)	24 m		
RAINE, Mary	58 f EG	237-1826			
John	60 m				
183-1387		MADELLA, Richard (B), laborer	25 m		
		Anna (B)	25 f		
McRUDD, Jas, barber	22 m	Cornelius (B)	9 m		
Laura	20 f	William (B)	7 m		
Fanny	8 f	Eliza (B)	6 f		
140-1024		Josaphine (B)	4 f		
		168-1260			
McSHERRY, Mary	49 f IR	MADISON, Elizabeth, seamstress	31 f		
Patrick, laborer	25 m	Mary, wash & iron	26 f		
McNALLY, P	30 m	James	12 m		
54-378		Alcinda	8 f		
		Martha	5 f		
McSIM, Ownen	35 m	Infant	7/12 m VA		
Catharine	27 f	56-400			
Mary	10 f MD				
Susznna	7 f NY				
Jimiama	6 f VA	MADOLITH, Henry, coach maker	47 m		
70-493		Alma	31 f MD		
		Henry	14 m		
McVANY, Owen, laborer	25 m IR	James	12 m		
Catharine	25 f	GETTY, Dominick, blacksmith	23 m IR		
Patrick	5 f WA	ALLISON, John, coach painter	24 m VA		
Ellen	1 f	CAWOOD, Sarah	50 f		
90-646		199-1524			

80

ALEXANDRIA VIRGINIA 1860 CENSUS

MACHEN, Coffer, RR engineer -/200	29 m	MANDEVILLE, Mary 4K/5K	78 f EG
Ann E	29 f	197-1501	
Mary	4 f		
ROBINSON, Emma (B), domestic	16 f	MANKIN, Chas, house carpenter -/100	37 m
153-1128		Sarah	32 f
		Charles	7 m
MAGINK, Henry, machinist	40 m IR	Wallace	4 m
Jane	36 f	41-275	
Margaret	11 f MD		
154-1139		MANKIN, Mark, ms carptr 5K/2K	55 m
		Elizabeth	49 f
MAHAFFEY, Thos G, coal agent 21K/1K	45 m ST	Alexander, grocer	26 m
......	35 f CN	Barbara	22 f
Emily	23 f CN	Charles	21 m
GIBSON, Matilda	7 f PA	Samuel, clerk comm merchant	19 m
83-594		George, plasterer appren	16 m
		Benjamin	13 m
MAHAN, Thos, coachman	25 m VA	Kate	8 f
Susan	23 f	191-1455	
Sarah	4 f		
42-285		MANKINS, Daniel, stone mason	49 m IR
		Sarah A	40 f VA
MAHONE, Jane, shoe bonder	36 f	DALLAS, Geo	14 m
Elinor	12 f	WILLIAMS, Mary, domestic	33 m
John	10 m	154-1138	
246-1913			
		MANKINS, Wm D, grocer 8K/1K	60 m
MAHONY, Samuel, laborer -/50	27 m MD	Dorcas	67
Mary	55 f VA	Elizabeth	28 f
KING, Annie, domestic	10 f GT	Martha	26 f
198-1518		Oscar	16 m
		Virginia	8 f
MAHUN, Thomas, coachman -/50	25 m VA	BRADSHAW, Mary (M), domestic	35 f
Susan	23 f	41-274	
Sarah	6 f		
42-285		MANLY, Francis, cord wanner -/40	41 m
		Helen	41 f
		CARSON,, H C	8 f
MALONEY, Cor, laborer	37 m	LEWIS, Selima	80 f PA
Ellen	30 f	SAINT, Joseph, house carpenter	26 m
Margaret	9 f	227-1748	
Jimmy	8 m		
Cornelius	5 m	MANSFIELD, Freeman, house carptr -/100	31 m NC
55-385		Precilla	18 f NC
		James	12 m NC
MALONEY, James, shoemaker	37 m IR	Susanna	10 f
Margaret	33 f	William	3 m VA
John	5 m	161-1194	
James	2 m		
MONAHAN, shoemaker	20 m IR	MANSFIELD, Henry, tobaconist 4K/700	63 m MD
174-1308		Lucy	63 f VA
		JACOBS, Amelia	36 f
MALORY, John, laborer	20 m IR	MANSFIELD, Mary	30 f
281-2147		Lucinda	28 f
		Ann	22 f
MANAHAN, Lou, laborer	37 m IR	JACOBS, Fanny	10 f AR
Bridgett	36 f	Thomas	4 m VA
John	12 m EG	Amanda	1 f
Mary	7 f VA	11-52	
Bridgett	3 f		
Lawrence	8/12 f	MARBERRY, Wm H, bank cashier 2K/1K	42 m
168-1262		Anna -/1200	32 f

ALEXANDRIA VIRGINIA 1860 CENSUS

Alice	13 f	Annie	4/12 f	
Anna		BLACK, Catharine (M), domestic	27 f	
Francis F	6 m	133-975		
Leonard	4 m			
Mary	2 f	MARKELL, George H, tanr & curr 9K/3K	49 m	
DENT, McGruder, grocer	19 m	Mary	40 f EG	
123-902		Sarah E	20 f VA	
		RAINE, Mary	58 f EG	
MARBLE, Israel (B)	50 m	John	60 m	
238-1838		183-1387		
MARCEY, Jas	27 m	MARKELL, Samuel W, tanner -/150	40 m	
Elizabeth	26 f	Elizabeth	39 f	
John H	3 m	Virginia	19 f	
James F	2 m	Amanda	14 f	
259-2014		George	12 m	
		Samuel	8 m	
MARCEY, Jas, farmer 600/200	53 m	Bettie	2 f	
Mary	50 f	199-1520		
Catharine	24 f			
Jane	20 f	MARKHAM, Mary -/50	46 f EG	
Mary	17 f	Mary, dress maker	20 f MD	
259-2012		Elizabeth	18 f	
		Frances	15 f	
MARCEY, Lewis, farmer 600/100	48 m	29-180		
Ann	60 f			
Robert H	48 m	MARKHAND, J, dairyman -/300	38 m EG	
Mary	30 f	Mary	40 f	
William	7 m	ALLEN, Sarah	8 f	
Robert	3 m	Sarah	66 f	
259-2013		RAMB, Edmond, laborer	20 m MD	
		281-2145		
MARCEY, Samuel, laborer	25 m			
Mary	23 f			
Matilda	6 f	MARKS, Robert, hotel keeper -/50	29 m VA	
Henrietta	3 f	Eliza	35 f	
Infant	4/12 f	George	10 m	
259-2011		John	7 m	
		Jimmy	2 m	
MARCY, Samuel, laborer	32 m	107-791		
Mary	25 f			
Matilda	7 f	MARROTT, John W, bridge builder -/50	46 m EG	
Henrietta	5 f	Jane	35 f	
Lucy	5/12 f	Wm H	13 m	
260-2015		Mary	12 f	
		SAVAGE, Mary	15 f	
MARCHER, Jas, gardner -/50	50 m EG	258-2004		
Temperance	50 f			
James, laborer	25 m	MARS, Jno (B), laborer	30 m	
Emanuel	23 m	Rebecca (B)	27 f	
Sarah	20 f	122-896		
John	16 m			
Emma	14 f	MARSHALL, James K, gr & comm mc -/1K	36 m	
Ann	6 f	Fanny	36 f	
Catharine	18 f	Claude	4 m	
Mary	1 f	Lucy	2 f	
273-2104		Jas I	9/12 m	
		Edward C, clerk	18 m	
MARK, Ann S 2K/200	60 f	24-140		
Ellen, teacher	46 f			
Lydia	31 f	MARSHALL, Sophia (M) -/30	20 f	
GREGORY, Douglas, dry goods merchant	34 m	Harriet (M)	8 f	

ALEXANDRIA VIRGINIA 1860 CENSUS

Emily (M)	10/12 f	MARTIN, John, sailor 3900/100	56 m	
240-1859		Sally	20 f	
		Mary	17 f	
MARSHALL, Thos, comm merch 5K/30K	35 m MD	Jack	15 m	
Henrietta E	33 f	Vigin..	11 f	
Anauna	12 f	Billy	8 m	
Denis	10 m	James	5 m	
Elenor	8 f	Helen	2 f	
Sallie	7 f	222-1712		
Thos	2 m			
Infant	1/12 m	MARTINE, Elizabeth	44 f IR	
104-766		James, sailor	23 m	
		Thomas, carter	17 m	
MARTIN, A C, freight agent -/100	46 m	Bridgett	15 f	
Susan	42 f	John	12 m VA	
Isabella	17 f	Michael	10 m	
CAWOOD, Catharine	16 f	56-393		
Ann	12 f			
MARTIN, Clara	4 f			
THOMPSON, Joseph, carpenter	19 m	MARY, Edward, house carpenter	33 m	
187-1415		Alice	30 f	
		REED, Alice	10 f	
		Ida	5 f	
MARTIN, Adam, farmer -/500	32 m	LOYD, Mary, domestic	15 f	
Ann	26 f EG	191-1454		
Maggie	4 f NJ			
Thomas	3 m	MARYNE, Mertin, agri 3K/2K	35 m	
Mary	9/12 f	Caroline	24 f MD	
SWANN, Wm, laborer	42 m	Chas B, clerk	21 m	
280-2139		105-778		
MARTIN, H S, brewer -/500	52 m NY	MASELLA, Armanda (B), laborer	38 m	
Clarissa	48 f	Elizabeth (M), wash & iron	31 f	
Hortense	19 f	41-277		
Mary	17 f			
Henrietta	17 f	MASON, Peter, RR fireman	25 m	
H Clay	15 m	Martha	21 f	
Fanny	13 f	MORRON, Jas, plasterer	22 m	
Leonard	9 m	Annie	21 f	
Emma	7 f	BLADEN, Georgana	16 f OH	
Ada	5 f	206-1572		
Ida	5 f			
142-1045		MASON, Sidney (B)	58 f	
		TOB, Phoebe (B)	16 f	
		172-1287		
MARTIN, James, boot & shoe mkr -/150	36 m MD			
Jane	40 f	MASSEY, John, laborer	32 m	
....., clerk leather store	15 m	Catherine	50 f	
Ann	12 f	252-1961		
Thomas	8 m			
Lavinia	7 f			
Ellen	5 f	MASSEY, Joseph, sailor	30 m	
Elenora, daily domestic	16 f EG	May	21 f	
181-1374		John	1 m	
		KING, Mattey H	52 f	
MARTIN, John, coal .... -/350	46 m	222-1715		
Hannah	33 f VA			
John	11 m	MASSEY, Robt (insane) 2K/1K	74 m	
Reper	4 f	Mary	62 f	
Wm H	1 m	WINSSELL, Helen	37 f	
BURNS, Mary A	12 f	John	10 m VA	
173-1295		107-794		

ALEXANDRIA VIRGINIA 1860 CENSUS

MASSEY, Rudolph, tailer -/300	37 m	Katie	6 f
Urusula	32 f	Willard	3/12 m
Virginia	13 f	190-1446	
Richard	12 m		
Harry	10 m	MAY, William H, agri store 20K/-	35 m
Helen	8 f	Sarah	30 f
Randolph	6 m	John	4 m
Mary	5 f	33-209	
Addis	1 f		
194-1480		MEAD, Catharine, seamstress	34 f MD
		Mary, seamstress	18 f VA
MASSEY, Wm L, merch tailor 1200/4K	46 m	William, appren printer	16 m
May E	44 f VA	Kate	12 m
Mary D	18 f	59-418	
Caroline K	16 f		
Gertrude	13 f	MEADE, Drayton G, agri store -/3500	29 m
Wm A	11 m	Annie	27 f NY
James	7 m	Frances	4 f VA
Sally	4 f	Bessie	2 f VA
MURRAY, Jane	65 f IR	HIRTE, Hugh S, clerk	21 m
LAWLER, Dennis, appren tailor	17 m	Kiddin M, clerk	19 m
120-884		105-779	
MASSIE, Mary 10400/-	67 f		
Maggie 2K/-	22 f	MEADE, Robert, baggage master -/50	28 m
Nancy	8 f	Rosia	26 f
Eugene	5 m	Edm	4 m
167-1248		Wilmar	1 m
		65-459	
MASTERS, John, coal agent -/350	46 m KY		
Hannah	33 f VA	MEAGHER, Elizabeth, grocer 1500/300	42 f IR
John	11 m	James, porter	26 m VA
Reper	4 f	Mary	2 f
Wm H	1 m	64-451	
BURNS, Mary A	12 f		
173-1295		MEAGHER, Patrick, laborer	27 m IR
		Catharine	22 f
MASTISSON, Mary 4350/100	63 f MD	Margaret	1 f
GLASCOE, Charlotte	13 f VA	150-1109	
213-1641			
		MECHOR, Ferdinand, hotel kpr 1500/100	32 m MD
MAURY, Maria -/100	55 f SL	Sophia	22 f SX
Elizabeth	21 f VA	Aurilea	5 f MD
George	16 m	Armine	3 f
Mary	11 f	KRONS, Arty, tunner	26 m SX
Harriet	5 f	SMITH, Chin, domestic	18 f
COONEY, Joseph, barkeeper	27 m MD	MELCHOR, Julius	2 m MD
PARSONS, John, laborer	22 m EG	110-817	
DEITZ, John, laborer	21 m NJ		
NOWLAND, John, laborer	21 m VA	MERAN, James, steam b engines -/100	35 m NY
DuVAL, John, laborer	25 m	Irma	31 f
BUSHBY, Joseph, wheelwright	25 m	May	2 f VA
71-501		132-962	
MAXWELL, Geo, plaster master 3K/150	46 m DC		
Erma	35 f	MERCHANT, Robt, varnisher -/150	40 m EG
Ella	18 f	Isabella	30 f MD
Geo, plasterer	17 m	James	11 m VA
Ada	15 f	Elizabeth	9 f
Frank	13	Saml	6 m
Agnes	10 f	George	2 m
Carrol	8 m	78-551	

ALEXANDRIA VIRGINIA 1860 CENSUS

MERNIK, Alfred (B) -/200	50 m	MILES, Jas L, bricklayer	45 m PA
Rebecca (B)	41 f	Delia	42 f
Jane (B)	19 f	Wm, blacksmith	18 m PA
202-1546		James	12 m
		Cordelia	4 f
MERTIMER, Ludwell, farmer 1500/150	63 m	Elleanor	8 f
Mary	57 f	Missouri	6 f
James	15 m	Laura	3 f
Frances	12 f	242-1879	
275-2116			
		MILLAN, Walter R, negro tr 2800/2K	36 m
MEYENBURG, S, dry goods merch 1K/10K	32 m HN	Columbia	26 f
Sophia	23 f HD	Eddie V	4 f
Max	8/12 m	John	2 m
Catharine	25 f HD	141-1041	
12-62			
		MILLER, Augt, laborer	26 m GR
MIDDLETON, Hanna (B)	40 f	Kate	20 f
David (B)	19 m	Lena	3 f
Haina (B)	23 f	Mary	1 f
Jane (B)	16 f	270-2083	
Mary (B)	13 f		
Isabella (B)	9 f	MILLER, Chas, laborer	38 m NY
Ulyses (M)	2 m	Christie	30 f
Laura (M)	9/12 f	Amanda	4 f VA
55-382		Charles	3 m
		79-561	
MIDDLETON, Henry, coach maker -/2K	47 m		
Alma	31 f	MILLER, Elisha, china store 4K/1500	32 m VA
Henry	14 m	Bettie S	27 f
James	12 m	CARTER, Jenny	11 f
GILLING, Dominick, blacksmith	23 m	EVANS, Charlotte (M), domestic	47 f
ALLISON, John, coach painter	24 m VA	SWANN, John H, clerk	18 m
CAWOOD, Sarah	52 f	6-40	
199-200-1524			
		MILLER, Fred, comm clerk	45 m
MILBURNE, B C, potter 10K/2K	45 m MD	Maria	41 f
Thinga	49 f	Willey, machinist	19 m
John, apothecary 1K/3K	29 VA	Susan	16 f
Stephen, potter	27 m	Annie	12 f
Washington, apothecary	19 m	Sara	9 f
Austin, grocer clerk	16 m	188-1424	
Florence	14 f		
Ethelbert	11 m	MILLER, Martin, laborer	27 m MD
Margaret	8 f	Fanny	26 f IR
207-1580		William	6 m PA
		Julia	3 f
MILBURNE, Lewis, apothecary -/300	24 m VA	Sylvester	10/12 m VA
Kate	20 f	59-418	
ETHERIDGE, Grace	8 f		
GRIMES, Julia, domestic	17 f	MILLER, Robert H, china merch 85K/75K	62 m
207-1582		Sue	57 f
		Caroline	19 f
MILBURNE, Timothy, gardner -/75	65 m EG	Eliza	17 f
TUNNING, John	40 m	Margaret A	29 f
253-1966		O'FLANNAGAN, Betty, domestic	18 f IR
		DOWNEY, Julia	50 f
MILES, Basel (B), drayman	36 m	Laune	20 m
Mary (B)	30 f	6-42	
Henrietta (B)	11 f		
Lucretia (B)	1 f	MILLER, Samuel 30500/20K	56 m
28-174		MARSHALL, Charles (M), domestic	45 m

ALEXANDRIA VIRGINIA 1860 CENSUS

Margaret (B), domestic	45 f	James	12 m
170-1273		Cordelia	11 f
		Ell...	9 f
MILLER, Sidney G, RR contr -/15962	40 m NY	Missouri	6 f
Fanny W	35 f MS	Laura	3 f
Cecilia	13 f CT	242-1886	
Kate	11 f		
Sidney	7 m	MILLS, John A, bar keeper -/30	33 m
Fanny	3 f VA	Sarah	4 m
Theodore	7/12 m	Ella	2 f
DAVIS, Cawhuie (M)	31 f	Winfield	5/12 m
85-609		183-1396	
MILLER, Sylvanis, RR contr	42 m NY	MILLS, Jno H, turner -/100	27 m MD
Mary	32 f MA	Catharine	25 f
Sylvanius	9 m CT	Alice	1 f
Rosalie	8 f	226-1741	
Ellen	7 f		
Thadeus	5 m	MILLS, Mary J, seamstress	38 f
Mary	2 f	Clarinda	15 f
14-76		28-170	
MILLER, William, grocer 16K/1K	35 m EG	MILLS, Milly (B)	61 f
Rebecca	35 f DE	RANDALL, Hester (M)	67 f
John	13 m	131-957	
Mollie	11 f		
105-776			
		MILLS, Sanford, laborer -/1200	42 m
MILLER, William D, hotel keeper	30 m MD	Savenia	37 f
Caroline	25 f VA	William	19 m
ROGERS, J C, clerk	26 m	Mary	18 f
AUGER, R H, shoe cutter	40 m MA	Amanda	15 f
HUNT, Danl, shoe cutter	35 m MA	Mark	12 f
CLEGGETT, E H, grocer clerk	25 m MD	John	10 m
MORGAN, Daniel, RR clerk	45 m	Elizabeth	8 f
SMITH, Wm W, hardware clerk	26 m	Susan	6 f
SANFORD, V, comm clerk	27 m	George	5 m
BOWMAN, J C, baggage man RR	24 m	Ann	4 f
COACHMAN, J, restaurant	35 m	Melvin	2 m
WRIGHT, Wm, sec insurance co	50 m	277-2129	
FISHER, Wm, shoe maker	30 m GR		
HISTER, Wm E, salesman dry goods	25 m VA	MILLS, Sarah	33 f
HEYMAN, H, clothing store	25 m	Ella	11 f
ZIMMERMAN, J R, clerk dry goods	23 m	Carey	2 m
CRANE, Peter, clerk drug store	21 m	219-1684	
RABE, A I, clerk comm store	33 m		
STICKLEY A S, clerk comm store	22 m		
BRYAN, James, clerk agri store	60 m	MILLS, Thomas, carpenter -/50	41 m
MARTIN, Bridgett, chambermaid	19 f IR	Laura	27 f
O'BRADY, Mary, washer woman	45 f	Bettie	5 f VA
CONNER, Mary, seamstress	35 f VA	Willie	3 m
MADDOX, J E	24 f	Maggie	1 f
SAUNDERS, S L	47 m	30-195	
Margaret	40 f		
JONES, William D (B), dining rm serv	60 m	MILLS, William (M), laborer	30 m
JACKSON, Damdiste (B), dining rm serv	50 f	Haney (B)	50 f
122-894		TATE, Jas (B), laborer	25 m
		28-172	
MILLS, James L, bricklayer -/50	45 m PA		
Delia	42 f VA	MILLS, Wm, cigar maker 600/50	61 m VA
Wm, blacksmith	18 m PA	Eliza	55 f
Delia	16 f	235-1811	

ALEXANDRIA VIRGINIA 1860 CENSUS

MINGO, Fred	45 m NA	Margaret	22 f	
Mary	42 f	Haremon C	5 m	
90-648		MOLAIR, James, machinist	23 m	
		Luther	20 m	
MINOR, John, hardware -/2K	51 m	Bettie	18 f	
Lydia	23 f	Roze, printer	16 m	
Ella	18 f	LYNN, Charley, clerk	22 m	
CUBIT, Kitty, domestic	25 f	GOODMAN, Robt, RR engineer	22 m	
Money	21 f	KEYS, Alexander, fireman RR	29 m	
35-224		SCOTT, machinist	21 m	
		John, shoemaker	40 m	
MINOR, Smith, farmer 3K/6K	69 m	COHEN, John, machinist	26 m	
Mary	69 f	LUCKITT, William, fireman RR	25	
Marcella	36 f	PIERSON, Joseph, printer	18	
Christian S	39 m	GOODMAN, John, bricklayer	26 m GR	
Elijabeth M	33 f	33/34-215		
Cornelia	29 f			
Mary J	26 f	MONCURE, Mary	20 f IR	
266-2061		95-695		
MINOR, Wm J, farmer	40 m	MONGO, Fred	45 m NA	
Catharine	72 f	Mary	62 f	
NEWTON, Margaret	20 f	90-648		
256-1985				
		MONROE, H L, constable 1K/3500	41 m	
MITCHELL, George (B) 800/50	50 m	Margaret	35 f MD	
Ellen (B)	45 f	William H	16 m VA	
Margaret (B)	21 f	John	12 m	
Harriet (B)	18 g	Thom H	3 m	
George (B)	13 m	249-1941		
Robert (B)	12 m			
WARE, Adaline (B), do-estic	25 f			
167-1253		MONROE, J C, pilot agent -/100	62 m	
		Mary	58 f	
MITCHELL, Margaret 600/20	40 f	Cornelius, steam RR engineer	25 m	
Thomas, machinist	17 m	Nancy	25 f	
Gertrude	16 f	Francis	5 m	
Florida	10 f	Mary	3 f	
52-363		175-1314		
MIX, C E, grocery clerk 13K/5K	50 m CT	MONROE, James T -/100	36 m VA	
Catharine	47 f	Amanda	36 f	
William, farmer	26 m	Mary	8 f	
Catharine	20 f	Anna	7 f	
Martha	18 f	Rebecca	1 f	
Franklin	16 m	178-1331		
Edward	16 m			
Frank	12 m	MONROE, John H	65 m MD	
Ella	6 f	Elizabeth	33 f	
GIBSON, Henry (M), laborer	30 m	Elizabeth	8 f	
Charlota (M), domestic	31 f	Samuel	6 m	
267-2066		George	4 m	
		67-470		
MOHALL, Robt, laborer	36 m EG			
Margaret	33 f	MONROE, Wm, huckster	79 m	
James	10 m VA	Sarah	57 f	
William	9 m	James	13 m	
Anne	6 f	108-796		
98-723				
		MONTJOY, Arrington, scavenger	60 m	
MOLAIR, Hebanon, brd house 800/300	55 f	Nancy	57 f	
JELIFF, G D, dry good merch	33 m CT	74-521		

ALEXANDRIA VIRGINIA 1860 CENSUS

MONTJOY, William, machinist -/75	25 m	Martha	3 f
Nancy	25 f	BROADBECK, Emily, domestic	19 f
Ada	3 f	233-1796	
Edgar	2 m		
BEACHANT, Sarah, monthly nurse	55 f	MOORE, William F, drayman 4800/-	40 m
79-559		Catharine	35 f
		Maria, appren millener	15 f
MOORE, A F, shoe maker -/300	36 m MD	Thomas	10 m
Cornelea	33 f VA	Adalisde	7 f
McMANN, Mary	16 f	Evaline	6 f
MOORE, Alvin, cigar maker	17 m MD	Willie	5 m
108-802		Katie	3 f
		28-168	
MOORE, Chas, tanner	37 m IR		
Mary	42 f	MOORE, Wm S, machinist -/100	38 m
Mary	12 f	Ann	35 f
James	6 m	Norman	16 m
Maggie	3 f	Charles	11 m
239-1852		William	9 m
		Allen	6 m
MOORE, Chas S, ms machinist 1K/500	36 m CN	Julian	5 m
Mary A	34 f PA	Ezekial	2 m
William	10 m	225-1734	
Frank	8 m		
Media	6 m	MORAN, Anthony, sadler -/3K	52 m IR
Charles	2 m	Charlotte	45 f
202-1541		Charlotte	16 f NY
		Henora	13 f MD
MOORE, Jno, capt watch -/100	43 m MD	Mary	10 f
Anna	38 f BM	119-880	
Sarah	15 f		
Julia	13 f	MORAN, James, stmb engineer -/100	35 m NY
George	11 m	Jenny	31 f
Mary	4 f	Mary	2 f VA
Emily	2 f	132-962	
WHITNEY, James, Sailor	30 m		
Elizabeth	28 f BM		
Jane	3 f	MORE, Alfred, laborer	49 m MD
81-582		Ellen	48 f
		DIXON, Frances	14 f
MOORE, Joseph, laborer	50 m IR	183-1393	
Margaret	50 f		
John	18 m	MORGAN, Dan (B), laborer	39 m
36-230		165-1229	
MOORE, Joseph C, pilot agent -/100	62 m	MORNE, Sophia 2K/10K	55 f
Mary	58 f	Elizabeth	21 f
Cornelius, steamboat engineer	25 m	Mary	19 f
Nancy	25 f	AFFEY, Kate, domestic	22 f IR
Francis	5 m	75-532	
Mary	3 f		
175-1314		MORRELL, Mary -/8K	63 f MA
		Mary	34 f
MOORE, Mary	35 f	Sarah	27 f
Vernon	7 m	Virginia	24 f
Clarence	6 m	William	22 m
Ida	3 f	SHERWOOD, Maria	50 f
225-1735		121-889	
MOORE, Robert S, laborer	27 m MD	MORRIS, Chas, laborer	42 m IR
Martha	22 f	Mary	85 f
May	5 f	137-1002	

ALEXANDRIA VIRGINIA 1860 CENSUS

MORRISFIELD, Freeman, house carpenter	31 m NC	Ella	9 m	
Precilla	28 f	Sessa	3 f	
James	12 m	16-88		
Susanna	10 f			
William	3 m	MULLEN, Catharine, wash & iron	36 f GT	
161-1194		George	12 m VA	
		John	10 m	
MORRISON, Sabasy (M), wash & iron	70 f MD	217-1670		
Eliza (M)	38 f			
127-928		MULLINS, James, laborer	36 m	
		Jane	34 f	
MORTIMER, Mary, seamstress	26 f	Benjamin	10 m	
George	10 m	Albert	9 m	
Charles	7 m	John	6 m	
THOMPSON, Elmira, seamstress	30 f	William S	3 m	
86-616		55-390		
MORTON, Rebecca (B)	25 f	MURDEN, Geo, laborer	47 m IR	
Fanny (B)	1 f	Jane	45 f VA	
173-1293		Joseph	7 m VA	
		SHIRKS, John, laborer	25 m NJ	
MOSS, Victoria, seamstress	23 f VA	135-991		
Matilda	70 f			
THOMPSON, Elenora, wash & iron	25 f	MURKLEY, John, laborer	32 m MD	
Ida	3 f	Jane	33 f VA	
189-1452		Sarah	10 f	
		HENDERSON, Lauretta	21 f	
MOTHERHEAD, Lewis, ship carptr -/100	35 m	111-824		
May	26 f			
John	11 m	MURNAIN, Richard, laborer	28 m	
Charles	6 m	Mary	21 f	
Catharine	4 f	Laura	5 f	
William	2 m	232-1789		
190-1447				
		MURPHY, F T, physician 20K/1K	53 m	
MOURAELL, Elizabeth	60 f	191-1456		
ADAMS, Charles, dry goods clerk	38 m			
Morietta	33 f			
Charles	7 m	MURPHY, John, laborer 20	45 m IR	
Edwin	5 m	Margaret	40 f	
Lewis	2 m	Jeremiah, carter	20 m	
GRAHAM, Mary	82 f	John, laborer	16 m	
178-1332		91-660		
MOXLEY, Oscar (B), laborer	35 m	MURPHY, Lloyd, laborer -/30	50 m MD	
Julia (M)	25 f	Nancy	52 f	
Mary (M)	3 f	Thomas	28 m	
Joseph (M)	4/12 m	Fanny	23 f VA	
Ann Ella (M), wash & iron	27 f	Mary, cotton mill	23 f MD	
28-178		Sarah, spinner	19 f	
		Saml, weaver	17 m	
		Robt	14 m	
MUIR, John, hardware -/2K	51 m	Lloyd, spinner	12 m	
Lydia	28 f	Joshua	8 m	
Ella	18 f	92-666		
CABIT, Kitty, domestic	25 f			
MUIR, Money	21 f	MURPHY, Michael, laborer	35 m IR	
35-224		Catharine	26 f	
		Dennis	6 m VA	
MUIR, Wm H, cabinet Maker 20K/10K	46 m VA	90-647		
Eliza A	31 f			
James F	13 m	MURPHY, Miles, laborer	26 m IR	

ALEXANDRIA VIRGINIA 1860 CENSUS

Mary	26 f		Sarah	27 f	
207-1581			Virginia	24 f	
			William	22 m	
MURPHY, Patrick, laborer	28 m IR	SLAWOOD, Maria	20 f	
Margaret	24 f	121-889		
Anatalia	2 f VA			
242-1877		MURTOUGH, Jas, laborer	50 m IR
		Mary	43 f	
MURPHY, Patrick 700/60	66 m	Mary	10 f NJ
Anastasia	66 f IR	201-1535	
Miles, laborer	36 m		
240-1866		MURTOUGH, Wm, laborer	57 m IR
		Ann	57 f	
MURPHY, Thos, drayman 300/200	33 m IR	Bridgett	22 f
Harriet	30 f	John	21 m
94-683		Mary, domestic	19 f
		Elizabeth	17 f
MURRAY, Alex, tailor -/3K	36 m	Thomas, brickmaker	15 m
Martha	38 f	Margaret	8 f
Thomasine	13 m	William	5 m
Ellen	8 f	201-1534	
Catharine	7 f		
Joseph	5 m	MUSE, William H (B), laborer	27 m
McGEE, Mary, domestic	16 f	Mary (B)	26 f
WITHERS, Margaret	52 f	WHEELER, Josephine (M)	24 f
114-843		Mary E (M)	10/12 f
		28-171	
MURRAY, Jas, laborer	48 m IR		
Bridgett	29 f	NAILOR, Barbara, huckster	52 f WB
Mary	7 f VA	John	15 m VA
John	3 m	60-425	
HENRETTY, Francis	41 m IR		
SAULS, John	54 m EG	NALLES, Serepta -/50	50 f VA
101-748		Boynton, nailor	22 f
		Willis, house carpenter	20 m
MURRAY, Levi, cabinet man	50 m VA	Ellen	17 f
Catharine	40 f	Ruberta	13 f
John, cabinet maker	23 m	Elvira	11 f
Levi, blacksmith	22 m	BLACK, Jane (B)	30 f
Arthur, appren cabinet maker	25 m	204-1563	
WIGGS, Jas, teacher	26 m		
James D	13 m	NALLS, Jas, ms carptr 4100/300	49 m
Betty	11 f	Ann	39 f
Mary V	8 f VA	Rowena	18 f
Richard	5 m	Lithia	13 f
Caroline	3 f	Benjamin	10 m
27-163		BLACK, Cecilia (B)	12 f
		246-1912	
MURRAY, Wm, tailor 800/4050	36 m IR		
Elizabeth	34 f IR	NALLS, Martin, hatter	38 m
Margaret	19 f IR	Harriet	36 f
John S, printer	18 m IR	Harriet	12 f
Jesse, appren carpenter	16 m IR	Lydia	12 f
James	12 m IR	Jane	10 f
Ann	9 f IR	151-1115	
Maria	8 f		
Bettie	7 f	NEALE, C L, stone cutter -/3K	60 m MD
Mary	3 f	Anna	40 f
124-910		Charles	30 m WA
		Indiana	19 f VA
MURRELL, Mary 8K/-	63 f MA	Susan V	18 f
Mary	34 f	Laura	17 f

ALEXANDRIA VIRGINIA 1860 CENSUS

Frances	16 m	NEWMAN, Wm, carpenter	50 m	
James	16 m	Elizabeth	40 f	
Emma	10 f	SHAP, Wm, cooper	65 m MD	
Anne	6 f	Anna	25 f VA	
175-1311		Eddie	3 m	
		Susan	22 f	
NEALE, Christopher, lawyer 40K/4K	67 m	Virginia	19 f	
Virginia C	36 f	140-1027		
Chapman	10 m			
CHAPMAN, Sidney	70 m	NICHELSON, John, huckster -/50	50 m	
196-1498		Percella	42 f	
		213-1640		
NELSON, George (B), porter	36 m			
Virginia (B)	27 f	NICKINS, Jno (M), bank runner -/20	46 m	
Alevin (B)	4 f	Lucy (M)	37 f	
John (B)	2 m	John (M), porter	18 m	
FULLER, Jenny (B)	91 f	James (M)	15 m	
200-1528		Lucy (M)	10 f	
		123-897		
NELSON, Geo W, police officer 800/150	50 m	NIGHTINGALE, John, ship carpenter	45 m	
Elizabeth	47 f	Isabella	44 f	
Maria	23 f	Amanda	16 f	
Elizabeth A, milliner	17 f	John	13 m	
George	15 m	Ann	11 f	
Mary E	12 f	Isabella	9 f	
69-487		May	7 f	
		Orlando	5 m	
NELSON, John, steam/engineer -/100	28 m	Maria	3 f	
Catherine	30 f IR	James	6/12 m	
Annie	10 f NJ	224-1726		
Samuel	5 m			
John	7/12 m	NIGHTINGALE, Joseph, grave dig -/150	45 m	
Mary	6 f	Emily	31 f	
Catharine	3 f NJ	John	18 m	
213-1642		William	16 m	
		Edgar	13 m	
		Ada	11 f	
NELSON, Patsy (B), wash & iron	40 f	Joseph	8 m	
Martha (B)	29 f	George	6 m	
Jinny (M)	27 f	Chas	2 m	
Georgiana (M)	23 f	Missouri	7/12 f	
Charlotte (B)	26 f	243-1883		
Billy (B), laborer	21 m			
Alice (B)	6 f	NIGHTINGILL, James, cutler -/100	83 m	
Caroline (B)	9 f	Mary	66 f	
John (B)	5 m	174-1305		
Haddie (B)	3/12 f			
Daniel (M)	4 m	NOEL, William, pilot -/50	45 m	
Ada (M)	2 f	Catherine	37 f	
210-1611		Arthur C, house & light painter	27 m	
		Cordelia	17 f	
NEVITT, James C, comm merch 400/250	45 m	Harriet	15 f	
Alevia	35 f	Isaac	13 m	
Henry	13 m	Andrew	10 m	
Mary Estelle	4 f	Alice M	2 f	
Angelina	3 f	110-820		
Julia	3/12 f			
Joseph	78 m	NOKES, Jane (M)	31 m	
Helen	37 f	George Thos (M)	7 m	
KENNEDY, Bridget	18 f IR	Jane (M)	2 f	
169-1270		111-823		

ALEXANDRIA VIRGINIA 1860 CENSUS

NOKES, Jesse (B), omnibus driver -/50	53 m	Patrick	26 m	
Melvina (M)	50 f	Maria	24 f	
Edwinia (B)	19 f	Ann	22 f	
Harry (B), waiter	16 m	John, laborer	20 m	
165-1233		KIGGING, Mary, weaver	22 f	
		89-637		
NORRIS, Albert, house carptr -/50	43 m NH			
Emiline	36 f VA	NUGENT, Owen, grocer -/300	36 m IR	
Jane	20 m	Mary	36 f	
Mary	17 f	John	7 m	
Nancy	16 f	WINSTON, John, appren baker	15 m	
208-1592		26-153		
NORRIS, Emiline, shoe binder -/20	48 f	NUTT, Ann M	49 f	
Edward, gas fitter	21 m	Alice	25 f	
Mark, appren carpenter	16 m	Wm H, grocer clerk	22 m	
James	11 m	Rebecca	20 f	
Willie	9 m	CHICHESTER, Sally	17 f	
216-1664		DUNN, John H, clerk dry goods	19 m	
		112-829		
NORSONG, Jno T, grocer -/1K	38 m MD			
Virginia	30 f	NUTT, Wm D, asst treas 8K/8K	57 m	
Jno W, clerk	19 m	WISE, Alice	29 f	
Francis	11 m	254-1978		
103-763				
		O'BRIEN, Edward, ms carptr -/300	38 m MD	
NORTON, George, Epis mn -/5K	36 m NY	Mary A	32 f MH	
Annie	27 f	William	11 M MD	
Clarissa	4 f	Mary	5 f VA	
Garfel..	2 f	Edward	2 m	
Keith	3/12 m	Harvey, laborer	36 m MD	
217-1669		49-338		
NORTON, Jas, carpenter -/50	25 m IR	O'BRIEN, John, carpenter -/50	41 m MD	
Nancy	25 f VA	Hannah	38 f NY	
James	7 m	Owen, appren carpenter	18 m MD	
John	5 m	Margaret	17 f PA	
Luke	1/12 m	Hannah	13 f VA	
79-564		Laura	6 f	
		John	2 m	
NOWLAN, Julia (B), wash	43 m	William, cigar maker	36 m MD	
James (M), bricksmith	20 m	Ida	4 f VA	
Alfred (B)	18 m	78-558		
John (B)	22 m			
Elizabeth (M)	16 f	OCCONOR, Jno -/50	34 m IR	
Harriet (M)	15 f	Margaret	26 f	
Ella (B)	11 f	Ellen	7 f	
201-1531		162-1202		
NOWLAND, Chas W, house painter -/100	40 m	OCCONOR, Patrick, laborer	29 m IR	
Susan	41 f	Catharine	26 f	
Thas S	15 m	Timothy	1 m VA	
George	7 m	Mary	60 f IR	
SKINNER, Thos, laborer	73 m	273-2102		
Ann	50 f			
Jane M	42 f	ODEN, Ann (M), wash & iron	38 f	
ROWLAND, R, cabinet maker	23 m	Nathaniel (M), sailor	42 m	
ASHLAND, Chris, grocer clerk	19 m	43-290		
226-1744				
		OGDEN, Andrew, shoemaker -/75	40 m	
NUGANT, Nancy -/30	60 f IR	Martha	39 f DC	
Michael, laborer	28 m	Melissa	18 f VA	

ALEXANDRIA VIRGINIA 1860 CENSUS

Mary	16 f		WOOD, Mary	10 f	
Emma	14 f		NEWMAN, Lena	10 f	
Alice	6 f		FREEMAN, Emily	9 f	
Virginia	4 f		HUNTER, Mary	8 f	
William	2 m		SAMUEL, Susan	8 f	
160-1186			HUTCHINS, Cornelia	9 f	
			STEELE, M Spring	8 f	
OGDEN, John, merchant 1500/-	37 m	PA	Mary C	6 f	
Charity	36 f	NY	HILCRULIN, Rose	5 f	
Mary	7 f		ARMSTRONG, Christena	8 f	
DONALLY, Ellen, domestic	35 f	IR	209-1599		
12-61					
			OSBERN, Luke, farmer 400/50	46 m	MA
OGDEN, Wm, carter -/50	49 m		Jane	45 f	
Julia	48 f		Henry, laborer	19 m	
PHILLIPS, Laura	11 f		Frances	16 f	
Ann	9 f		Laura	11 f	
207-1583			Matilda	14 f	
			Harriet	9 f	
O'HEARON, David, laborer	35 m	IR	265-2055		
Catharine	25 f				
Catharine	10 f				
Bridgett	8 f		OSTERBERG, Fred, watchmaker -/150	48 m	WB
Annie	7 f		Cellestine	48 f	VA
James	2 m		6-37		
Andrew, laborer	40 m				
66-467			O'SULLIVAN, Daniel, gardner -/800	47 m	IR
			Mary	49 f	
O'LEARY, Cornelius, porter -/500	45 m	IR	William, dairyman	25 m	
Bredgett	38 f		Mary	23 f	
Cornilus	6 m		John, gardner	21 m	
Daniel	2 m		Bridgete	19 f	
45-305			Johanna	17 f	
			James	18 m	
OLK, Nathaniel (B), laborer	49 m		283-2165		
Sarah (B)	39 f				
Elizabeth (B)	15 f		O'SULLIVAN, Drake, laborer -/75	38 m	IR
George (B)	13 m		Mary	28 f	
Horns (B)	4 m		Timothy	6 m	
246-1916			Solonia	9 f	
			Mary	4 f	
ONEIL, Harriet, boarding -/200	45 f	VA	Elen	2 f	
Susan	30 f		KELLY, Catharine	61 f	IR
CRUPPER, Boston, clerk grocery store	32 m		Aurosa	24 f	
Elizabeth	32 f		RYAN, Timothy, laborer	28 m	
WHITING, Ella	31 f		McDEVITT, Thos, laborer	28 m	
NEWMAN, Effin	44 f		LOUDLEY, Michael, laborer	35 m	
John, clerk comm	47 m		RYAN, Cornelius, laborer	31 m	
COLTER, Sarah	29 f	NY	159-1183		
KELLY, Edward, clerk drug	18 m				
LUTRELL, Thos, clerk dry food	21 m		O'SULLIVAN, Mary, seamstress	31 f	ST
POITOZE, Victor, french teacher	28 m	FR	Jane	10 f	
113-834			Daniel	6 m	
			229-1763		
NEUMAN, Ellen, matron orp asym 3K/300	56 f				
PRICE, Fanny	58 f		OWENS, Jas, rag merchant -/25	26 m	VA
LYLES, Emily	16 f		Sarah	23 f	
FLETCHER, Fanny	16 f		181-1373		
DYER, Esther	15 f				
BAYNE, Francis	13 f		OWENS, Mary	50 f	IR
SAUL, Emma	12 f		Mary	9 f	VA
THOMAS, Mary	12 f		79-565		

ALEXANDRIA VIRGINIA 1860 CENSUS

OXLEY, E J, farmer -/200	61 m VA	
Elizabeth	62 f	
Susan	31 f	
Sophia	25 f	
272-2093		

OWENS, Richard, machinist -/100   46 m EG
  Sarah   38 f MD
  Richard, stone cutter   24 m
  William   22 m
  Sarah J   4 f
  Martha   1 f
DAIE, Georgana, ward   10 f
43-288

PADGETT, Edwin, paper hanger   22 m
  Mary   19 f
  Mary   1 f
242-1879

PADGETT, Geo R, grocer -/1400   40 m MD
  Sarah   30 f
  Franklin   14 m
  Samuel   3 m
  Rebecca   8/12 f
BAYLISS, Malinda   23 f
2-11

PADGETT, James, bricklayer   29 m
  Sarah   23 f MA
189-1433

PADGETT, Jas, shoemaker -/50   63 m MD
  Ellen   60 f
  Elizabeth   24 f
CLARRIAGE, Mary   38 f
  James, appren apothecary   16 m
  May   16 f
  Willie H   10 m
129-941

PADGETT, John G, clerk agri store   32 m
  Susan   48 f
  Wm F, tailor   20 m
  Benjamin, printer   20 m
  Emma   17 f
WESBERY, John, appren tailor   15 m
  Franklin   8 m
  Ida   16 f
  Martha   19 f
195-1488

PADGETT, John W, sailmaker 1K/200   40 m
  Libby Ann   35 f
  John   15 m
  Chas   12 m
  Robert   9 m
  Wilmer H   5 m
GRAHAM, Sarah   22 f
GENTRY, Malinda   12 f
63-446

PADGETT, Joseph, constable -/50   51 m
  Mary   42 f
  Virginia   19 f
  Jane   17 f
  Laurence   14 f
  Edwin   10 f
  Edgar   7 m
  Mildred   5 m
  Infant   9/12 f
42-280

PADGETT, Joseph, bricklayer -/30   24 m
  Sarah   23 f MA
189-1443

PADGETT, Wm F, sdlr/hrns mkr 7K/5K   37 m
  Harriet E   25 f VA
DAVIS, Sarah, domestic   18 f
18-104

PADGETT, Wm H, bricklayer -/20   26 m
  Sarah   22 f
  Alice   6 f
  Mary   10/12 f
147-1088

PADGETT, Wm L, post off clk 700/150   35 m MD
  Rachael   30 f VA
77-544

PAFF, Fred -/150   23 m HS
  Lousie   23 f HN
139-1021

PAGE, Elijah, boarding -/5K   22 m MD
  Philis..   25 f
  Bett..   22 f
  Mary   20 f
  John   16 m
  Emily   27 f
  Edgar   5 m
  Charles   2 m
CLEGETT, Ann   60 f
  Kate   35 f
JOHNSTON, Wm, bankers clerk   21 m
SULLY, Robert, civil engineer   23 m
TAYLOR, Ann   45 f
CAMPBELL, Sarah   65 f
WRIGHT, Anna, house keeper   18 f VA
SMITH, Baky (B), cook   45 f
BECKLEY, Katy (M)   19 f
172-1291

PAINE, John (B), laborer -/30   27 m
  Elizabeth (B)   22 f
  Sarah (B)   5 f
  James (B)   3 m
  Helen (B)   4/12 f
241-1870

PAPPS, Fred, shoemaker -/150   23 m

ALEXANDRIA VIRGINIA 1860 CENSUS

Lousie	23 f HN	PATTERSON, Edward, soapmaker -/60			30 m IR	
139-1021		Ann			26 f	
		Mary			12 f	
PARK, Philip, plumber -/150	38 m EG	James			2 m	
Catharine	27 f	Catharine			3/12 m	
Jimmy	1 m	93-674				
123-900						
		PATTERSON, Jas W, shoemaker -/50			43 m	
PARROTT, John H, music store -/1K	48 m	Ann			39 f	
Elizabeth E	45 f	Mary E			15 f	
Helen	20 f	Margaret			2 f	
Billie	18 f	152-1120				
Bertie	16 f					
John	12 m	PATTON, Hezekiah, cigar maker -/50			35 m	
22-128		Margaret			42 f	
		BASHBY, John, teacher -/50			20 m	
PARSONS, John, house carpenter -/60	63 m	PATTON, Ann			15 f	
Elizabeth	55 f	Masson			8 f	
Joseph, laborer	28 m	Willemena			5 f	
WEST, John	29 m PA	William			3 m	
Asma	19 f	BOYER, John			76 m	
John	2 m	133-972				
SHERWOOD, John	16 m					
281-2146		PATTON, Larkin, watchman -/50			39 m	
		Jane			28 f	
PARSON, Jno H, laborer -/30	36 m	Mary			9 f	
Sarah	36 f	John			3 m	
Winniford	12 f	Kate			4/12 f	
Mary V	9 f	73-514				
Henry	7 m					
Margaret	5 f	PAUL, Isaac, comm merch -/300			56 m MD	
Alice	5/12 f	Mary J			42 f	
49-340		William J, bookkeeper			21 m	
		Robert, salesman			19 m	
PARTLOW, Milton Y, comm merch 8K/3K	36 m	Joseph, salesman			16 m	
Mary E	30 f MD	Virginia			14 f	
Louis L	3 m	Isaac			12 m	
Willie	4/12 m	Louisa			8 f DC	
Benjamin, clerk	26 m	Arthur			4 m VA	
104-772		Martha			2 f	
		67-474				
PASCOE, Jno L, RR clerk 3K/385	50 m					
Ann R	47 f	PAULER, Wm, RR construction -/300			48 m FK	
Margaret	24 f	Immogene			42 f VA	
Virginia	14 f	Mary			19 f	
Sally (M), domestic	14 f	Benjamin, brakeman			17 m	
128-935		Maria			10 f VA	
		HOLLINGER, William (B), domestic			13 m	
PASPER, Wm H, sailor	29 m MD	MELVIN, Jennie (M), domestic			10 f	
Mary	17 f	45-313				
NALORY, James	18 f					
Mary	2 f VA	PAYNE, Cecilia (B)			68 f	
222-1713		Cecilia (B)			14 f	
		159-1177				
PALSEY, ..., seamstress	19 f					
Jimmy	16 f VA	PAYNE, Chas, carpenter			40 m	
222-1716		Elizabeth			36 f	
		Chas			15 m	
PATTERSON, Catharine	31 f	Catharine			12 f	
George	8 m	Anna			9 f	
Joseph	3 m VA	John			5 m	
138-1008		At..e?			3 m	

ALEXANDRIA VIRGINIA 1860 CENSUS

George	6/12 m	Edward	5 m
260-2022		66-466	
PAYNE, John (B), porter	40 m	PENN, Mark L, cabinet mkr -/100	41 m MD
Mary (B)	48 f	Mary E	19 f VA
Alexander (B), ship caulker	21 m	Benjamin, upholster	18 m
Virginia (B)	16 f	Alice	13 f
Isaac (B)	16 m	Margaret	11 f
242-1876		Sarah	10 f
		Consillo	7 f
PAYNE, John, shoemaker	33 m	18-103	
Elizabeth	28 f		
Mary	12 f	PENN, Thomas, laborer	36 m
John	7 m	Rebecca	31 f
Alice	4 f	Virginia	10 f
Henry	3 m	John	5 m
Ada	2/12 f	Walter	1 m
195-1484		RYE, Jesse	50 m
		102-756	
PAYNE, John (B), laborer	46 m		
Maria (B)	38 f	PENN, Walter, shoemaker -/150	45 m
SMITH, Griffith (B)	77 m	Mary	46 f
Dalia (B)	690 f	Mary R	17 f
John (B), carter	24 m	Virginia	15 f
WILLIAMS, James (B), laborer	25 m	Walter M	4 m
49-343		Charlotte	6 f
		24-139	
PAYNE, Mary (B), wash & iron	40 f		
159-1179		PENSE, Allen, farmer 8K/1K	49 m
		Harriet	45 f
PAYNE, Thomas, shoemaker -/50	43 m MD	Augusta	16 f
Mary	40 f	HALL, Mary	22 f
Dan R, appren	16 m	PEARL, Thomas S, laborer	22 m
Emma	13 f	PENSE, Andrew	6 m
Saml C	11 m	EAGAN, Samuel	48 m
John	8 m	261-2026	
51-368			
		PENTZ, Elijah B, carriage mkr -/200	32 m PA
PEACH, Jno G, lawyer 12K/5K	35 m	Mary	28 f
Millie	26 f	Ella	4 f
Helen	10/12 f	OVEAR, Wm, carriage mkr	26 m OH
141-1033		Annie	22 f PA
		McKNIGHT, Mary	18 f DC
PEACH, W Selden, druggist 4K/800	27 m	CARSON, John, moulder	40 m
Rebecca	53 f	BEACH, Mason, brakeman	23 m
CRANE, Peter	21 m	NUTCH, Charles, cabinet maker	45 m
12-57		OVEAR, Charles	4/12 m
		31-199	
PEARL, Elijah C, farmer 3500/100	77 m CT		
Polly	73 f	PEPER, Jas E (M), brickmaker 100/50	39 m
Marcus	50 m	Ann (M)	30 f
Jane	40 f NY	William (M)	7 m
Helen	12 f VA	Sarah (M)	5 f
263-2041		Ann (M)	3 f
		Infant (M)	3/12 m
PEARSON, Jesse, sailor -/400	52 m	84-604	
Mary E -/4K	52 f		
223-1720		PERKING, Henrietta	60 f
		Mary E	28 f
PEEL, Henry, druggist -/332	31 m EG	Jane	20 f
PELL, Mrs	31 f	WIBERT, Garret, fireman RR	30 m
Ella	7 f	16-87	

ALEXANDRIA VIRGINIA 1860 CENSUS

PERKINS, James H, clerk RR off -/150	32 m		George	15 m	
Mary	34 f		Mary E	16 f	
James	13 m		Taylor	6 m	
Charles	4 m		Mary E	9 f	
160-1187			Lewis M	3 m	
			WALLACE, Adam, pilot	67 m	
PERKINS, Warren 1500/200	71 m CT		John, pilot	30 m	
Dorthia	69 f MA		107-787		
SQUEAR, Geo C, house carp 600 insane	40 m NY				
Emily	29 f		PEVERELL, Isaac, cabinet mkr -/100	30 m EG	
Rocetta	12 f		Mary	26 f NY	
Perkins	9 m		Ellen	9 f VA	
Ann	4 f		188-1430		
275-2115					
			PEYTON, Mary A 600/100	40 f KY	
PERRY, Elizabeth 5K/4K	48 f MD		Mattie	19 f VA	
William, comm merch	25 m		Craven	9 m	
Joseph, comm merch	23 m		John F	11 m	
ARNOLD, Bettie	20 f		KEMPF, Amanda, seamstress	23 f MD	
104-770			DELPH.., John (B), machinist	21 m VA	
			158-1174		
PERRY, Jno, lumber merch -/5K	30 m MD				
Mariana	27 f		PHILIPS, George, bricklayer -/50	30 m VA	
Chas S	5 m		Ann	27 f	
SMOOT, Adalaide	18 f		James	10 m	
Florence	16 f		Sarah	8 f	
JULIUS, Elizabeth (M)	35 f		Ellen	2 f	
129-940			Sarah K	55 f	
			JONES, Kitty, domestic	16 f	
PETITT, Mary A, seamstress	26 f		87-628		
Kate, dress maker	22 f				
Sista	9 f		PHILIPS, James, bricklayer -/75	23 m	
212-1632			Mary	20 f	
			Emily	7/12 f	
PETTIT, Artewiesa	41 f		37-237		
Frances, laborer	22 m				
Virginia, seamstress	21 f		PHILIPS, Jas B, farmer 3300/600	55 m MD	
Mary, cotton mill	19 f		Mary C	50 f	
Amanda	17 f		James, house carptr -/6K	30 m DC	
John, sailor	15 m		Samuel, farmer	22 m	
Ann	12 f		Ainett	19 f	
Barbara	11 f		Ansley	17 m	
Infant	2/12 f		Stephen	15 m	
91-662			Hamilton	5 m	
			Catharine, domestic	14 f	
PETTITT, George, machinist -/20	26 m		255-1983		
Amanda	27 f				
Elizabeth	4 f		PHILIPS, Lucy	50 f	
James	2 m		Richard, porter	27 m	
John, laborer	17 m		Julia	29 f	
201-1533			Albert	8 m	
			James	6 m	
PETTY, Catharine, seamstress	46 f		Benjamin	4 m	
Jeremiah, laborer	27 m		HUDSON, Robert, sailor	16 m	
William	23 m		185-1404		
Edmonia, seamstress	18 m				
Elizabeth	16 f		PHILLIPS, Cornelius, carter -/50	29 m	
220-1697			Sarah	29 f	
			William	8 m	
PETTY, Eli, tavern keeper -/1500	67 m VA		Oscar	7 m	
Sarah	33 f MD		Cornelius	5 m	
Thos	17 m VA		Jane	3 f	

ALEXANDRIA VIRGINIA 1860 CENSUS

GREENWELL, Geor	17 m	Edward	5 m
225-1731		Albert	3 m
		Frank	4/12 m
PHILLIPS, Jas G, carter -/500	40 m	54-376	
Catharine	32 f		
Catharine	17 f	POLLARD, John H	32 m
John	13 m	Marion	30 f
Francis	7 m	William	11 m
Henry	4 m	Frances	8 m
Charles	1 m	Bettie	6 f
JESPER, Andrew (B)	26 m	44-304	
192-1465			
		POLLARD, Nancy, seamstress	56 f
PHOENIX, Alice (M), wash & iron	33 f	Emallie	16 f
Laura (B)	16 f	23-131	
241-1871			
		POORS, W A, pilot -/80	50 m
PIERPOINT, John, apothecary 7K/10K	60 m VA	Amelia	34 f
Mary	57 f	Sophia	16 f
Edward	20 m	183-1397	
WANTON, Hannah	65 f		
ELLIOTT, Lucinda, domestic	35 f	POPE, William B, engineer RR	25 m
129-942		Leuoxy?	60 f
		30-188	
PILES, Walter A, cabinet maker -/30	44 m		
Sarah	22 f	PORTER, Nicholas, omnibus agent -/100	37 m MD
Maria	21 f	Eliza	27 f
Samuel	6/12 m	Alice	13 f
Elizabeth	12 f NY	Susan	5 f
27-162		Mary	3 f
		George	10/12 m
PIPER, Wm H (M), brickmaker 1K/1300	36 m	LEADLY, Dan, machinist	23 m MD
Sarah (M)	28 f	Amelia	20 f DC
James (M)	10 m	113-835	
Elizabeth (M)	7 f		
Alice (M)	3 f	POSEY, Thomas, cashier -/100	24 m
George (M)	1 m	Agnes	23 f
94-678		BARNWELL, Sarah	21 f
		214-1654	
PITTS, Benjamin, shoemaker -/25	33 m		
Elisa	28 f	POSS, John, baker 800/50	50 m FK
Francis	10 m	Henry, carpenter	19 m
Mary	8 f	Harriet	45 f
Josephene	4 f	Anna	17 f
Charles	2 m	John	14 m
160-1192		Margaret	11 f
		40-269	
PITTS, Robert T, shoemaker -/100	25 m		
Ann D	55 f	POTZCHAUDS, Jerer, laborer	30 m IR
Patsy	23 f	Catharine	30 f
Mildred	30 f	Catharine	9 f
Aurilea	13 m	56-397	
SMATHERS, Lucy, seamstress	21 f		
114-840		POWELL, Ann M, farmer	60 f
		Alfred	20 m
PLUMBER, Burwell, bookkeeper 1700/250	38 m	Annie	15 f
Ann C	34 f	Fanny	16 f
Sarah T	16 f	282-2153	
Lucy	13 f		
Annie	12 f	POWELL, Cuthbert, clerk RR co -/200	29 m
Clara	9 f	Mary	26 f
Sally	7 f	Ella	4 f

ALEXANDRIA VIRGINIA 1860 CENSUS

Anna	2 f	Merietta	11 f	
PARIS, Rebecca (B), domestic	18 f	Nathan	9 m	
SAYRES, Matilda	54 f	Benjamin	6 m	
Virginia	18 f	Kate	9/12 f	
118-872		COOKLY, Rubin, appren	19 m	
		HUMPHREY, Lucy, monthly nurse	60 f	
POWELL, E B, clk insurance co 13K/1K	36 m	196-1489		
Ardelia	31 f MD			
Anne	8	PRICE, Charles, ms carptr -/150	46 m	
William	7 m	Mary	40 f	
Salley	5 f	Margaret	22 f	
Brooke	3 m	Charles	14 m	
Lewellen	2 m	Orlando	12 m	
SMITH, Geo (B), domestic	16 m	Janet	10 f	
119-878		197-1504		
POWERS, Fred, laborer -/20	43 m SX	PRICE, Ellis, steam boat capt -/200	43 m	
Helen	32 f SL	Judith	35 f	
William	2 m VA	Mark, comm h clerk	24 m	
153-1136		Elizabeth	18 f	
		Millie	16 f	
POWERS, Lindsay, carpenter -/30	24 m	Maggie	14 f	
Henry	55 m	Kate	12 f	
Ann	65 f	Samuel	10 m	
SMITH, Alan S	12 m	Harris	8 m	
TATE, Columbia (M), domestic	12 f	WILSON, Margaret, teacher	33 f	
152-1125		176-1317		
POWERS, Mary	42 f NF			
Francis, plumber	20 m	PRICE, Geo, dom house tavern keeper	55 m	
Anthony, appren bricklayer	19 m	Mary	44 f	
Martina, appren gas fitter	17 m	Susanah	27 f	
Vicent, house painter	15 m	James, machinist	25 m	
Thomas	12 m	Edgar, carter	19 m	
Mary	10 f	Mary	18 f	
SULLIVAN, Mary, seamstress	4 f PA	Louise	17 f	
52-369		Sarah	16 f	
		Emma	12 f	
PRAWLE, Charles, cabinet maker -/50	39 m GR	Frank	8 m	
Margaret	33 f	Alice	5 f	
Dennis	13 m	Ir... Terry	5 f	
George W	10 m	Ida	3 f	
52-364		THOMAS, Martha, domestic	14 f	
		67-471		
PRETTYMAN, Robert, coach mkr 9K/600	39 m			
Margaret	36 f	PRICE, Wm, laborer 2K/200	59 m	
David	16 m	Sarah	57 f	
Robt	12 m	Wilmer, laborer	20 m	
Margaret	9 f	MULLICAN, Saml	30 m	
Mary	6 f	123-901		
Lillie	4 f			
MORGAN, Wm	76 m IR	PRICE, Wm B, architect 1000/200	48 m	
13-66		Sarah	47 f	
		Wm H, carpenter	20 m	
PREYS, John, tailor -/151	29 m	Ella	16 f	
Esther	29 f	Charles	11 m	
Emma	6 f	Harry C	9 m	
197-1503		SMITH, Catharine (M), domestic	20 f	
		Dick (M)	12 m	
PRICE, Benjamin F, pls carptr 1600/200	32 m	Samuel (M)	6 m	
Mary	30 f	PRICE, Virginia	20 f VA	
William	13 m	144-1064		

ALEXANDRIA VIRGINIA 1860 CENSUS

PRINCE, Rachael (B)	35 f	John	8 m
Catharine (B)	13 f	Mary	6 f
Upton (B)	7 m	Jimmy	2 m
Arthur (B)	3 m	Nicholas	7/12 m
William (B)	7/12 m	55-387	
237-1831			
		RADCLIFF, Ann, doctress -/150	52 f
PROCTER, Rose	48 f VA	Richard, laborer	37 m
Henry, grocer clerk	16 m	William, machinist	22 m
Samuel, telegraph operator	14 m	214-1651	
CRAIG, Gotlieb, upholster	26 m GR		
HEALY, Alexander, cam.....	23 m VA	RAMSEY, Eliza 5K/300	60 f
GLENROY, Peter, harness maker	26 m IR	BALLES, Mary	20 f VA
LOGE, John, house carpenter	20 m MD	179-1333	
BOTHERTON, Lewis	23 f VA		
GILMAN, James, upholsterer	36 m IR	RAMSEY, G W, bank clerk	52 m
DAVIS, Jane (B), domestic	12 f VA	Millie	44 f
177-1326		Geo W	16 m
		Margaret	14 f
PROCTOR, James -/200	24 m	Allen T	12 m
Fanny	21 f	Anna	10 f
40-271		Dennis	7 m
		BARTLEMAN, Mrs 20K/1K	85 f IR
PROGAM, Malinda -/500	53 f	Rebecca J	53 f VA
Mary	26 f	153-1135	
Ellen, teacher	23 f		
Maggie	20 f	RANDOLPH, Lucy (B)	35 f
Carrie	18 f	141-1039	
SUTTON, Fanny	40 f		
ATWELL, Lucy	29 f	RANTON, Saml, laborer 400/30	56 m
130-949		Elizabeth	53 f VA
		Thomas	22 m
PRUTLER, Peter, farmer 2K/100	47 m NY	99-729	
Emma	46 f		
Giles	12 m	RATCLIFF, John, house carptr -/200	41 m MD
Hennan	10 f	Mary	37 f
...man	6 m	Conway	7 m
Caroline	2 f VA	Hannah	9/12 f
268-2074		219-1689	
PURCELL, Julia	20 f	REARDON, Wm, clerk comm store -/2500	21 m
Ella	16 f	Catharine	27 f
174-1301		Mildred	25 m
		Adalaide	23 f
PURCELL, Randolph, laborer	27 m DC	218-1681	
Mary	28 f		
68-478			
		REAVES, Washington, sailor	40 m MD
PURCELL, Richard, turner -/50	27 m IR	Frances	29 f VA
Margaret	28 f	229-1761	
Mary	4 f		
John	1 m	REDDIN, Thomas, laborer	39 m MD
HUGH, Mary	65 m IR	Mary	38 f
166-1241		William	14 m
		Sarah	11 f
QUAID, Jas, gardner -/30	55 m MD	Ann	8 f
Rebecca	43 f	Infant	5/12 m
George, laborer	16 m	Purce	7 m
247-1920		BENNER, Wm, brickmaker	40 m PA
		CARRICK, Godfrey, laborer	35 m GR
QUAIN, James, laborer	32 m IR	ESKRIDGE, Thomas, laborer	22 m VA
Jane	26 f	MURRAY, Edward, laborer	38 m IR

ALEXANDRIA VIRGINIA 1860 CENSUS

KELLY, Thomas, laborer	16 m NY	BUNTNY, Mary N, tailoress	20 f NY	
HENTON, Isaac	13 m GT	49-337		
274-2109				
		RICHARDS, Caleb, carter 50/1700	40 m VA	
REED, Dortia (B), wash & iron	28 f	Amanda	30 f	
Ben (B), laborer	26 m	John	13 m	
Edward (B)	4 m	Annie	11 f	
Albert (B)	2 m	Lizzie	11 f	
GRAY, Susan (B), domestic	27 f	Caleb	8 m	
44-301		Addie	7 f	
		Blank	5 f	
REED, George, laborer -/50	27 m	BLACK, John (B)	40 m	
May	30 f	232-1792		
Laura	8 f			
Georgana	6 f			
Mary	4 f	RICHARDS, Johanna	35 f IR	
Catharine	2 f	Jerry	15 m	
259-2010		John	8 m VA	
		Anne	5 f	
REED, Jas H, RR treas 1800/682	53 m	Thomas	3 m	
Ann D	47 f	96-700		
James	15 m			
127-927		RICHARDS, Wm B, fancy store	28 m VA	
		Louisa	29 f	
REED, Samuel R, bricklayer 2K/1K	33 m VA	Cora	9 f	
Mary	26 f	Eva	8 f	
Mary A	3 f	Lula	7 f	
Leona	3/12 f	Edith	6 f	
George, bricklayer	25 m	Wm B	3 m	
FAISONS, Wm, appren	15 m	MERCER, Sarah	35 f EG	
189-1448		DAVIS, Georgiana (M), cook	25 f VA	
		BILL, Joseph (B), porter	14 m	
REMINGTON, Wm, house carpenter	23 m	SMITH, Larinia (M), nurse	18 f	
Maria	28 f	121-892		
MANKIN, Virginia	11 f			
William	7 m	RICHARDS Sr, Wm B 9200/65	63 m	
Bertrand	5 m	Priscilla	59 f	
George	4 m	Addie	18 f	
199-1523		160-1191		
RENO, Wm J, machinist 12K/50	36 m	RICHARDS, Wm C, boss coal wf 1500/1600	42 m	
Louise	30 f	Mary	35 f	
John	7 m	Catharine	10 f	
Ann	5 f	Jane	6 f	
Samuel	3 m	Anna	3 f	
Ida	3/12 f	HERRISH, Wm T, harness mkr -/600	34 m NY	
Louise	17 f	Jane -/500	33 f VA	
247-1927		Mary C	2/12 f	
		145-1066		
REUNOE, John R, blacksmith -/20	37 m			
Sarah	35 f MD			
Eunice	4 f DC	RICHARDSON, Elisha, brakeman	27 m MA	
John	2 m	Mary J	23 f NY	
195-1486		Ellen	5 f	
		Mary	2 f	
REYNOLDS, Wm, collector 800/50	55 m	Wm	2/12 m	
Grace	43 f	38-253		
245-1906				
		RICHARDSON, John, grocer 2K/500	39 m	
RHODES, Wm H, tailor -/50	37 m VA	Elizabeth	32 f	
Concordia	30 f	Alfred	10 m	
William	11 m	Marietta	8 f	

ALEXANDRIA VIRGINIA 1860 CENSUS

```
    Alethia                        6 f      ROBINS, Fanny                   55 f IR
    Thomas                         4 m      CARROLE, May N                  30 f
34-220                                      ROBINS, Nicholas                11 m
                                         162-1209
RICHMOND, Jas, butcher 3K/500     30 m
    Majah                         38 f      ROBINS, John, laborer -/3K      30 m ME
    Harriet 1800/1500             55 f MD 192-1461
    Jack (B)                      12 m
281-2149                                    ROBINSON, Geo H, comm merch 500/20K  42 m
                                                Mary                        35 f
RIDGELY, John, tobacconist 2500/500  35 m MD  Josaphine                    18 f
    Mary                          27 f PA     John P                        15 m
    Elizabeth                      5 f MD     Sarah D                        6 f
    John                           1 m        Thomas                         3 m
39-258                                      RICE, Mary                      29 f
                                            PAYNE, Jas R, clerk             16 m
                                         106-786
RIDGELY, S E, tailor -/75         32 m MD
    Mary                          26 f      ROBINSON, John, plasterer 800/500  24 m MD
    Singleton                     10 m          Sarah                       20 f
    Annie                          6 f          William                      4 m
    David                          1 m          John                         2 m
169-1268                                 198-1519

RILEY, Wm, laborer                28 m IR  ROBINSON, John, farmer -/300     60 m MD
    Mary                          27 f          Elizabeth                   62 f
    Mary                           4 f          Elizabeth, dressmaker       24 f VA
    Jas A                          2 m          Sally, teacher              23 f
258-1998                                 131-958

RISTON, Sarah 600/150             78 f      ROBINSON, Moses, restaurant -/50  38 m PA
    Alvin                         28 m          Christina                   27 f MD
WALKER, Harriet                   54 f          Samuel                      10 m VA
208-1590                                        Emily                        7 f MD
                                                Moses                        5 m VA
ROACH, Jas, farmer 85K.5K         45 m IR       George J                     3 m MD
    Elizabeth                     40 f          Roxena                    4/12 f VA
    James                         21 m      CONNER, Ann, domestic           23 f MD
    Mary                          19 f   99-734
    Ursula                        17 f
    Philip                        16 m      ROBINSON, Richard, tailor 2K/200  36 m
    Elizabeth                     13 f          Alice                       15 f
    Dora                          11 f          Korell                      13 m
    John                           8 m          Hester                      11 f
    Carrie                         6 f          Mary                         9 f
    Charles                     9/12 m          Kate                         6 f
DONALLY, Rose                     30 f          Carrie                       4 f
CARSON, John                       2 m      PADGETT, Georgia, seamstress    22 f MD
275-2117                                    COOPER, Matilda                 75 f
                                         46-314

ROACH, Michael, laborer -/30      50 m IR  ROBINSON, Robert H (M), laborer -/50  38 m
    Catharine                     41 f          Mary A (M)                  28 f
98-722                                          Robert (M)                  12 m
                                                Agnes (M)                    7 m
ROBERTS, Jeff, laborer            30 m IR 176-1318
    Mary                          24 f
    Willie                         3 m VA  ROBINSON, T B, lawyer 45K/60K    45 m VA
    Mary                        6/12 f          Martha J                    32 f
BIRMINGHAM, Thom, laborer         25 m IR       Mary V                       9 f
FLARITY, Andrew                   40 m          Thomas                       8 m
60-420                                          Bolmy W                      6 m
```

102

ALEXANDRIA VIRGINIA 1860 CENSUS

John W	4 m		Lilly	9/12 f
Mercer	2 m		81-578	
WILLERSON, Bettie	38 f			
135-987			ROSENCRANTZ, John, saper-cotton mill	50 m NJ
			Caroline	40 f PA
ROBY, Ann	70 f		91-655	
133-970				
			ROSS, Amy (B)	60 f
ROBY, Barton, house carpenter	61 m MD		190-1445	
Emily	34 f			
Samuel	14 m		ROSS, John (B), laborer -/30	47 m VA
Barbara	13 f		Mary (B)	37 f
Joseph	8 m VA		John (B)	19 m
Francis	2 m		Catharine (B)	18 f
156-1159			Lacy (B)	17 f
			Richard (B)	15 f
ROBY, Hannah	64 f		Joseph (B)	12 m
Catharine	32 f		George (M)	9 m
John, laborer	28 m		Charles (B)	5 m
Joshua	9 m		James (B)	3 m
William, appren joiner	12 m		244-1891	
Chas	6 m			
Mary	4 f			
38-248			ROSS, Wm H, merchant 20K/200K	40 m ST
			Caroline	26 f
ROBY, John E, house carpenter	25 m		Gudalope	4 f
Neilirma ?	32 f		John	3 m
Lucian	10/12 m		James	6/12 m
193-1466			CAMPBELL, Alexander, farmer	26 m EG
			DAZE, John, laborer	18 m VA
ROGERS, Jas S, clerk -/300	32 m MD		GARDNER, Chas, gardner	26 m
Monia	32 f		Frances (M), laborer	26 f
Caroline	5 f		William (B)	12 f
Juliett	5 f		GARDNER, Mary	23 f
Isabella	3 f VA		261-2029	
James	7/12 m			
TATE, Mary (M), domestic	45 f		ROTCH, Sarah	50 f
Daniel (M)	10 m		Mary A	30 f
106-783			CARROLL, Frances (B), domestic	20 f
			193-1466	
ROLLS, Andrew, laborer	30 m			
Louise	30 f		ROTCHFORD, Richard, shoemaker 800/100	36 m
Ann	6 f		Mary J	30 f
Harriet	2 f		81-581	
Samuel	2/12 m			
149-1099			ROWEN, Mary	38 f IR
			Ellen	13 f
ROLLS, Wm, laborer -/100	40 m		Michael	8 m
Ann	36 f		150-1106	
Richard Lovelace	16 m			
CHESHIRE, James, baggage master	28 m		ROWLAND, R, cabinet maker	23 m
248-1933			227-1744	
ROSE, Henry, brakeman -/30	30 m			
Mary	30 f		ROXBERRY, Jacob	46 m VA
Johanna	3 f		Elizabeth	42 f
Henrietta	2 f		Asa, fancy store clerk	18 f
Charles	4/12 m		George	16 m
248-1932			Virginia	11 f
			Alice	8 f
ROSE, Jas, brakeman -/50	24 m		FISHER, Annie -/2K	72 f EG
Sarah	22 f EG		120-885	

ALEXANDRIA VIRGINIA 1860 CENSUS

RUDD, Jno A, house painter 3K/100	62 m EG	TIMBERLAKE, J M, clerk	40 m	
Sally	58 f	S..., Tim, chandler	40 m MD	
Charles	33 m	TAYLOR, Chas, piano tuner	30 m VA	
Amanda	27 f	SAYLER, Chas, moulder	22 m GR	
Alice	12 f	KULER, E S, clerk	25	
Charles	9 m	31-196		
Anne	4 f			
Eva	2 f	RYAN, Stacey, grocer -/30	29 f IR	
June	33 f	Mary Ann	10 f MD	
Margaret	18 f	Maggie	2 f GT	
174-1299		70-494		
RUDD, Richard A, brick mkr 2K/300	59 m EG	RYLE, Benjamin, wheelwright	24 m MD	
Elizabeth	59 f VA	Mary	22 f	
RUDD, Isaac W, brick maker	23 m VA	72-508		
Georgana	19 m			
119-881		RYON, Alfred, huckster -/50	32 m	
		Frances	26 f	
RUDD, Richard H, house painter -/100	36 m	Samuel	20 m VA	
Elizabeth	35 f	Josephine	18	
Alice	11 f	Theodor	15 m	
Kate	6 f	Larry	15 m	
Adalaide	1 f	John	12 m	
SCHWARTZ, Emma	18 f	Infant	1/12 m	
BARNESS, Frank, appren house painter	16 m	RYON, Mary (M), domestic	22 f	
50-352		James (M)	1 f	
		31-201		
RUSHMAN, Wm, pilot -/50	45 m			
Harriet	43 f	ST CLAIR, Thomas, ms carptr 1K/500	28 m	
Ann, ... knitter	19 f	Becilla	24 f	
Sarah	17 f	Virginia	2 f	
William	16 m	McMAHAND, Wm, appren	21 m	
Elizabeth	9 f	52-367		
223-1800				
RUSSELL, Moses (B), coachman -/100	62 m	SAMPSON, Henry, moulder -/50	28 m EG	
Mary (B)	50 f	Sarah	25 f VA	
Moses (M), brick maker	16 m	William	7 m	
CHIM, Jas (M)	9 m	James	4 m	
123-898		Francis	2 m	
		226-1739		
RUSSELL, Robert, wharf builder	46 m DC			
Ann	35 f	SAMPSON, Henry, shoe maker 5K/1K	54 m	
John	17 m VA	Julia	48 f	
Jacob	16 m	Richard	23 m	
George	11 m	Julia Tubman	21 f	
Joseph	4 m	French R Simpson, clerk	20 m	
100-742		Sarah E	18 f	
		Selina	16 f	
RYAN, Daniel, laborer -/50	33 m IR	Geo L	15 m	
Eliza	27 f	Mary A	13 f	
Anthony	3 m VA	Arthur	11 m	
Edward	2 m	Ernest	10 m	
CALON, Ann	22 f IR	Winfield	8 m	
163-1218		11-54		
RYAN, John W, tavern keeper -/300	50 m	SAMPSON, Peter W, cabinet mkr 900/100	29 m	
Ellen	40 f	Mary	28 f DC	
John, bar keeper	33 m VA	Julian	2 f VA	
Durcas	16 f MD	MAHLER, Catharine	30 f DC	
Nora	10 f VA	HAYS, Lucy (M), domestic	9 f VA	
Susan	33 f	23-134		

ALEXANDRIA VIRGINIA 1860 CENSUS

SANDFORD, John, ms carpenter	32 m MD	SCHOOLER, Louis, clothier -/2K	30 m BV	
Louisa	36 f	Sarah	20 f	
Ella	6 f	121-891		
Henry	2 m			
Malinda (M), domestic	16 f	SCHWARTZ, Henry, dry good merch -/2K	27 m BV	
32-206		Jenny	24 f	
		BROWN, Betty	22 f	
SANGSTER, Ed, farmer -/5200	55 m	SCHWARTZ, Fanny	3 f VA	
Mary	50 f	BROWN, Wolff, clerk	17 m BV	
James, farmer	27 m	SCHWARTZ, Jane, clothier -/200	26 m	
Betty	25 f	HASS, David, daguerre -/500	40 m HL	
Mollie	5 f	FRANK, Hannah, domestic	35 f HD	
George	3 m	126-920		
Bessie	2 f			
Infant	1/12 f	SCOLON, Adolphus (B), laborer	31 m	
Thomas	25 m	BOLL, Mary Ann (B)	27 f	
John, lawyer	22 m	LURUES, Ellen (B)	49 f	
Mary	18 f	ROBINSON, ... (M), laborer	29 m VA	
21-123		?, Haywood (M)	27 m	
		161-1200		
SAUDERS, Addison, grocery clerk -/400	20 m			
Nellie	22 f			
Barbara	17 f	SCOTT, Anna (M), wash & iron	30 f	
James	13 m	Martha (M)	8 f	
Mary	13 f	Charles (M)	6 m	
Kate	10 f	Willie (M)	4 m	
WOODHOUSE, Wm, electrician	25 m	Minnie (M)	2 m	
118-874		143-1050		
SAVOY, Mary (B), grocer 600/100	50 f	SCOTT, Charles (B), foreman steamboat	41 m	
BERRY, Jane (B)	33 f	Sarah (B)	38 f	
Fanny (B)	12 f	CYES, Maria (B), wash & iron	21 f	
David (B)	7 m	James (B)	5/12 m	
WHITING, Mary (B)	31 f	161-1198		
Jane (B)	4 f			
SAVOY, James (B)	13 m	SCOTT, Daniel, farmer	40 m NY	
DIGGS, Mary (B)	42 f	Autha	40 f PA	
SAVOY, Mary (B)	31 f	Lucinda	16 f NY	
211-1622		Emmond	12 m	
		Emily		
SAXTON, Timothy, laborer	50 m IR	May	6 f	
Ellen	40 f	Ida	2 f	
May	12 f	Ira	2 m	
Ellen	3 f	270-2089		
Timothy	4/12 m			
248-1929		SCOTT, Sylvester, teacher -/700	55 m MA	
		Lydia	32 f	
SCARCE, Wm B, farmer 800/530	42 m PA	Lucy	4 f VA	
Mary	44 m	Benjamin	8/12 m	
155-1152		SOLOMAN, Mary (B), cook	40 f	
		Eveline (B), domestic	34 f	
SCHAFER, Christian, confect -/1500	23 m GR	PAYNE, Helen (B), nurse	20 f	
Susanna	43 f VA	THOMPSON, Amanda (B), domestic	18 f	
Laura	17 f	132-968		
George	13 m			
SIGHT, George, journey confect	22 m			
3-19		SEAL, David (M), laborer	22 m	
SCHARTZ, Mary	23 f	Elyabeth (B)	28 f	
90-653		William (B)	4 m	
		Mary (M)	2 f	
SCHILER, Edward, fence painter -/200	40 m PR	RONALD, Lucinda (B)	60 f	
109-812		198-1516		

ALEXANDRIA VIRGINIA 1860 CENSUS

SEAL, Henry (M), domestic	56 f	SHAY, S King, custom house 900/100	59 m MD	
Annie (M)	16 f	Jane	6 f	
198-1517		Amelia V	23 f	
		A.lena	17 f	
SEARS, Annie	52 f EG	209-1598		
James, baker	32 m NF			
Jane	20 f	SHELLDRAKE, Wm, grocer 300/130	48 m EG	
Robert	17 m	Louise	49 f	
16-84		William, joiner	23 m	
		Matilda	16 f NY	
SEATON, George (M), ms carptr 4K/300	34 m	Louise	14 f NY	
Maria (M)	33 f	Eliza	11 f NY	
Geo C (M)	13 m	Edward	8 m NY	
Catharine (M)	10 f	158-1168		
Edwin (M)	8 m			
Sallie (M)	6 f			
Constance (M)	5 f	SHERDEN, Peter, laborer	22 m IR	
Colcote (M)	11/12 m	Catharine	17 f	
197-1505		Rose	17 f	
		Michael, laborer	45 m	
SEATON, Lucinda (B) 1700/60	60 f	56-395		
239-1853				
		SHERWOOD, Henry, farmer -/500	30 m	
SELDNER, P, grocer 3K/1K	40 m BD	Henrietta	22 f	
Amelia	26 f FK	Andrew	4 m	
WAGG, H...	56 f	KIRBY, John, laborer	17 m	
10-51		267-2065		
SELF, James, blacksmith -/75	30 m VA	SHERWOOD, Louis A	45 m	
Margaret	26 f	May	35 f	
Ema	2 f	Jesse	18 m	
205-1569		Joshua	14 m	
		Frank	12 m	
		Elizabeth	16 f	
SEMMES, Samuel (B), ship carpenter	60 m	Mary	8 f	
Indiana (M)	9 f	280-214		
231-1785				
		SHEVERS, Patrick, laborer	35 m IR	
SHAKELFORD, John, house painter -/150	65 m VA	Ann	32 f	
Maria A	50 f	Patrick	3 m VA	
Kate	25 f	97-714		
Martha	23 f			
Susan	21 f	SHINN, Stephen, grocer & comm 1500/1K	59 m EG	
14-75		Mary	50 f	
		Robert, liquor inspector	30 m	
SHAKES, Jno, brush store -/500	86 m MD	Jas W, n......	26 m	
Amanda	48 f	George R, grocer clerk	21 m	
Mary	35 f	Mary	14 f	
John	23 m	BROCKETT, Kitty (M), cook	55 f	
Ruberta	16 f	WHITE, Ben (M), domestic	10 m	
130-952		180-1371		
SHAMROCK, Bertram, sailor 250/30	38 m PA			
Elizabeth	26 f NY	SHIRLEY, Wm H	28 m	
Henry	7 m PA	Martha	23 f	
Virginia	9/12 f VA	Wm H	1 m	
100-736		257-1996		
SHAW, Charles P, tobacconist 12K/6K	53 m	SHOEMAKER, Lewis, coppersmith -/75	35 m MD	
Jane	76 f	Mary	23 f	
Catharine	58 f	Laura	7 f	
3-18		226-1738		

ALEXANDRIA VIRGINIA 1860 CENSUS

SHOEMAN, Mary, wash & iron	30 f GR		SIMMONS, Joseph, butcher -/50	21 m VA	
Mary	60 f		Jane	21 f	
John	13 m		Alice	1 f	
124-907			72-509		
SHORT, Oliver, laborer	45 m		SIMMONS, Thomas,, farmer 1K/200	72 m	
Catharine	40 f		Teresa	60 f	
James	10 m		259-2009		
John	7 m				
RICE, Owen	45 m IR		SIMMS, Douglas R, bank clerk -/300	38 m	
John	13 m		Virginia	36 f	
101-750			Marion	1 f	
			BLACK, Ann, domestic	37 f	
SHUSTER, Owen 900/100	39 m SX		168-1263		
Mary	40 f PA				
Mary	12 f VA		SIMMS, Margaret	40 f	
80-568			Adamia A, spinner	19 f	
			Emma, warfer	16 f	
SHUTE, William, sailor	39 m		82-592		
Sarah	29 f				
James	19 m				
Emma	60 f		SIMMS, Randolph, plasterer	23 m	
William	3 m		Sarah	18 f	
Infant	9/12 f		85-611		
229-1764					
			SIMON, Chas A, French cook -/100	27 m FR	
SIDEBOTTOM, Ann, hotel keeper 2K/100	70 f		Lucinda	21 f	
Jane	30 f		Lucy	1 f WA	
5-32			178-1327		
SIDEBOTTOM, Samuel, ms carptr -/130	30 m		SIMONS, Edward, laborer	38 m IR	
Margaret	25 f		Bridgett	30 f	
Louise	30 f		Patrick, appren cabinet maker	18 m	
Mary	6 f		Margaret	7 f VA	
Isabella	3 f		Michael, laborer	28 m IR	
Clara	9/12 f		81-583		
169-1269					
			SIMPSON, A M, grocer -/350	43 m	
SIGGERS, Geo, book binder -/500	34 m EG		Maria	42 f	
Mary	28 f NY		Maria	13 f	
Harriett	5 f		Julia	10 f	
George	3 m VA		Josephine	5 f	
115-848			ELKIN, John	10 m	
			187-1423		
SIGLER, John, carpenter	36 m PA				
SCHWARTZ, Mary	23 f		SIMPSON, Gilbert, grocer 6500/1K	51 m	
Rosannah	6/12 f		Margaret	48 f	
90-653			Margaret	22 f	
			Thomas	21 m	
SILLIKS, Mary A, seamstress	43 f		Gilbert	17 m	
Frances	18 f		Mary	15 f	
James, clerk	16 m		Henry	8 m	
Thomas	5 m		MITCHELL, Kate, domestic	14 f	
Margaret	2 f		4-24		
37-240					
			SIMPSON, Jas H, ms baker 3500/1K	24 m VA	
SIMMON, Wm A, laborer -/30	32 m		Thomas, clerk	21 m	
Susan	43 f		THOMAS, John, baker	20 m	
Sarah	5 f		MISER, Geo	35 m DC	
May	1 f		ROADSTEIN, Dan	24 m GR	
WILSON, Mary	16 f		CONNIFFY, John, drover	16 m IR	
248-1931					

ALEXANDRIA VIRGINIA 1860 CENSUS

THOMAS, Richard, bakers appren	17 m	SIPPLE, John H, cigar & tobacco -/400	28 m VA
ALLEN, Margaret, cook	30 f	Anna	20 f
113-833		George	2 m
		GREGG, Cym, appren	13 m
SIMPSON, James W, banker -/150	48 m VA	24-142	
Ann	48 f		
Anne V	15 f	SIPPLE, Mary -/50	36 f VA
Jane E	12 f	Charles, clerk grocery	23 m
Chas A	10 m	Sarah	68 f
AXGTOWN, Augustus, appren	15 m GR	Mary, teacher	17 f
17-92		107-1247	
SIMPSON, John	48 m	SISSON, John, laborer	48 m
Margaret	38 f	Margaret	38 f
John	17 m	John	17 m
Billy	15 m	Billy	15 m
Jimmy	13 m	Jimmy	13 m
George	7 m	George	7 m
Sarah	5 f	Sarah	5 f
Eddie	5 m	Eddie	5 m
232-1790		232-1790	
SIMPSON, John W, house carptr -/100	32 m VA	SISSON, John A 4K/2500	46 m
Catharine	32 f NY	Jane	45 f
Kate	2 f VA	Alberta	21 f
213-1636		Jane	16 f
		John	13 m
SIMPSON, Lewis, shoemaker	34 m MD	Townsly	5 m
Matilda	44 f VA	HARRISON, Robt, laborer	22 m
282-2156		260-2020	
SIMPSON, peter W, laborer -/100	56 m	SISSON, Wm A, ms carptr 2K/100	48 m
Mary	52 f	Lucretia	44 f
Mary	19 f	TAYLOR, Caroline	23 f
VINCENT, Wm, carpenter -/150	27 m MD	148-1048	
Lenora	24 f VA		
William	4 m		
134-978		SKIDMORE, Samuel	46 m VA
		Louise	41 f WB
		101-747	
SIMPSON, Peter W, cabinet mkr 900/100	29 m		
Mary	28 f DC	SKIDMORE, Sarah 1200/-	68 f
Julian	2 f VA	John, carpenter	40 m
MAHLER, Catharine	30 f DC	Maria	38 f
HAYS, Lucy (M), domestic	9 f VA	Lewis, house painter	33 f
23-134		Andrew, laborer	30 m
		Emma	31 f
SIMPSON, William G, baker	27 m VA	39-256	
Erma	23 f		
Margaret	3 f	SKINNER, John T, hotel keeper -/50	41 m
William	1 m	ALLISON, Geo A, bar keeper	33 m
WELSH, Joseph, journey baker	23 m IR	ENGLISH, Thomas, fisherman	50 m
Ellen, domestic	19 f VA	WILLIAM, Sophia, cook	30 f GR
MITCHELL, Juith, domestic	16 f VA	4-29	
FOX, George, Journey baker	36 m		
26-152		SKINNER, Martha A, candy stall	65 f
		136-997	
SINCLAIR, Thomas, ms carptr 1K/500	28 m		
Pricella	24 f	SLACK, James, mail carrier -/30	23 m
Virginia	2 f	Mary	19 f
MAHANDX, Wm, appren	21 m	Adelia	6/12 f
52-367		140-1028	

ALEXANDRIA VIRGINIA 1860 CENSUS

SLATER, John, gardner 9K/1500	49 m EG	Clifton H	19 m	
Matilda	36 f	Mary D	16 f	
Joseph	23 m	Francis	14 m	
Elizabeth	20 f	Alice C	12 f	
John	19 m	Courtland	9 m	
William, appren apothecary	16 m	Sarah G	9 f	
Mary	13 f	BELL, Nora (M)	45 f	
ROACH, Mary, domestic	31 f IR	173-1297		
277-2133				
		SMITH, Geo, gardner -/100	47 m BD	
SLAYMAKER, A H, dry good merch -/6K	38 m PA	Frances	27 f	
Faithful May	30 f	Margaretta	3 f	
Elizabeth	10 f	Infant	1/12 f	
Alexander	5 m	155-1149		
Willie	1 m			
BLACK, Sarah (M), domestic	28 f	SMITH, George A, Epis clergy 9K/5K	56 m	
Henrietta (M)	19 f	Aphilia	56 f	
249-1940		Elizia W	25 f	
		Isabella	20 f	
SMITH, Andrew, horse trader -/150	45 m IR	Henry M	16 m	
Lucy	27 f ME	21-121		
Helen	2 f VA			
92-665		SMITH, Jas, carter 2K/600	33 m	
		Mary	33 f	
SMITH, Ann (B), wash & iron	35 f	Annie	10 f	
Joseph (B), laborer	19 m	Slater	4 m	
Henry (B)	18 m	Mary J	7 f	
Charlotte (B)	7 f	Infant	3/12 m	
256-1983		COX, Louisa (M)	59 f	
		Lucy (M)	11 f	
SMITH, Betsy (B), cook -/50	50 f	Levis (B)	3 m	
Adelia (M), domestic	18 f	79-566		
ALLEN, James (B), house carpenter	36 m			
237-1827				
		SMITH, John, gardner	50 m NA	
SMITH, Cornelia (B)	30 f	Odelia	53 f BD	
Elizabeth (B)	21 f	Martin, laborer	21 m NA	
Augustus (B)	6 f	Elizabeth	14 f	
Cornelia (B)	1 f	John	8 m	
HONESTY, Lavinia (B)	17 f	100-740		
256-1984				
		SMITH, John L, shoemaker 1600/2K	56 m VA	
SMITH, D B, coal dealer 16K/700	47 m	Mary	35 f	
Harriet	44 f	James	15 m	
Lacy	19 f	Mary E	13 f	
Boyd W	16 m	George	11 m	
Eliza	16 f	Fanny	6 f	
Rebecca	11 f	Emma	3 f	
Harriet	2 f	MITCHELL, Julia (M)	18 f	
DAINGERFIELD, Eliza	53 f	5-31		
216-1668				
		SMITH, John P 45K/500	46 m VA	
SMITH, Elizabeth (B), wash & iron	30 f	May	45 f	
Hamilton (B)	10 m	Fanny	19 f	
Caroline (B)	7 f	James	12 m	
Alice (B)	4 f	Thomas	8 m	
Ada (B)	2 f	251-1948		
131-954				
		SMITH, Lewis, laborer	28 m IR	
SMITH, F L, Lawyer 13K/3K	50 m	Mary	24 f	
Sarah G	45 f	John	2 m VA	
Margaret	21 f	57-401		

ALEXANDRIA VIRGINIA 1860 CENSUS

SMITH, Michael		30 m	SMITH, S A, sadler -/50	40 m	
Mary		22 f	Lavenia	26 f	
DONALLY, William		45 m	Ann	2 f	
CASEY, Milton		30 m	Eleanora	10/12 f	
94-686			171-1281		
SMITH, Patrick		72 m IR	SMITH, Thomas, lime burner 6K/3K	56 m	
Mary		70 f	Maranda	50 f	
Hugh		70 m	Laura	21 f VA	
138-1011			HARRISON, Virginia	23 f	
			John	m	
SMITH, Peter, shoemaker		51 m HD	109-805		
Catharine		40 f			
Lena		15 f	SMITH, Thomas Wm, super gas wk 5K/500	52 m	
90-652			Ellen	46 f	
			Seabring, clerk	19 m	
			Catharine	17 f	
SMITH, R M, Editor 20K/628		46 m	Elizabeth	13 f	
Ellen		40 f	Mary	9 f	
Rebeca		16 f	WATTLES, Sarah	76 f	
William		14 m	21-117		
Nannie		3 f			
WILLIAMS, Jas E, reporter		20 m	SMITH, William, ship carptr -/100	50 m MD	
SMITH, Jas M, co-editor		36 m	Susan	40 f	
118-571			HOWARD, Louise	19 f	
			REED, Martha	20 f	
SMITH, Rachael B		47 f MD	226-1742		
Rachael		24 f			
Hesselius		21 m	SMITH, Wm H, grocer 1900/800	30 m	
Eric		16 m	Frances	21 f	
DICKMAN, Bettie (B), domestic		10 f	82-589		
141-1040					
			SMOOT, Alleghany, lumber merchant	26 m VA	
SMITH, Rebecca, boarding house 2K/100		48 f MD	Susan	23 f	
Noble		27 m	Henley	2 m	
Sarah		22 f	2-8		
Robt		19 m			
Saml		17 m	SMOOT, C C, tanner 47K/27K	62 m MD	
CAWOOD, Joseph, fisherman -/1K		66 m	Charles	36 m	
Benjamin, fisherman		39 m	Susan	30 f	
Andrew, fisherman		30 m	Ellen	5 f	
Thomas, fisherman		32 m	Clinton	3 m	
Robert, carpenter		38 m	Cora	1 f	
Wm H, baggage master		22 m	KING, Chas	16 m	
KULON, Frank, cooper		28 m HY	2-14		
FREIDLY, Geo, tanner		26 m DC			
GRAVES, Henry, farmer		30 m	SMOOT D L, lawyer -/300	25 m	
HURTLE, Thos, fisherman		27 m	Laura W	23 f VA	
ELLIOT, Margaret		5 f	Walter C	6/12 m	
Fanny		2 f	143-1054		
Chas		28 f MD			
68-480			SMOOT, George H, lmb mc 10600/30375	59 m MD	
			Catherine	50 f	
			Catherine A	19 f	
SMITH, Richard H, fireman RR -/50		30 m	FRENCH, Ca.. W	7 f	
Janet		26 f	1-5		
Catharine		5 f			
JEFFERSON, Emily, domestic		16 f	SMOOT, J H D, lumber merch -/10K	28 m	
154-1140			Frances P	25 f	
			Kate W	6 f	
SMITH, Robert J, lawyer -/7K		42 m	French	4 m	
115-850			Minnie	2 f	

ALEXANDRIA VIRGINIA 1860 CENSUS

SHEARS, Sarah, domestic 12 f
1-6

SMOOT, James R, butcher 3K/500 30 m
  Mijah 38 f
  Harriet 55 f
  Jack (B) 12 m
281-2149

SMOOT, John B, tanner/curring -/1300 30 m
  Sarah 28 f MD
  Henry 4 m VA
  William 2 m
3-15

SMOOT, Phebe 3K/10K 50 f
  Jas R, lumber merch 30 m
  Kitty 27 f
  Laura 23 f
  William A, clerk 19 m
  Carrie 16 f
  Laura 12 f
25-146

SMOOT, Thomas S, butcher -/200 27 m
  Sarah E 24 f
  Mary M 3 f
  Isabel 1 f
281-2148

SMYTHE, Susan 5K/9K 62 f MD
  Elizabeth 41 f VA
LAURENS, Catharine 12 f
CARROLL, Mary (B), domestic 20 f
21-119

SNOWDEN, Edgar, editor 7K/6K 50 m
  Louise 44 f
  Harold, physician 23 m
  Joanna 20 f
  Annie 18 f
  Cedi... 16 f
  Osman 14 m
  Willie 12 m
  Mary 10 f
  Herbert 8 m
  Powell 5 m
  Mary 70 f
231-1786

SNOWDEN, Edgar, editor -/200 27 m
  Clarence 26 f
  John H 3 m
  Edgar 1 m
FORD, Louisa (B), domestic 18 f
DYSON, Ellen (B) 30 f
23-129

SNYDER, Robt R, tinner 11K/6K 49 m
  Ellizabeth 35 f
  Margaret 15 f

  Ellen 11 f
109-810

SOLOMAN, Ann 3K/1K 77 f MD
PADGETT, Sarah 75 f
  Lucretia 60 f
129-944

SOLOMAN, Nelson (B) 28 m
  Amelia (B) 20 f
  Charles (B) 3 m
  Alfred (B) 2/12 m
168-1256

SOLOMAN, Townsend (B), laborer 65 m
  Susan (B) 61 f
  Jane (B) 25 f
  Sarah (B) 16 f
  Theophilus (M) 13 m
  Jane (M) 7 f
  Towsend (M) 3 m
  James (M) 2 m
151-1116

SOMBY, Mary (B), domestic 59 f
168-1257

SOPER, John H, shoemaker -/50 27 m MD
  Matilda 24 f VA
  William 6 m VA
  Ed Duncan 4 m
  Mary 2 f
  Infant 3/12 f
HUNTINGTON, Elizabeth, domestic 18 f
24-143

SOUTHARD, John H, laborer 48 m
  Eliza 40 f
  Delany 11 m
  Mary 6 f
  William 3 m
276-2124
* see page 115 for SOUTHARD

SPEEKS, Sarah (M) 28 f
  Josaphine (B) 5 f
  Herbert (B) 3 m
  Jerome (B) 2 f
GIBSON, Lewis (B) 80 m
253-1971

SPELLMAN, Wm C, shoemaker -/30 77 m
  Annie 65 f
  Frances 18 f
204-1562

SPENCER, James, caubler -/25 27 m
  Ann 19 f
195-1485

SPRIGG, Mary (B), wash & iron 34 f
  Ann (B) 3 f

ALEXANDRIA VIRGINIA 1860 CENSUS

Margaret (B)	1 f	BLACK, Mary (B)	30 f
240-1862		197-1507	
SPILLMAN, Wm C, shoemaker -/30	77 m	STABLER, Richard H, drug/chm 14K/6K	40 m
Ann	65 f	Jane	36 f
Frances	18 f	Edward	13 m
204-1562		Mary	10 f
		Lawrence	5 m
SPINKS, Albert, parior -/250	40 m VA	Caroline	2 f
Mary	30 f	FAWCETT, Edward	16 m
James, butcher	20 m	HAYS, Nora, domestic	19 f IR
George	18 m	STABLER, Rebecca	45 f
Mary	18 f	SYPHAX, Frances (B), domestic	66 f
Alice	14 f	18-105	
Thomas, laborer	17 m		
Chas	6 m	STALLING, Vincent, laborer -/30	60 m
WOOD, Frank, carter	18 m	Eliza, seamstress	30 f
235-1816		Harriet	19 f
		78-552	
SPINKS, Cynthia	73 f		
JOHNSTON, Mary (M), domestic	23 f	STANDIFORD, John, ms carptr -/300	32 m MD
33-213		Louisa	36 f VA
		Ella	4 f
SPINKS, Elizabeth, domestic	55 f	Henry	2 m
ALLEN, Nancy, seamstress	55 f	Malinda (M), domestic	16 f
Harriet, stocking --	40 f	32-206	
151-1118			
		STANLEY, James T, steam engineer -/50	
SPINKS, Jas, negro trades -/500	63 m	Elizabeth	53 f
Sarah	53 f MD	William	16 m
Emma	19 f VA	Robert	12 m
Alexander	16 m	Jane	10 f
148-1092		Julia	10 f
		Julia	8 f
SPINKS, Rebecca 500/50	67 f	George	5 m
Thomas, RR fireman	26 m	Inno...	10/12 f
Julia	32 f	194-1476	
WEST, Rebecca	40 f		
Mary	28 f	STANSBERRY, Joseph, turner -/50	37 m MD
GALLAHER, Mary, weaver	24 f MD	Georgiana	26 f VA
FAIRFAX, Karissa, warper	40 f VA	Daniel	8 m
72-504		Francis	5 m
		Mary E	3 f
SPOTTS, Abraham, RR fireman -/30	32 m P[	John M	7/12 m
Louise	21 f MD	16-89	
Aphelia	3 f VA		
157-1162		STANTON, Elihu, bricklayer --/100	46 m
		Isabella	32 f
SPRIGG, D F, Epis minister 3K/7K	36 m	Richard	12 m
Emily	36 f	Ruberta	11 f
Tracy	5 f	John	7 m
BLACK, Eliz, domestic	19 f VA	Edgar	5 m
140-1026		Isabella	2 f
		220-1699	
SPRIGG, Joshua, shoemaker	53 m MA		
Ann	29 f VA	STARK, Jas, mail carrier	2 m
KELLY, William, house painter	25 m	Mary	19 f
May	22 f IR	Adelia	6/12 f
245-1903		140-1028	
STABLER, Deborah 6K/5K	60 f	STEARS, Annie -/40	52 f EG
REESE, Balak	15 f MD	James, baker	32 m NF

ALEXANDRIA VIRGINIA 1860 CENSUS

Jane	20 f		STILTON, Henry, machinist -/50	53 m EG	
Robert, baker	17 m NY		Margaret	54 f IR	
16-52			Mary	3 f VA	
			Elizabeth	9/12 f	
STEARS, Wm, steam engineer -/40	51 m		146-1078		
Sarah	53 f				
Ames	21 f		STINER, Jonathan, carpenter	48 m	
Harriet	17 f		Sarah	46 f	
George W	1 m		George, cigar maker	23 m	
185-1403			Elizabeth	19 f	
			James, appren	16 m	
STEDMORE, Samuel	46 m VA		Annie	15 f	
Louisa, watchkeeper	41 f		Marietta	13 f	
101-747			Sallie	11 f	
			Charles	8 f	
STEELE, Jas, laborer -/50	27 m		Porterfield	6 m	
Catharine	25 f		51-354		
Laura	7/12 f				
80-572			STOLLINGS, Theodore, blacksmith -/50	32 m	
			Hanora	28 f	
STEPHENS, J M, druggist 4500/5000	33 m		Benjamin	8 m	
Susan J	34 f		Mary	4/12 f	
Willie	4 m		187-1421		
Minnie	3 f				
JONES, Margaret (M), domestic	25 f		STONE, Jane, seamstress	35 f	
105-774			John, fisherman	18 m MD	
			Robt, clerk	16 m	
STEPNEY, Wm (B), laborer	40 m		109-803		
Margaret (B)	26 f				
William (B)	2 m		STONE, Joseph, sailor	48 m MD	
147-1084			May	36 f	
			Annie, appren dressmaker	16 f	
			Alerne	13 m	
STEVES, Morgan	30 m NY		Emma	8 f	
Amanda	21 f		Margaret	5 f	
TODD, David	73 m VT		John	2 m	
265-2054			192-1458		
STEWART, Eliza	61 f IR		STONELL, John W, merchant -/50	35 m	
William, carpenter	33 m VA		Sarah	27 f	
Mary Jane	21 f		Cecilia	5 f	
57-404			Infant	5/12 f	
			236-1819		
STEWART, John W, whsale tbco 15K/50K	50 m				
Margaret	40 f		STONELL, Wm, farmer 1K/300	57 m	
Bettie	18 f		Margaret	37 f	
Annie	15 f		William, laborer	23 m	
John C	11 m		Anna	20 f	
Elmira S	7 f		Virginia	19 f	
111-826			William	20 m	
			273-2101		
STIFF, Wm W, clerk comm store -/150	31 m		STOOPS, Belinda J, grocer	39 f	
Sarah	26 f		Alice	16 f	
Walter	4 m		Columbus	11 m DC	
James	1 m		John M	9 m	
220-1698			William H	9 m	
			KUTCHER, Anna	26 f WB	
STILLMAN, Tobias, express man -/200	28 m NY		24-137		
Eliza	25 f				
Mary	2 f		STOUTENBERG, Jas A, groceries 1K/1500	39 m NY	
45-310			Esther	36 f	

ALEXANDRIA VIRGINIA 1860 CENSUS

Seymour	7 m VA		Elizabeth	25 f	
Katie	5 f		Amelia	21 f	
Jenny	3 m		DAVIS, William (M), domestic	15 m	
MAHONY, Susan (B), domestic	21 f VA		DYSON, Mary (B)	12 f	
Josaphene (B)	2 f		BROWN, Emma, adopted dau	16 f	
131-961			3-17		
STRAWBURY, Joseph, turner	37 m MD		STUDD, Fred -/100	30 m EG	
Georgiana	26 f		Virginia	26 f VA	
Daniel	8 m		Jane	13 f NY	
Francis	5 m		Mary	9 f	
Mary E	3 f		John	5 m VA	
John M	7/12 m		Laura	2 f	
16-89			99-732		
STRIDER, Geo, laborer -/50	36 m		SULLIVAN, Daniel, laborer	60 m IR	
Phebe	33 f		Mary	59 f	
Bernie	5 m		HUGHES, Mary	69 f	
Janett	2 f		SULLIVAN, Thomas, machinist	18 m	
SCOTT, Sarah, domestic	54 f		202-1542		
225-1732					
			SULLIVAN, Dennis, laborer	31 m	
STRIDER, John L, tailor -/200	40 m MD		Margaret	23 f	
Catharine	31 f		Violet	3 m	
John	15 m		...	9/12 m	
Anne	14 f		CLARKE, James	30 m IR	
Elenor	12 f		184-1398		
Hugh	9 m				
Margaret	3 f		SULLIVAN, Elizabeth, seamstress	56 f	
Fannie	2 f		Emma V	46 f	
KING, Wm W, tailor	21 m		Charles	7 m	
Margaret	17 f		60-424		
15-80					
			SULLLIVAN, Maria, female nurse	50 f	
STUART, Ann L	70 f		John, carpenter	25 m	
Albert, lawyer 9500/1K	38 m		Andrew, huckster	20 m	
Charles, lawyer	36 m		George	12 m	
Henry	34 m		51-359		
Sarah	24 f NC				
Chas	10 m		SUMMERS, J W, farmer 3K/1500	35 m	
Richard	8 m		Virginia	25 f	
Meta	6 f		John	3 m	
Kate	2 f		chas F	2 m	
Infant	1/12 f		Simon	33 m	
19-110			253-1969		
STUART, Cornelia (B), wash & iron	25 f		SUMMERS, Jas, carriage maker	30 m	
May (B)	5 f		Sarah	26 f	
Lindon (B)	6/12 m		Edgar	1 m	
228-1759			33-214		
STUART, James M, dr gd merch 30K/2K	48 m		SUMMERS, Jno, coach maker 5K/6K	58 m	
Susan	40 f GT		Mary C	35 f	
Carrie	11 f		William	31 m	
Mary	8 f		John	27 m	
Donald	6 m		Rafalo	19 m	
BROOK, Georgiana, domestic	25 f		Charles	5 m	
12-60			Laura	14 f	
			Annie	3 f	
STUART, Wm, printer 18K/500	28 m VA		EDELIN, Louise, coach maker	25 m DC	
Sarah	38 f		TROFIT, Jacob, appren	18 m VA	
Mary	29 f		128-934		

ALEXANDRIA VIRGINIA 1860 CENSUS

SUMMERS, Mary C -/4K	45 f		SUTTON, William, shoemaker -/25	34 m
Joseph	16 m		Sarah	30 f
Florence	10 f		Mary	12 f
29-183			William	10 m
			George W	8 m
SUMMERS, Susan (B), wash & iron	36 f		Ruberta	6 f
141-1038			Cornelia	4 f
			John	1 m
SUMMERS, Wesley 13K/400	60 m		157-1164	
Margaret	45 f			
Emma	18 f		SWAIN, Geo, 9K/2K	68 m MA
Alice	16 f		Mary	60 f VA
Rotchford	14 m		WOOD, Laurson,	18 F
Susan	10 f		214-1646	
Philip	8 m			
Sidney	6 m		SWAIN, George Jr, house carpenter	34 m
30-187			Eliza	36 f PA
			Horace	8 m VA
SUPPLY, Mary -/50	24 f VA		Mary	63
Charles, grocer clerk	23 m		194-1474	
Sarah	68 m			
Mary, teacher	17 f		SWAIN, Julia, shoemaker 1500/50	47 m
167-1247			Francis, clerk comm store	19 m
			Mary	9 f
SOUTHARD, Mary A -/20	26 f		MITCHELL, William, house carpenter	23 m
John	10 m		188-1428	
Sarah	7 f			
William	6 m		SWAIN, Stephen, ms carptr 1400/150	41 m
Charles	2 m		Mary	35 f
BRYANT, John J, ship carpenter	57 m		Edgar	17 m
233-1799			George	14 m
			Mary	12 f
SUTHARD, John H, laborer	45 m		Sally	10 f
Eliza	40 f		A..?	2 f
Delaney	11 m		Benjamin	7/12 m
Mary	6 f		191-1452	
William	3 m			
276-2124			SWAIN, Walter, carpenter -/50	29 m
			Sarah	25 f MD
SUTHARD, Sylvester, machinist	26 m		William	5 m
Elizabeth	26 f		Erma	20 f
Rossaline	1 f		182-1379	
WELLS, Julia	26 f			
37-239 (there are two 239's)			SWAN, Frances B, farmer 9K/?	44 f
			Mary	41 f
SUTHARD, Thomas, laborer	40 m		Rosina	30 f
HOSKINS, George, carter	16 m		Sally	9 f
276-2123			William	7 m
			Mary	3 f
SUTTLE, C F, comm merch -/30K	44 m		272-2099	
ADELE, Thos, clerk	20 m			
106-784			SWAN, James, shoemaker -/100	38 m MD
			Martha	26 f
SUTTON, Stephen, blacksmith	28 m		James T	4 m
Mary	28 f		43-287	
Saul	7 m			
Mary	5 f		SWAN, Thomas W, farmer 20K/15K	39 m
Jane	4 f		Ellen	42 f
Johanna	3 f		Susanna	7 f
Ann	4/12 f		SWANN, William T, lawyer	42 m
HEART, Thos, pump maker	49 m		280-2140	
186-1410				

115

ALEXANDRIA VIRGINIA 1860 CENSUS

SWAN, William G, shoemaker	41 m	Douglas (M)	6/12 m
Sarah Ann, monthly nurse	42 f	Eliza (B)	36 f
Ann	14 f	167-1251	
William	10 m		
Marion	7 f	SYPHAX, Maria (M)	56 f
27-161		Bertha (M)	35 f
		Maria (M)	16 f
SWANN, Robert, laborer	45 m VA	Annie (M)	80 f
Catharine	50 f	Mary (M)	9 f
HILLCOLME, Billy, laborer	40 m GR	Washington (M)	7 m
183-1394		264-2044	
SWARP, Fred, baker -/50	25 m	TACEY, Jefferson, paper hanger -/2500	30 m EG
Cornelia		Maud	30 f
Katy	7/12 f	GEORGE, H, appren	16 m VA
FRAZIER, S A, cabinet maker	30 m	TACEY, Masy	9 f
Isabella	22 f	17-93	
Arthur	2 m		
146-1073		TACKER, John, brickmaker	36 m
		Nancy	40 f
		244-1892	
SWEENEY, Mickie, laborer	48 m IR		
Margaret	40 f	TAILER, Eliza	33 f
Mary	15 f VA	Laura	13 f
Hanora	10 f	Augustus 18K/2K	3 m NY
John	7 m	269-2081	
242-1878			
		TAILOR, Jas, plasterer -/50	28 m
SYMES, Alexander (B), plasterer	55 m	Laura	25 f
Sophia (B)	56 f	Augusta	4 m
236-1821		James	1 m
		HIBBINS, Maria	58 f
SYMMES, Noble, plasterer	23 m	222-1710	
Frances	19 f		
Willie	2 m		
82-591		TARLTON, Henry, boot & shoe mkr -/50	56 m VA
		Susanna	47 f
		Henry C, printer	20 m
SYMMS, E M -/100	42 f	Victoria	22 f
Josaphene	22 f	Margaret	17 f VA
Christopher, dry goods clerk	18 m	Sarah	7 f
HICKEN, John, house carpenter	29 m	SMITH, Margaret	79 f
Mary	8/12 f	225-1736	
STEWART, Mary	69 f MD		
McCLOSAND, Michael, silversmith	22 m IR	FASSETT, Jas, livery keeper 3700/300	56 m MD
218-1678		Catharine	40 f DC
		Henry	22 m
SYMS, Margaret (M), wash & iron	27 f	Emma	20 f
FRAZIER, Caroline (B)	12 f	Mary	18 f
164-1227		Marion	15 f VA
		John	13 m
SYNCOX, Aaron, laborer	37 m	Kate	9 f
Mary, grocer	39 f	Louise	8 f
Edward, laborer	21 m	Ida	2 f
John, appren bricklayer	19 m	MULLIGAN, Mary, domestic	12 f
Susanah	15 f	131-959	
William	7 m		
48-331		TARYTON, Henry, shoemaker -/400	52 m
		222-1714	
SYPHAX, Lewis (M), laborer	22 m		
Martha (M)	24 f	TATE, Hewella, wash & iron 600/-	48 f
Julia (M)	3 f	45-319	

ALEXANDRIA VIRGINIA 1860 CENSUS

TATE, Samuel (B)	68 m		Julian	6 m
Cassandra (B)	69 f		Annie	4 f
156-1156			250-1947	
TATSAPAUGH, Henry, hs of prost -/250	73 m		TAYLOR, Ashley (B)	38 f
Margaret	69 f		William (B)	13 m
Hanna, prostitute	23 f		Mary (B)	10 f
Mary, prostitute	18 f		John (B)	7 m
Laura, prostitute	16 f		210-1608	
181-1375				
			TAYLOR, C, farmer 20K/5K	39 m
TATSAPAUGH, Julia, dress maker -/50	31 f		Harriet	33 f
Clarence	10 m		Chas S	13 m
Paulena	9 f		Esther	5 f
Edwin F	7 m		131-960	
Charles	4 m			
DIXON, Ch, dress maker	35 f		TAYLOR, Cor, grocer 800/200	65 m VA
174-1300			Susanna	53 f MD
			Susanna	26 f VA
TATSAPAUGH, Susan 500/50	57 f		Elisha P	23 m
Rebeca	54 f		James M	21 m
WILLIAMS, Martha (B)	16 f		Mary	17 f
235-1812			Lucinda	15 f
			Cornelius	9 m
TATSAPAUGH, W H, shoemaker -/100	29 m		142-1046	
Laura	26 f MD			
Annie	8 f VA		TAYLOR, George, laborer 800/-	37 m IR
Mary	5 f		Alice	34 f
Laura	2 f		Joseph	3 m
TAYLOR, John, shoemaker	23 f HN		94-684	
Rose	18 f BV			
115-851				
			TAYLOR, Geo W, asst flour inspector	50 m IR
TATSPAUGH, Virginia, prost -/30	27 f		Valerie	56 f VA
Wallace	4 m		Robt, miller	18 m
Geo W	2 m		Thomas, appren tailor	16 m
GATES, Eliza, hs of prost	41 f		104-765	
WILLIAMS, George (B)	14 m			
210-1612			TAYLOR, Henry, shoemaker -/400	52 m
			222-1714	
TATTERSON, Francis, boot mkr -/20	43 m			
Mary	35 f		TAYLOR, J H C, merchant -/50	31 m MD
Matilda	2 f		Martha	30 f VA
Rosalie	13 f		Marion	7 m MD
150-1111			Emma	4 f VA
			Alice	8/12 f
TATTERSON, James, cabinet mkr	39 m		80-569	
Ella	40 f IR			
Emma	12 f VA		TAYLOR, Jimmy (B), domestic	26 f
William, appren printer	11 m VA		Mary (B)	6 f
158-1173			William (M)	3 m
			Ann (M)	6/12 f
TAYLOR, Alfred, machinist -/30	22 m MD		PAYNE, Louis (M), shoemaker	25 m
Amelia	21 f		41-278	
William	1/12 m VA			
James, carpenter	24 m MD		TAYLOR, John T, shoemaker 700/300	63 m
Mary	19 f		Mary E	25 f MD
89-640			Susan	23 f
			Valentine, shoemaker	19 m
TAYLOR, Alice E B	33 f		Rebecca	2 f
May	10 f		HOOE, Margaret (M)	14 f
Archie	8 m		5-36	

ALEXANDRIA VIRGINIA 1860 CENSUS

TAYLOR, Joshua (B)	69 m	TENNISON, Charles E, hotel kpr -/200	36 m	
Cornelia (M)	55 f	Laura	26 f	
247-1919		Mary C	10 f	
		Emson B	9 f	
TAYLOR, Julia A, notion shop	37 f	Laura	7 f	
Charles	16 m	John	6 m	
Franklin	13 m	James	3 m	
Annie	8 f	Margaret	6/12 f	
Ada	2 f	MITCHELL, Matilda	44 f	
CAVILLEAR, Samuel, huckster	24 m WA	ROCK, Wm R, blacksmith -/600	43 m VA	
Jane	18 f	1-4		
Joseph	1/12 m			
192-1459		TENNISON, Samuel, restuarant -/1500	46 m	
		Margaret	37 f VA	
TAYLOR, Lawrance B, lawyer 5K/1K	22 m	Charles	18 m	
Virginia	36 f	Charlotte	14 f	
Nancy	13 f	Samuel	7 m	
Rosalie	8 f	David	2 m	
Brook	6 m	Catharine	13 f	
166-1243		TATSPAUGH, Richard, machinist	32 m	
		62-44		
TAYLOR, Robt, flour inspector -/500	48 m			
Mary E	38 f MD	THOMAS, Geo T, comm merch -/500	50 m	
Thomas	13 m	Maria	45 f	
Jean	6 m	Mary	17 f	
Robt	3 m	HARPER, W A	39 m	
Mary	2 f	Jane	60 f	
COWAN, Thomas, express clerk	26 m MD	Alice	8 f	
Sally	26 m	Emma	7 f	
103-765		Frank	6 f	
		Willie	4 m	
TAYLOR, W Arthur, lawyer 10K/3800	35 m	124-908		
Mary E	69 f			
Harriet C	31 f	THOMAS, Jane, soap mfc 3300/1000	41 f	
173-1298		Ellen	20 f	
		Joshua, clerk	19 m	
TAYLOR, William, laborer	28 m NJ	Emma	17 f	
Elizabeth	30 f VA	Alice	13 f	
Alice	2 f	George	11 m	
RIDGWAY, Maria	8 f	Ada	8 f	
116-858		Florence	5 f	
		33-210		
TAYLOR, Wm 5K/2K	48 m			
Elizabeth	54 f	THOMPSON, Betty 500/3K	75 f	
Fairfax	21 m	Kitty	73 f	
Charles	18 m	145-1065		
Manadier	17 m			
TRAVIS, Henry	25 m			
271-2094		THOMPSON, Christina, boarding -/100	50 f MD	
		Joseph, ship carpenter	19 m VA	
TAYLOR, William, carpenter 850/75	65 m	Sarah	17 f	
Lucinda	30 f	HODGES, Elizabeth	16 f	
Charles	3 m	COLDER, John, machinist	32 m ST	
William	1 m	Adona	28 f	
Mary, nurse	12 f IR	Isabella	5 f	
81-576		Willie	4 m	
		COLE, Emma (M), domestic	15 f	
TEBBS, Elizabeth, teacher 6K/1K	31 f	228-1757		
GURBER, Ledia, teacher 6K/-	20 f			
SIMS, Caroline (B), domestic	27 f	THOMPSON, Ella (M), baker	40 m	
Roxalena (B), cook	50 f	Martha	26 m	
76-536		John (M), brickmason	22 m	

ALEXANDRIA VIRGINIA 1860 CENSUS

James (M)	12 m	THOMPSON, W W, turner	29 m VA	
Samuel (M)	11 m	Mary	23 f	
203-1556		Emma	5 f	
		Joseph	3 m	
THOMPSON, Jas 1500/75	33 m MD	Mary	5/12 f	
Lucinia	31 f VA	39-259		
Elmira	7 f			
James B	3 m	THORM, Clay, carter	25 m MD	
64-450		59-416		
THOMPSON, John, watchman	38 m	THORM, Will J, huckster -/30	27 m MD	
Emiline	39 f	Agnes	22 f ST	
Luther	13 m	Frank	2 m VA	
Maria	11 f	John	5/12 m	
Eveline	10 f	60-423		
Mildred	7 f			
Clay	5 m	THORNTON, John (M), laborer	35 m	
Edgar	3 m	Lucinda (M)	22 f	
FONCE, George, shoemaker	45 m MA	Mamy (M)	3 f	
232-1791		Margaret (M)	3/12 f	
		38-249		
THOMPSON, John (B), wash & iron	48 m			
Richard (B), laborer	17 m	THORNTON, Major (B)	70 m	
36-232		Sally (M)	49 f	
		266-2060		
THOMPSON, John, carter 5K/500	50 m MD			
Margaret	45 f MD	THORNTON, Sarah (B) 400/30	68 f	
PARISH, Mary	25 f	243-1888		
Frances	5 f			
Ella	3 f			
812-585		THRIFT, John, laborer	70 m	
		Peggy	60 f	
THOMPSON, John W, turner -/200	29 m VA	255-1987		
Mary	23 f			
Emma	5 f	THURSTON, Elizabeth, brd House -/600	45 f NH	
Joseph	3 m	Eunice G	57 f	
Mary	3/12 f	Sally	35 f	
39-259		CAWOOD, Daniel, comm merch	73 m VA	
		Mary	68 f	
THOMPSON, Rudolph, cooper -/20	28 m VA	STUART, Miss	73 f	
Eugina	28 f	HOWARD, David, clerk	35 m	
Rudolph	5 m	Mary	35 f	
Aurilea	3 f	John	15 m	
Sarah	7/12 f	Robert	6 m	
94-681		FRANK, Mr, coal agent	30 m NY	
		Georgia	20 f	
THOMPSON, Samuel, laborer	40 m VA	ARMSTEAD, Phebe	55 f	
Sarah	30 f	ARMSTEAD, Will	53 m	
Sally	4 f	PRETTYMAN, Mrs	24 m	
Thomas	2 m	HORNER, Robert, dry good clerk	28 m VA	
Susan	1 f MA	DOWNEY, Mis	25 f NY	
283-2166		ANLSNIL, Mr, house carpenter	23 m GR	
		SMITH, David (B), domestic	53 m VA	
THOMPSON, Susanna, seamstress	53 f MD	MIRRETT, Mrs	35 f	
Jane, spinner	19 f	19/20-111		
George, barber	18 m MD			
92-669		TITUS, Samuel, farmer 2K/200	45 m VA	
		Martha	46 f	
THOMPSON, Thomas H, laborer	45 m VA	Joseph	16 m	
Mary J	40 f	Laura	7 f	
Sarah	16 f	India	4 f	
253-1967		257-1990		

ALEXANDRIA VIRGINIA 1860 CENSUS

TODD, Samuel, house carpenter	47 m	Robt	15 m	
Mary	33 f	Joseph	12 m	
Eliza	3 f	John	9 m	
Sarah E	4 f	William	4 m	
25-144		Ann	7 f	
		George	3 m	
TOLBERT, John (B)	24 m	Amelia	4/12 f	
Mary (B)	25 m	CLARK, Elizabeth	61 f	
John (B)	4 m	TRAVIS, Ann	55 f	
Wm (B)	2 m	103-761		
165-1231		TRAVIS, Thomas, harbor ms 1500/300	70 m MD	
TOLL, James, laborer	35 m IR	Henrietta	51 f	
Annie	27 f	John, ship carpenter	29 m	
Rosea	12 f	Mary E	27 f	
Margaret	9 f	Elenor	24 f	
Jane	5 f VA	Jas A, machinist	18 m	
Frances	2 f	Christina	13 f	
90-645		Alonzo	11 m	
		THOMAS, Edward	3 m	
TOMLINE, Robert, restaurant	49 m	Lucy V	2 f	
Sarah	38 f	BROWN, H C, house carpenter	30	
Mary A	15 f	Ann	6	
Beuia Vista	12 f	Henry	4	
Acamia	9 f	183-1390		
Margaret	8 f			
Robert, appren carpenter	17 m	TREACLE, James, pilot -/30	56 m	
William	6 m	Elizabeth	53 f	
Rawlton	3 m	Henry, clerk dry goods	20 m	
WALKER, Dan (B)	18 m	Henrietta	17 f	
FERGUSON, Polly	74 f	224-1728		
10-48				
		TREACLE, William H, pilot -/30	36 v	
TOPER, John H, shoemaker	27 m MD	Jane	33 f	
Matilda	26 f VA	William	6 m	
William	6 m	Infant	6/12 m	
Ed Duncan	4 m	223-1722		
Mary	2 f			
Infant	3/12 f	TRIPLETE, Wm H, bookkeeper	53 m	
HUNTINGTON, Elizabeth, domestic	18 f	Charles, locksmith	17 m VA	
24-143		100-738		
TOTTEN, Lauria	83 f	TRIPLETT, Susan	35 f	
233-1798		Virginia, domestic	19 f	
		Isabella	9 f	
TOWNSBY, Thomas, house caprentr -/30	35 m	Franklin	5 m	
Mona	30 f	Rebecca	1 f	
Charlotte	8 f	207-1586		
Katie	5 f			
Charles	3 m	TRIPLETT, Thornton 1K/100	38 m	
Sally	2 f	Mary	8 f	
212-1625		Isadore	14 f	
		Sally	12 f	
TRAVIS, John, farmer 1K/200	32 m VA	Savinia	6 f	
Rachael	25 f	Mary	4 f DC	
Chas	9 m	Sarah	71 f VA	
Margaret	6 f	Ann	38 f	
John	4 m	176-1316		
269-2080				
		TRUSSELL, Susan	35 f	
TRAVIS, Jno W, cooper -/50	38 m	Virginia, domestic	19 f	
Amelia	f VA	Isabella	9 f	

ALEXANDRIA VIRGINIA 1860 CENSUS

```
  Franklin                              5 m      James                                 5 m VA
  Rebecca                               1 f      Ellen                                 2 f
207-1586                                        150-1112

TUBMAN, Jas, grocer 2500/1K            50 m MD  TURNER, Zach, RR foreman             22 m MD
  Salena                               46 f       Ann                                19 f WA
  Oscar, house painter                 23 m    65-460
  Salona                               10 f
  Maguder, paper hanger                19 m     TWAIN, James, laborer                32 m IR
40-270                                            Jane                               26 f
                                                  John                                8 m VA
TUCKER, Caesar (B), wood sawyer        50 m       Mary                                6 f
  Maria (B)                            55 f       Jimmy                               2 m
40-263                                            Nicholas                         7/12 m
                                                55-387
TUCKER, H, 1800/200                    52 m MD
263-2042                                        TYLER, Thompson, plasterer           57 m
                                                  Mary                               46 m
TUCKER, Jas W, farmer 10K/300          22 m       Charles, plasterer                 26 m
  Thomas                               21 m       John Edward                        21 m
DAY, Lewis (B)                         15 m       Jane                               13 m
255-1982                                          Thompson                           10
                                                  Rachael                             8 f
TUCKER, Samuel, brickmaker 4700/200    63 m DC    Annie                              16 f
  Elizabeth                            67 f       Eliza                              17 f
  John, brickmaker                     35 m VA  36-229
  Elizabeth                            24 f
  Samuel                                3 m     UHLER, Peter G, lumber merch 6200/10K 57 m PA
LIPPEL, John                           14 m       Catherine                          42 f MD
GRAY, Mary, domestic                   31 f       Alfred G                           14 m VA
225-1733                                          Lycurgus                           12 m
                                                  George                             16 m
                                                  Kate                                8 f
TUCKMAN, Gasper, lawyer 20K/6K         55 m     GRIFFITH, Alfred, Meth Epis mn -/10K 77 m
  Apollinaire                          30 f     1-7
INGALLS, Edward                        29 m
  Monia                                22 f     VACCARI, Rose, grocer 4K/-           64 f IR
  John                                  9 m       Kinzer Lou, carpenter              27 m VA
  Sally                                25 f VA    Sarah                              21 f
272-2100                                          Mary                             1/12 f
                                                COOK, Jas F, grocer clerk            18 m DC
                                                  Mary                               16 f
TURLEY, Hinsin (M), gardner            77 m       Rose                               13 f
  Catharine (M)                        56 f     TAYLOR, Rose                         17 f PA
  Andrew (M), laborer                  22 m     110-818
  James (M)                            12 m
  Catharine (M)                        16 f     VALENTINE, Edward, oyster house -/100 50 m
282-2161                                          Delila                             40 f
                                                63-447
TURNER, Albert A, brakeman 600/50      29 m
  Lucinda                              26 f     VALENTINE, Thomas (B)                70 m
  Henry                                 5 m       Lydia (B)                          64 f
  Jane                                  2 f     240-1864
77-549
                                                VALENTINE, William, pork btch -/2500 45 m BD
TURNER, Lucy L 12500/3K                60 f VA    Lucinda                            54 f VA
LEE, C(assius) F                       16 m     SUTTON, George                        9 m GT
87-622                                          26-156

TURNER, Patrick, laborer               33 m IR  VAN BUREN, E B, Hotel keeper 2500/300 60 m NY
  Betsy                                33 f       Mona                               55 f
  Betsy                                11 f ST    John                               19 m
```

ALEXANDRIA VIRGINIA 1860 CENSUS

SMALL, Henrietta, house keeper	22 f		VENDEVERKING, G, farmer 34200/5K	50 m NY	
O'NEAL, Thomas, barkeeper	35 m		Jane	45 f NJ	
BENNETE, John, laborer	35 m NY		Jane	16 f	
GRIST, A A	20 m		Emma	12 f	
273-2108			Ella	3 f GT	
			GOLSOY?, Cornelia	17 f GR	
VANDERFRIGHT, N W, super RR -/8K	39 m NJ		256-1997		
Caibanne	32 f				
Joseph	11 m NH		VENEY, Maria (B), wash & iron	52 f	
Amy	9 f VA		Eliza (B)	18 f	
Charles	7 m PA		Laura (B)	13 f	
169-1267			Romulus (B)	9 m	
			68-476		
VANDERBURGH, Gilbert 6K/200	40 m NY				
Sarah	33 f				
Eveline	16 f		VERMILLIM, Mrs -/100	36 f	
Charlotte	11 f		Nancy	50 f	
Maria	9 f		James, machinist	19 m	
DAY, John, laborer	16 m		237-1825		
256-1986					
			VERNON, John, tanner 400/50	38 m IR	
			Ann	29 f	
VANNARRE, Joshua, tailor 2K/100	40 m NY		Catharine	2 f VA	
Aletta	40 f		244-1893		
Mary	17 f				
Ann	15 f		VIOLETT, Cloa 800/150	50 f	
Jane	14 f		Robt E, house painter	26 m	
Elinor	9 f		Alfred	19 m	
Clarence	2 m		Cloa Ann	26 f	
205-1568			Georgiana	22 f	
			69-485		
VANSANT, James 13400/25300	69 m MD				
Sarah	71 f				
Mary	71 f		VIOLETT, Robt G, comm merch 22750/750	60 m	
Elizabeth	37 f VA		Amanda	47 f	
122-895			ANDERSON, Jas H, comm merch	54 m	
VAUGHN, James H, upholstery -/30	43 m EG		BEATIE, Emma	15 f MD	
Eda	40 f MA		VIOLETT, Jno	57 m VA	
Frederick	10 m RI		ANDERSON, Elenor	67 f	
Edith	7 f		146-1077		
Joseph	5 m				
128-933			VOGELSANG, D, farmer 1K/200	37 m BV	
			Elizabeth	67 f PR	
VEITCH, A, house carpenter -/100	29 m		Anna	24 f MD	
Mary	23 f		279-2138		
William	3 m				
John	6/12 m		VOGELSANG, Philip, baker -/500	29 m	
261-2025			Henrietta	26 f	
			Catharine	3 f VA	
			Geo W	2 m	
VEITCH, Jno A 3600/100	36 m		217-1675		
Clara	38 f				
Florence	11 f		VORCE, Nelson, farmer 4K/300	40 m NY	
Franklin	5 m		Sarah	25 f	
Chas, cabinet maker	40 m VA		Sarah	13 f	
145-1072			John	9 m	
			275-2113		
VEITCH, Wm C, farmer -/200	58 m				
Sarah	49 f		VOWELL, Elizabeth -/100	60 f EG	
Robt	16 m		MILLS, John, sailor	29 m VA	
Andrew	16 m		Harvey	25 m	
261-2024			VOWELL, Hollie	17 f	

ALEXANDRIA VIRGINIA 1860 CENSUS

WELLS, George	5 m		WALKER, Jas, shoemaker 3500/100	69 m
Kate	3 f		Catharine	64 f
53-372			Ann E	42 f
			Adaline	20 f
WADDEY, James, machinist -/75	27 m		Sarah	8 f
Mary	26 f		James	2 m
Frank	2 m		15-82	
Jenny (B), nurse	12 f			
79-560			WALKER, Jas W 500/50	45 m
			Catharine	44 f
WADDY, John, cabinet maker -/100	29 m		George, laborer	21 m
Nelitia	58 f		Sarah	18 f
Josaphine, teacher	23 f		Frank	18 m
HODGES, Mary	17 f		William	13 m
WADDY, Thomas, cabinet maker	28 m		223-1723	
218-1682				
			WALKER, Levin T, shoemaker -/100	28 m
WADE, Robt H, porter -/30	40 m MD		Virginia	24 f SC
Jane	28 f		Acadenia	6 f VA
Martha	16 f VA		Emma	5 f
Robt	16 m		Isadora	4 f
Charles	12 m		Andrew	2 m
Isabella	10 f		48-334	
Francis	8 m			
Samuel	6 m		WALKER, R W, laborer	32 m
64-452			Amegia	25 f
			SARTAM, James	8 m
WAITER, Anna -/50	40 f MD		42-279	
Louise	45 f			
Christina	30 f		WALKER, Samuel, gardner	36 m VA
128-936			Anna	23 f
			Sarah	7 f
			Randolph	5 m
WALKER, Andrew J, shoemaker	32 m VA		Mary	3 f
Elizabeth M	26 f MD		Marta	3 f
HEKEUDAFFER, Mary	21 f		George F	62 m
Frederick, baggage master	29 m		34-219	
BUTLER, James, shoemaker	70 m MD			
Washington, axe maker	23 m DE		WALKER, Wm 500/150	40 m
Jas... Jarvis	12 m VA		Louise	35 f
Infant	1/12 f		Wm	18 m
47-322			David	16 m
			John	13 m
WALKER, Ethelbert, shoemaker -/30	31 m		Joseph	11 m
Anne	26 f		Martha	7 f
Ida	6 f		Sarah	5 f
Francis M	5 m		Ellen	2 f
Albert	3 m		257-1995	
41-276				
			WALKER, William T, shoemaker	49 m
			Martha	34 f
WALKER, Francis, shoemaker	31 m		Jane	13 f
.illie	25 f		Fanny	11 f
48-335			Frances	8 f
			Billy	6 m
WALKER, George W	45 m		Florence	8/12 f
Catharine	44 f		179-1334	
George, laborer	21 m			
Sarah	18 f		WALL, William, RR contractor -/400	70 m IR
Frank	16 m VA		Dora	50 f
William	13 m		Augustus	22 m MA
Laura	9 f		Arthur	12 m NY
223-1723				

ALEXANDRIA VIRGINIA 1860 CENSUS

Emma	17 f MA	WARD, Zed, cook	35 m	
Dora	13 f NY	Ann	28 f	
Jane	13 f	Arty	7 f	
163-1215		Willie	2 m	
		175-1313		
WALSH, John, grocer 900/100	40 m IR			
Margaret	35 f	WARE, Alexander, laborer	49 m MD	
James, plumber	25 m	Ellen	48 f	
Mary	18 f	DIXON, Frances	14 f	
Elizabeth	2 f	184-1383		
Virginia	7/12 f			
211-1614		WARE, C A, livery keeper -/1800	37 m VA	
		Elizabeth	36 f	
WAMER, Hannah (B)	30 f	Sally	15 f	
Lawrence (B)	10 m	MUIR, Jane -/3K	50 f	
Alice (B)	5 f	Mary	48 f	
Delaware (B)	3 m	Elizabeth	40 f	
54-381		18-98		
		WARE, Isabella (M), wash & iron	27 f	
WANTON, Mary E, teacher -/75	47 f	Addison (M)	5 m	
Mary	19 f	Betsey (B)	3 f	
Hannah	18 f	Inf (B)	3/12 f	
Julia	13 m	PEARSON, Fanny (B), domestic	67 f	
Virginia	12 f	27-159		
197-1499				
		WARFIELD, A D, dyer -/200	42 m MD	
WARD, Bright, laborer	35 m IR	Sarah	40 f DC	
Bridgett	35 f	Geo T, dyer	21 m	
57-402		Edgar, apothercary appren	18 m	
		Billy	15 m VA	
WARD, Charles (B), hackman -/30	37 m	Roberta	13 f	
Marion (B)	30 f	Andrew	10 m	
237-1829		Ada	7 f	
		Alice	5	
WARD, Elizabeth, seamstress	50 f DE	Frank	3 m	
BOYER, Elizabeth	12 f	115-846		
110-814				
		WARNER, Basil, church sexton -/50	55 m VA	
WARD, James T, Prot Meth mn	40 m DC	Julia	37 f	
Catharine	37 f	Ann M	12 f	
Mary	8 f	Arthur	5 m	
20-113		Cilcilia	4 f	
		Saml	3 m	
WARD, Jonathan, plasterer -/100	60 m	Amanda	9/12 f	
Julia	20 f	Margaret	26 f	
Jonathan, moulder	17 m	Fanny, hucker	38 f	
WEBSTER, Jas, plasterer	22 m	Edward, plasterer	26 m	
28-169		57-409		
WARD, William, drayman -/30	36 m	WARNER, H, ship carpenter -/75	52 m VA	
Louisa	30 f MD	May	50 f DC	
Mary	17 f VA	John, machinist	26 m VA	
William	13 m	Henry, sealer	22 m GT	
Charles	11 m	May	17 f MD	
James	6 m	Enj	12 m	
Ellen	3 f	Elizabeth	10 f	
Infant	2/12 f	218-1677		
KELL, Arthur, house painter	22 m			
COOK, Ellen	50 f MD	WARNER, Jane (B)	45 f	
58-410		55-383		

ALEXANDRIA VIRGINIA 1860 CENSUS

WARREN, Thomas, night scavenger -/150	62 m MD	WATERS, Thomas A, lumber merch -/500	43 m	
Phamia	67 f VA	Cordelia	30 f	
Thos, hatter	34 m	Georgiana	19 f	
Elizabeth	24 f	Virdiex	17 f	
HENING, Basil	17 m	Hally	4 m	
77-543		Grace	2 f	
		22-126		
WASHINGTON, Geo, gr/comm merch 300/-	36 m VA			
Sallie	28 f	WATKINS, David, house carpenter	40 f	
Henry	6 m	Elizabeth	39 f	
CHASE, Mary (M), domestic	26 f	David	16 m	
SOLMER, Caroline (B)	23 f	Virgia	16 f	
HARRIS, Eliza (B)	19 f	John	11 m	
JOHNSTON, Alice (M)	8 f	Frank	8 m	
22-125		Jimmy	6 m	
		A...a?	1 f	
WASHINGTON, Geo (B), fireman boat	57 m VA	245-1908		
Mary (B)	59 f			
HOOE, Augustus (M)	8 m	WATKINS, Jas W, farmer 500/50	32 m	
124-911		Nancy	56 f	
		George	18 m	
WASHINGTON, Mary (M)	54 f	Emily	16 f	
Billy (M), tailor	30 m	258-1997		
238-1839				
		WATSON, Hariet (B), nurse	49 f	
WASTON, Isaac, physician -/7K	76 m VA	Adaline (M)	30 f	
177-1323		Edgar (B), blacksmith	21 m	
		Sarah (M)	16 f	
WATERMAN, Simon, clothing -/5K	51 m BV	John (M)	14 m	
Caroline	38 f	Lewellen (M)	11 m	
Bettie	12 f VA	165-1236		
Rosie	7 f			
Moses	5 m	WATSON, Laura 250/50	29 f	
Boswick	2 m	236-1823		
Irman	11/12 m			
ROSENFIELD, Mike, clerk	17 m	WATTLES, C W, lawyer 4500/2K	36 m	
121-887		Harriet	26 f CT	
		Willie	4 m	
WATERS, Benjamin, lmb merch 30K/15K	70 m MD	Harriet	1 f	
ZIMMERMAN, Mary	42 f VA	DIGGS, Mary (B), domestic	50 f	
William, clerk	19 m	BROOK, Frances (M)	12 f	
Adaline	17 f	250-1942		
Walter	16 m			
Dora	13 f	WATTLES, H S, coal dealer 4K/500	35 m	
Alice	8 f	Caroline	27 f	
McCARRIE, Julia, seamstress	24 f	Sarah E	4 f	
13-73		Caroline	3 f	
		Infant	1/12 m	
WATERS, John (B), brickmaker	23 m VA	DAVIS, Mammy (B), domestic	30 f	
Elizabeth (B)	19 f	67-473		
Jonathan (B)	13 m			
Hennson (B)	1 m	WATTS, Sarah (B), wash & iron	59 m MD	
Marion (B)	53 m	ASHE, Lucy (M), domestic	18 f VA	
Almarissa (M)	16 f	Hugh (M)	8/12 m	
Billy (M)	12 m	BLACK, Jas (B), laborer	20 m	
206-1578		138-1012		
WATERS, Richard, constable -/100	34 m	WAUF, George, laborer	27 m HD	
May Ann	31 f	Elizabeth	21 f	
William	6 m	Augto	4 m VA	
Frank	3 m	Catharine	9/12 f	
214-1652		100-741		

ALEXANDRIA VIRGINIA 1860 CENSUS

WAUSBERRY, Eliza, grocer	49 f HC	WEEDEN, Francis M, lock smith -/100	45 m VA
George, cigar maker	19 m VA	Sarah J	41 f MD
MILES, Amelia	20 f JM	Frances C	22 f VA
Mary	11 f VA	Richard, lock making	20 m
MILLS, Chamberlain, house carpenter	27 m MD	Chas M	15 m
Ada	2/12 f VA	Walker G	13 m
165-1232		Caroline	11 f
		John	8 m
WEAVER, Wm (M), laborer	40 m	Henry	6 m
Letty (M)	48 f	Harriet	3 f
Chas (B)	19 m	126-923	
Hannah (B)	16 f		
212-1623		WELL, Alfred, shoemaker	28 m EG
		Sarah	30 f VA
WEBB, Emanual, gardner	35 m	39-255	
Anna	26 f		
Alice	9/12 f	WELLS, Cornelius, shoemaker	22 m VA
243-1886		Frances	22 f
		49-339	
WEBB, Rebecca (B)	35 f		
CARROLE, Harriet (B)	20 f	WELLS, Elizabeth	54 f
Thomas (B)	28 m	John, laborer	19 m
13-70		FISHER, Billy, laborer	19 m
		146-1080	
WEBB, W B, depot agent -/50	34 m		
Richard	12 m	WELLS, Joseph, shoemaker	25 m VA
Martha	8 f	Sarah	22 f
Mary	8 f	Richard	1 m
Pocahantas	7 f	230-1775	
99-727			
		WELLS, Joseph, laborer	50 m EG
WEBSTER, Hiram, carpenter -/100	60 m GT	Susan	40 f
Virginia	35 f MD	Lucy	15 f
187-1416		Jimmy	13 m
		269-2078	
WEBSTER, James (M), hs carptr 1400/50	40 m		
La... (M)	48 f	WELLS, Mary	75 f
Alvina (M), appren	15 m	Amanda, seamstress	26 f
Lucy (M)	15 f	Virginia	23 f
Hornet (M)	9 f	Levin	11 m
Robert (M)	12 m	Mary	9 f
Hannah (M)	7 f	157-1165	
Emanuel (M)	3 m		
EDWARDS, Amy (M)	50 f	WELSH, John, laborer	45 m IR
200-1525		Mary	30 f
		James	10 m
WEBSTER, Jas (M), lawyer	67 m	Mary	6 f
27-160		Mike	3 m
		Kate	8/12 f
WEBSTER, Margaret	60 f VA	191-1457	
George, house carpenter	22 m		
Chas Edd	15 m	WEST, Elizabeth, seamstress	39 f
William	13 m	145-1069	
Thomas	10 m		
Lucinda	17 f	WEST, Jacob, baker	23 m GR
113-836		Caroline	22 f
		Margaret	6 f VA
WEBSTER, Palsey (B)	50 f	Caroline	4 f
Harriot (B)	13 b	John	3 m
Helen (B)	27 f	Henry	8/12 m
Carrie (B)	25 f	GROSS, Jacob, shoemaker	28 m WR
90-644		139-1020	

ALEXANDRIA VIRGINIA 1860 CENSUS

WEST, Jacob, cobler	75 m BV	WHEATLY, Julia	55 f
Margaret	76 f	James	25 m
153-1130		134-977	
WEST, Jno, laborer 650/30	36 m BV	WHEATLY, James H, pilot -/30	52 m MD
Elizabeth	37 f	Silena	38 f VA
Jacob	10 m VA	John	14 m
Christopher	8 m	Mary	10 f
Mary	4 f	215-1659	
George	8/12 m		
153-1129		WHEELER, Edgar (M), laborer	25 m
		Mary (M)	18 f
WEST, John, chancery 10K/300	45 m	MITCHELL, Lucy (B)	25 f
Paulina	45 f CT	William (M)	8 m
Theodore, medical student	20 m VA	Joseph (M)	9 m
LEE, Rebecca	74 f	47-327	
DYSON, Jane (M)	39 f		
THOMPSON, Samuel	10 m	WHEELER, Lydia (B), wash & iron	30 f
4-28		Mary (B)	13 f
		James (B)	5 f
WHALAN, Jas	40 m IR	Emma (B)	3 f
Margaret	35 f	Edgar (B)	8/12 m
James	17 m	155-1151	
Margaret, domestic	15 f		
Michael, appren soap maker	14 m	WHEELER, Medira (B)	33 f
John	7 m	43-291	
84-603			
		WHITE, Ann S, hs of prost 1200/100	50 f EG
		JONES, Ann, prostitute	34 f MD
WHALEY, Bushrod, farmer -/50	36 m	McCAIN, Margaret, prostitute	23 f IR
Martha	30 f	ROBBS, Jeremiah, sailor	22 m VA
Alice	9 f	68-479	
William	5 m		
Hallie	1 f		
43-286		WHITE, John, laborer	40 m
		60-421	
WHEAT, Benson, merchant 25K/5K	37 m VA		
Matilda	25 f	WHITE, Nancy (B), wash & iron	61 m
Clarence	5 m	202-1545	
Emily J	2 f		
1-37		WHITE, Robert -/25	27 m IR
		Ann	25 f
WHEAT, J J, retail merch 32K/43K	48 m	Robert	1 m VA
Emily	40 f	79-730	
Milton	17 m		
DIXION, Geo O, retired merch -/30K	42 m	WHITE, Thomas M, clerk gas works -/150	52 m VA
3-23		Providence	59 f
		Laura	26 f
		Bettie	24 f
WHEAT, Robert, comm merch 10K/5K	40 m	Chris, deputy clerk construction	21 m
Susan M	28 f	Harrison, clerk coal office	19 m
Fanny	8 f	Frank	15 m
Robert W	6 m	CHELDON, Frank	13 m
Marrie	3 f	STOUTENBURG, Cora	29 f
Infant	3/12 m	Maria	3 f
104-768		242-1873	
WHEATLY, Benedict, undertaker -/500	31 m VA	WHITE, Wm, clerk comm merch -/75	45 m
Martha	21 f	Mary	39 f
Julia	5 f	Landon, house carpenter	20 m
Elcon	2 m	Rebecca	10 f
REED, Edwin	5 m	218-1679	

ALEXANDRIA VIRGINIA 1860 CENSUS

WHITEMORE, J P, shoemaker	52 m
Jane	49 f
Rachael	22 f
Hamson, tailor	19 m
Pascal, carter	18 m
Alice	14 f
Martha	13 f
32-208	

WHITING, Fairfax H, plstr grindr -/100 67 m
  Margaret 35 f
  Charles 14 f
  Fairfax 7 m
  Douglas 5 m
  Joseph 2 m
148-1091

WHITMORE, Edmund T, dry gds merch 1K/- 40 m PA
  Isabella F 38 f
  Richard J 26 f
JEWELL, Hannah, music teacher 27 f MA
SLAYMAKER, H, clerk 27 m PA
12-58

WHITMORE, J P, shoemaker 52 m
  Jane 49 f
  Rachael 22 f
  Hamson, tailor 19 m
  Pascal, carter 18 m
  Alice 14 f
  Martha 13 f
32-208

WHITMORE, John F, carpenter 29 m VA
  Sarah 26 f
  Mary 9 f
  Ella 4 f
  Wm 2 m
37-242

WHITTESBY, L, 2500/200 64 m
  Elizabeth 54 f NC
  Sarah 56 f
  Oscar, teacher 30 m
198-1509

WHITTINGTON, George T, clerk 46 m
8-46

WHITTINGTON, Thomas, clerk of market 61 m
  Margaret 57 f ME
  Charles 21 m
  Harriet Lo.. 26 f
  Jas, grocery clerk 33 m
  Sidney 4 m
  Henry 11/12 m
WHITINGTON, Sarah 18 f
  Mon... 16 m
  Edward 14 m
173-1296

WIDLINDLAY, Jane 65 f
  Mary E 23 f

WIGGS, Sonia, dress maker 700/30 31 f
COLE, Laura (M), domestic 11 f
213-1638

WILBECK, Dan -/200 60 m NY
  Sarah 53 f CT
  Elizabeth 36 f NY
  John, machinist 27 m
  James 26 m
  Emma 19 f
ELDRED, Hester 27 f MD
  Harry 6 m VA
226-1744

WILBNAE, Henderson, ms station 1K/200 44 m MD
  Lucinda 32 f VA
  William 18 m
  Thompson 14 m
  Mary 9 f
  Mary Ida 5 f
  Arthur 2 m
McKINDNER, Mary 50 f
83-595

WILKINS, John, steam engineer -/150 30 m MD
  Laury 30 f VA
  John 2 m
202-1540

WILKINSON, Jas, laborer 1K/500 36 m IR
  Jane 28 f
  William 6 m
  Mary 3 f
  Joseph 9/12 m
94-682

WILLIAMS, Ann 50 f VA
213-1633

WILLIAMS, David, cabinet mkr 1500/600 40 m
  Mary 35 f
  Annie 15 f
  Chas 12 m
  Ida 6 f
  Mary 9 f
132-964

WILLIAMS, George, book maker 57 m
  Maria 36 f OH
  Leonard 14 m OH
  Louis 8 m IN
  James 3 m VA
158-1171

WILLIAMS, Geo R, house painter -/25 28 m
  Elizabeth 22 f
  Jas H 4 m
  Martha 15
189-1447

ALEXANDRIA VIRGINIA 1860 CENSUS

WILLIAMS, Georgiana (M), wash & iron	29 f	WHITELY, Fred, wood carver	29 m	
Mary (B)	2 f	Ellen	29 f	
William (M)	6/12 m	238-1845		
202-1549				
		WILLIAMS, Samuel, dentist 8K/1K	45 m	
WILLIAMS, John, cooper -/50	18 m	May E	26 f	
Lucy	45 f	Alice V	15 f	
Andrew, house painter	23 f	John	12 m	
Mary	18 f	Robert	10 m	
COLINS, Joseph, cabinet maker	23 m GR	Ashby	7 m	
William	10 m	BUTLER, Anna, domestic	55 f	
103-759		249-1938		
WILLIAMS, John (B)	50 m	WILLIAMS, Samuel (B), laborer -/150	56 m VA	
Catharine (B)	40 f	WARNER, Mary (B)	40 f	
Hannah (B)	26 f	203-1554		
Joseph (B)	17 m			
George (B)	15 m	WILLIAMS, Sanford, carter	36 m	
Laura (B)	7 f	Elizabeth	60 f	
Sarah (B)	5 f	157-1164		
Infant (B)	6/12 f			
227-1750		WILLIAMS, Thomas, hs painter 800/50	65 m	
		John M	43 m	
WILLIAMS, John, house painter	34 m	Rahael	37 f	
Sarah	40 f	Virginia	27 f	
Thomas	18 m	Dennis	15 m	
Simpson	3 m	Amelia	12 f	
201-1532		Annia	9 f	
		Ella	10/12 f	
WILLIAMS, Julia (B)	30 f	DUNCAN, Jas	4 m	
John (B), porter	18 m	164-1224		
Sarah (B)	16 f			
243-1890		WILLIAMSON, Wm -/2K	38 m	
		Mary	23 f	
WILLIAMS, Lucy (B), blksmith 1200/50	73 m VA	227-1751		
Frances (B)	50 f			
HORN, Lizzie (B)	17 f	WILLS, Elizabeth	54 f	
BROWN, W Car (B)	80 m	John	19 m	
201-1536		FISHER, Betty	19 m	
		146-1080		
WILLIAMS, Richard, farmer 4K/300	31 m			
Alecia	24 f DC	WILSON, Chas F, shoemaker -/100	62 m HV	
William E	3 m	Mary	30 f VA	
Richard	1 m	John C	6 m	
DRUMMOND, Virginia	29 f	Micea	3 f	
251-1956		KEYS, Millie, weaver	23 f	
		YOUNG, Lizzie	19 f	
WILLIAMS, Robert (M), laborer	42 m VA	82-590		
196-1493				
		WILSON, Hannah -/20K	60 f	
WILLIAMS, Robert, cooper	44 m	IRVING, Mary -/7K	55 f	
Robt, appren	18 m	SAILAIN, Abbie, domestic	50 f	
Thomas	15 m	SHONE, Jane (B)	18 f	
Virginia	16 f	18-99		
Jane	10 f			
Ann	18 f	WILSON, Robert J T, grocer -/3500	56 m VA	
103-760		Mary	49 f	
		David R	49 m	
WILLIAMS, Samuel, house carptr -/25	28 m EG	Mary	27 f	
Sarah	26 f	Fanny	16 f	
Samuel	6 m	ALLISON, Ann	60 f	
Joseph	3 m	183-1385		

ALEXANDRIA VIRGINIA 1860 CENSUS

WINDSOR, James, sailor -/250	29 m VA	WOLF, W, clothier -/500	26 m	
Mary	21 f	Margaret	25 f BD	
William	4 f	Samuel	4 m	
Hamilton (?)	2 f	Amelia	10/12 f DC	
George, sailor	18 m	3-20		
185-1405		WOLF, William, baker 1K/100	60 m PR	
WINDSOR, Maria (B), cook	35 f VA	Sophia	36 f BV	
George (B)	14 m	William	15 m DC	
Lafayette (M)	7 m	Margaret	12 f VA	
LEE, Ritta (B)	53 f	141-1034		
175-1309		WOLKER, William L, shoe maker	49 m	
WINDSOR, Wm H	28 m VA	Martha	34 f	
Amanda	38 f	Jane	13 f	
Richard	3 m	Fanny	11 f	
36-216		Billy	6 m	
		Florence	8/12 f	
WISE, Geo A, plasterer	35 m	179-1334		
Hester J	25 f			
Margaret	12 f	WONDER, Henry S, physician 7K/1K	69 m	
George A	4 m	Ann	58 f	
78-554		Julia	31 f	
		George	38 m	
WISE, George P, coal merch 8K/600	53 m	Ann	22 f	
Sally	52 f	Wm C	1 m	
Peter, teller bank	30 m	BLOGGER, Barbara, domestic	24 f	
Alice	29 f	TURNER, Daniel (B), laborer	33 m	
Jane	26 f	PAYNE, Cecilia (B)	15 f	
Edwin, civil engineer	25 m	266-2057		
Martha	21 f			
George	20 m	WOOD, Franklin, machinist	24 m	
Frank, clerk	18 m	Eliza W	19 f MD	
William, clerk	15 m	Francis	10/12 m VA	
Mary	13 f	BALEMAN, Mary	16 f	
James	11 m	208-1591		
25-148				
		WOOD, Hiram A, machinist -/25	28 m	
WISE, Savena, wash & iron	40 f PA	Nancy	26 f	
Elizabeth, domestic	22 f	Emma	5 f	
Barbara	19 f	William	2 m	
213-1634		140-1030		
		WOOD, Isaac, custom house -/200	57 m	
WISELOILLER, Geo, butcher 2500/100	44 m HC	Nancy	54 f MD	
Mary	43 f	WADDY, Amanda	25 f VA	
Betsy	17 f MD	WOOD, Edgar, sailor	27 m	
George	12 m VA	James, sailor	23 m VA	
146-1075		Fanny	13 f	
		WADDY, Walter, clerk shoe store	25 m	
		181-1378		
WITMER, Edmond T, dry goods merch -/1K	40 m PA			
Isabella	38 f	WOOD, John, shoemaker	42 m DC	
Rachel J	26 f	Ann	33 f VA	
JEWELL, Hanna, music teacher	27 f MA	Francis, carter	18 m	
SLAYMAKER, H, clerk	27 m	Sarah J	16 f	
12-58		Margaret	16 f DC	
		37-239		
WOLF, Joseph, tailor 300/30	25 m GR			
Mary	16 f JM	WOOD, John, cooper 10K/300	78 m NJ	
POTTER, Nancy	40 f VA	Elizabeth	79 f MD	
236-1822		Harriet	40 f	

ALEXANDRIA VIRGINIA 1860 CENSUS

Susan	35 f		Ellen, weaver	16 f
Alice	30 f		Anna	12 f
SEALS, Namei (M)	50 f		Peter	16 m
109-806			Charles	6 m
			174-1306	
WOOD, John Charles, laborer	29 m			
Mary	25 f		WREN, Julia -/1200	51 f
193-1473			Jas W, dry good clerk	23 m
			Anna E	21 f
WOOD, Thom, laborer	35 m		May V	19 f
Ellen	26 f		Wallace, grocer clerk	17 m
Ida	5 f		Gablana	15 f
Cora	3 f		144-1059	
50-348				
			WRIGHT, H D, plaster mill -/5K	47 m
WOODEY, Mary (B)	30 f		Charlotte	37 f
Ann (B)	9 f		William	20 m
James (B)	7 m		Henry, clerk insurance office	17 m
86-620			197-1506	
WOOLS, Jas, plasterer	33 m		WRIGHT, Jas, farmer	51 m
Mary	33 f IR		Elizabeth	51 f
James	10 m VA		Ann	16 f
Alice	4 f		Laura	6 f
Mary	2 f		283-2163	
239-1848				
			WRIGHT, Jane, boarding house	51 f
WOOLS, William, grocer 800/1K	43 m MD		Emily	26 f
Hannah	30 f IR		Catharine	19 f
Maria	17 f		KERR, John, sail maker	60 m
William	15 m		BRADSHAW, H R, wharf builder	41 m NY
Stephen	10 m		EASY, Charles, cigar maker	22 m PA
Sarah	7 f		LOCKLAND, John, tailor	31 m IR
Cilcelia	7 f		BOULDEN, Edwood, printer	19 m MD
Stephen	68 m NC		BROADWOOD, Chris, miller	25 m
Alfred, plasterer	30 m VA		BARTROM, Wm, bridge builder	28 m CT
75-526			HEALEY, Pat, bridge builder	26 m IR
			GETTS, Joseph, tailor	28 m GR
WOOLS, William 2500/2200	70 m		REDD, Charles, miller	30 m MD
193-146			REDD, Josephine	3 f MD
			TOLBERT, Elizabeth, house keeper	51 f VA
WORE, Philip (B), cooper	35 m		DELCHOY, Julia, sales woman	29 f MD
Jane (B)	29 f		NEULIR, Elizabeth, sales woman	24 f
Caroline (M)	7 f		178-1329	
SCOLS, William (B), laborer	22 m			
161-1199			WRIGHT, Leonia (B)	55 f
			Frank (B), ship caulker	25 m
WORTHAM, Wm R, steam engineer -/50	50 m MD		Joe (B)	18 m
Mary	45 f		BELL, Mary (B)	90 f
William, appren carpenter	16 m		227-1747	
Laura	10 f			
John	8 m		WRIGHT, Moses (B), laborer	57 m
Myra	4 f		Kelly (B)	50 f
217-1674			JOHNSTON, Fanny (M)	13 f
			238-1841	
WORTHINGTON, Catharine	58 f			
Mary, teacher	30 f		YEATON, William C, lawyer -/11775	39 m BM
Anne E	11 f		Mary	32 f
44-303			John	10 m
			Alexana	7 f
WORTHINGTON, Mary, shoe binder	37 f		Ruth	5 f
Frances	17 f		William	3 m

ALEXANDRIA VIRGINIA 1860 CENSUS

May F	5/12 f	YOUNG, Robert 2500/600	60 m ST
Ruth	55 f BM	Eleanor	50 f VA
Louisa	31 f	James, tailor	30 m
Eliza	28 f	Robert	28 m
87-621		Graham	13 m
		George	12 m
YOUNG, Albert, house carptr 500/50	34 m	John	8 m
Susan	28 f PA	Annie	20 f
Mary	10 f	133-974	
Emma	8		
James	6 m	ZIMMER, Nancy A 3K/100	33 f
Alice	2 f	Thomas, butcher	17 m
246-1914		George	14 m
		Wm H	12 m
YOUNG, Catharine (B), huckster	60 f	Alfred	7 m
David (B), baker	19 m	157-1163	
Frank (B), laborer	17 m		
43-292		ZIMMERMAN, John, laborer	27 m
		Leoma	29 f
YOUNG, John, farmer	59 m PA	Belle ...	11 m
Sarah	47 f MD	William	8 m
Cornalia	17 f DC	155-1147	
Cordilia	15 f		
Margaret	13 f VA		
Lucy	6 f		
Wm	5 m DC		
WALKER, Samuel, gardner	36 m VA		
34-218			

ALEXANDRIA VIRGINIA 1860 CENSUS

WARD INDEX TO 1859 POLL BOOK

NAME	WARD	NAME	WARD	NAME	WARD
ADDISON, J F	2nd	CORRY, Robert S	4th	GOINS, Randolph	3rd
ADMAS, Chas L	1st	CORSON, E J	2nd	GRAHAM, J W	3rd
ALEXANDER, W B	2nd	CORSON Jr, Job	2nd	GRAVES, Thos L	5th
ALEXANDER, W B	5th	COTTON, W	3rd	GRAY, Robert	2nd
AMOS, A J	3rd	COX, Oliva	5th	GREY, H	3rd
ANDREW, Chas	4th	CRANFORD, Chas	1st	GRIFFITH, Henry C	2nd
ARRINGTON, John	3rd	CROOK, Wm	4th	GRIGG, Sam	3rd
ARRINGTON, W L	3rd	CROSS, Thos	2nd	GUISENDAFFER, John B	1st
ATWELL, Ewel C	2nd	CROSS, W J	3rd	GUIZENDAFFER, F J	3rd
AUDLEY, John T	1st	CROUSE, John P	1st	GUY, James	1st
BAKER, Geo H	3rd	CRUPPER, A D	2nd	HALL, E	4th
BALL,, L T	5th	CRUPPER, J W A	3rd	HALL, Wm T	4th
BALLENGER, F S	4th	CRUST, Geo	3rd	HAMPTON, Henry	2nd
BARNES, Geo	5th	DAINTY, J N	1st	HANCOCK, Chas W	1st
BARTLETT, Peter A	2nd	DANIELS, F	1st	HANSLEY, Wm	4th
BARTMAN, C	3rd	DARLEY, Chas	4th	HARDEY, H W	3rd
BEACH, Jas T	3rd	DARNELL, Jas M	1st	HARRISON, L E	2nd
BEACH, Wm H	3rd	DAVIS, Zimmerman	4th	HART, N R	4th
BENNETT, W S	2nd	DAY, Harrison	1st	HART, Patrick	4th
BIRCH, Jas H J	5th	DEEVERS, C	1st	HAVENNER, H	3rd
BIRCH, W R	5th	DELAHUNT, John	3rd	HAYES, N	1st
BLONDHEAM, H	3rd	DELOZIER, A	3rd	HERBERT, Wm	3rd
BOARD, Thos C	4th	DEVITT, Thos	4th	HICKS, John T	2nd
BOYER, Henry	1st	DEVEY, Wm	1st	HICKS, Wm A	1st
BOYER, John A	1st	DOBEY, Alfred	1st	HIGDEN, J H	3rd
BOYNTON, A S	1st	DONALDSON, H D	5th	HILL, John T	1st
BRADT, A H	3rd	DOUGLAS, R S	3rd	HITCHCOCK, Thos	5th
BREEM, Patrick	4th	DUDLEY, Chas	3rd	HOOE, P B	3rd
BREMER, John	2nd	DUDLEY, John	4th	HOOFF, John	1st
BRODBECK, H	3rd	DUFFEY, Geo	5th	HORNSTEIN, Wm	3rd
BRODERS, Jas M	3rd	DUFFEY, Sam P	4th	HOUGH, Hez	1st
BRUIN, Sydney	3rd	DUNNINGTON, S M	1st	HOWISON, Albert R	3rd
BURGESS, Wm	4th	DYE, Amos	5th	HOWISON, Jas	3rd
BURKE, John W	1st	EASTLACK, A W	2nd	HOWISON, Sydney	1st
BURKLEY, Wm N	4th	ELLIOTT, Geo F	3rd	HUDSON, Thos	4th
BURLEY, Wm	3rd	ELMORE, W	4th	HUGELY, Geo F	3rd
CAMPBELL, John S	3rd	ENCOTT, Wm	5th	HUTCHINGS, Jas	1st
CANE, John	2nd	ENGLISH, C W	2nd	IRWIN, James	3rd
CARNE, Wm (Dane)	1st	ENTWISLE, Wm B	1st	JACKSON, E	1st
CAWOOD, Moses O B	4th	FAIRFAX, E B	1st	JACKSON, Robert W	1st
CHANCELLOR, Chas W	3rd	FEBREE, John E	5th	JAMIESON, A	3rd
CHILDS, R	3rd	FIELD, H C	3rd	JANNEY, John S	4th
CLARE, J P	1st	FITZGERALD, J	3rd	JAVENS, Chas	4th
CLARK, J H	3rd	FLOCKER, J A	2nd	JAVENS, John	4th
CLARK, Peyton	4th	FORD, E	3rd	JAVINS, R	3rd
CLEMENS, Jas	2nd	FORD, S P	3rd	JAVINS, Thompson	4th
CLEMENTS, Ed	5th	FORMAN, Geo W	3rd	JAVINS, Wm	4th
CLIFF(T), Ed B	1st	FRANCIS, Thos H	4th	JEMAN, Jacob	4th
CLIFFORD, Patrick	3rd	FRANKLIN, Jas	2nd	JENKINS, B H	3rd
COLLINS, Wm	3rd	FRAZIER, Richard	2nd	JENKS, W	3rd
COOK, Thos	2nd	FRENCH, D M	3rd	JENNINGS, John	4th
CORBETT, Michael	4th	GANH, J L	4th	JEWIT, Joseph	3rd
CORNELL, John D	4th	GAREY, Wm J	5th	JOHNSTON, Robert	4th
CORNEY, John	2nd	GOBERT, J A	3rd	JONES, Henry C	1st

ALEXANDRIA VIRGINIA 1860 CENSUS

Name	Ward	Name	Ward	Name	Ward
JONES, Walter	1st	MOORE, Wm A	1st	SORRELL, R	3rd
KELL, J	2nd	MORRISSEY, Jas	3rd	SOUTHERN, Richard	5th
KENNERSON, D	1st	MUIR Jr, John	3rd	SPINKS, Albert	4th
KIDWELL, G W	3rd	MULLEN, John	4th	SPOUTH, John	1st
KIDWELL, John	3rd	MULLIN, Henry	2nd	SPRINFIELD, Phillip	3rd
KINCHELOE, Owen	2nd	MURPHY, Jas	1st	STALLINGS, Thos	1st
KING, Chas	3rd	NASH, Robert H	1st	STATLER, W M	2nd
KIRCHELOE, E W	1st	NEWTON, A C	2nd	STIFF, Walter	1st
KIRCHELOE, Thomas	1st	NICKLEN, J R	4th	STONNELL, Benj	3rd
KNOX, Robert	4th	NORRISS, Benjamin	1st	STONNELL, Dan	3rd
LARKIN, J F	3rd	NORRISS, John E	1st	STONNELL, Vincent	3rd
LASH, Hugh	2nd	NORTON, Michael	3rd	STOOPS, Jas	3rd
LASLETT, Jesse	1st	OGDEN, H	4th	STOUTENBERG, T A	3rd
LATHROPE, J H	4th	OGDEN, Jackson	4th	STUART, W D	3rd
LAURENCE, Richard	1st	OSBORN, Jas	4th	SUMMERS, Geo L	4th
LAWRENCE, Henry	1st	PADGETT, Henry	3rd	SWAINE, J G	1st
LAWSON, Jas E	2nd	PAGE, C C	2nd	TALEFERO, John C	4th
LAWSON, Josephus	4th	PATTERSON, Daniel	2nd	TARLTON, Henry	1st
LEADBEATER, John	4th	PAYNE, Thos H	3rd	TATSAPAUGH, Chas R	1st
LEDONER, John	2nd	PENNYBACK, J S	3rd	TATSAPAUGH, J P	1st
LEE, Daniel M	3rd	PERRY, E	3rd	TATSAPAUGH, Jas W	1st
LENOIR, Wm J	4th	PERRY, Jas	4th	TAYLOR, Geo B	3rd
LESLIE, Abram	1st	PEYTON, A M	3rd	TAYLOR, Josh P	1st
LEWIS, John B	4th	PICKEN, Jos H	4th	TAYLOR, Robert	3rd
LOCKWOOD, J Wells	4th	PIERCE, Allen	5th	TENNYSON, W M	5th
LONGSTON, Jas	5th	POST, John P	3rd	THOMAS, Hiram	3rd
LOVEJOY, Jas B	1st	POWERS, Sam	3rd	THOMAS, Jas W	1st
LOVELACE, Wm	1st	PRICE, G E	2nd	THOMPSON, Henry	1st
LUGENBEALE, John	1st	PRICE, John T	2nd	THOMPSON, Wm W	3rd
LYLES, Geo H	3rd	PRICE, Wm	2nd	THORNE, Thos J	1st
McALLEN, Thos	4th	PURCELL, W T	2nd	TICER, Lewis	3rd
McBELL, George	1st	RATCLIFFE, R B	1st	TRAVISEE Sr, Thomas	4th
McCANN, Patrick	3rd	REED, Sam J	1st	TRIPLETTE, G S P	2nd
McCORMICK, T M	3rd	RIDGELY, S E	4th	TUBMAN, Wm J	2nd
McCUIN, Albert	3rd	RIGGEE, George	3rd	TURNER, Wm	1st
McCUING, Sam M	1st	ROBERTS, John S	2nd	UNDERWOOD, Wm	3rd
McDERMOTT, Patrick	3rd	ROBEY, Lemuel	1st	UPTON, E P	5th
McEWING, Thos	3rd	ROBEY, Wm	1st	VEITCH, George	5th
McKENZIE, Jas	1st	ROBINSON, A S	2nd	VIOLETT, W A	2nd
McLAIN, Andrew	3rd	RODEY, Wm	2nd	WALLACE, H S	2nd
McMUNAN, C H	3rd	RUDD, Jas T	1st	WALLS, Augustus	4th
McMUNAN, E M	3rd	RUDD, Robert	1st	WALSH, John	1st
McNALLY, M	2nd	RYE, Wm H	2nd	WARD, Hez	1st
McNARA, Mike	2nd	SANGSTER, A J	3rd	WARDER, Richard	1st
McSHERRY, Frank	3rd	SAVAGE, R	4th	WARE, Elkaner	1st
McSHERRY, R	2nd	SCOTT, Jos R	3rd	WARING, T B	2nd
McVEIGH, E T	3rd	SEIBERT, J L	2nd	WARNING, T E	2nd
MADDOX, Jas H	3rd	SHAFFER, H	3rd	WARNING, Thos	2nd
MAHONE, Joseph	1st	SHINGLING, Wm	4th	WARRING, Basil	2nd
MANGIN, D O B	4th	SHINN, S R	2nd	WEBSTER, J B	1st
MANKIN, Wm	3rd	SHOCK, Wm	3rd	WEBSTER, Jas	2nd
MARBURY, F A	1st	SHUSTER, F	3rd	WHALAN, D	2nd
MARCY, John	5th	SHUTZ, Wm H	1st	WHIPPLE, E A	5th
MASDEN, John	1st	SILLICK, James	3rd	WHITMER, Edwin	4th
MASSEY, George	5th	SIMPSON, Henry S	2nd	WHITTINGTON, H B	2nd
MASSEY Jr, Wm J	5th	SIMPSON, Rich H	3rd	WILLIAMS, John A	2nd
MEAGHER, T N	2nd	SISSON, John	2nd	WINSTON, Isaac	1st
MILLS, Alonzo	2nd	SISSON, Wm A	3rd	WOOD, Douglas	1st
MILLS, C	2nd	SKINNER, Thos	3rd	WOOD, Olander	1st
MILLS, Daniel	5th	SLAMACHER, Julius	3rd	WOODWARD, A J	4th
MINE, G S	4th	SMITH, Calvin A	4th	YOUNG, Benjamin	5th
MONROE, J M	2nd	SMITH Jr, John L	3rd	YOUNG, Edward	1st

CROSS INDEX

This cross index cites all persons in the text whose surname is different from that of the head of the household.

ABENSHEIN Christina 13 Jas 13
ADAMS Charles 89 Edwin 89 J H 55 Lewis 89 Mary 3 Morietta 89
ADELE Thos 115
AFFEY Kate 88
AGNEW J 48
ALLEN David 41 Harriet 112 James 109 Jane 3 10 Margaret 108 Nancy 112 Sarah 41 82
ALLISON Ann 129 Geo A 108 John 80 85 Robert 41
ALT S 55
AMDERSON Elenor 122 Jas H 122 Mary 64
ANLSNIL Mr 119
ANTHONY James 50 Mrs 50 Willec 50
ANUALINE Henry 68
APPICK John 16
ARCHIBALD Mary 6
ARMSTEAD Phebe 119 Will 119
ARMSTRONG Christena 93 Eliza 29
ARNOLD Bettie 97
ARRINGTON Chas 9 Ellen 9 James 9 Yeaton 9
ASAUS Emily 72
ASHE Hugh 125 Lucy 125
ASHLAND Chris 92
ATKINS Margaret 64 ___ 53
ATWELL Benjamin 38 John 3 38 Lucy 100 Milton Michelle 45 Pamelia 38 Susan 45
AUDISON Fanny 8
AUDLEY T 41
AUGER R H 86
AVERETT Wm H 55
AVERY Francis 37 J Q 55 Maranda 37
AXGTOWN Augustus 108
BADEN Alexander 45 Amanda 45 Reverdny 45
BAGNE Agnes 31
BAILOR Harriet 43
BAILY Peter 41
BAKER Phebe 45 Susana 68

BALDWIN Henry 34
BALEMAN Mary 130
BALL David 63 Elizabeth 40 Sarah 3
BALLES Mary 100
BALLINGER Eliza 69
BANKHEAD Louise 72
BANKS Wm H 41
BARBER J 48
BARKER H S W 55
BARLEY Wm H 48
BARNESS Frank 104
BARNWELL Sarah 98
BARRES Kate 48
BARTLEMAN Mrs 100 Rebecca J 100
BARTROM Wm 131
BASHBY John 95
BATT... John 3
BAUBACK Ann 55
BAYLESS James 11 Malinda 94
BAYNE Catharine 72 Francis 93 Louisa 72 Paterson 72
BEABE Virginia 8
BEACH Docia 69 John 80 Levi 27 Mason 96
BEACHAM Joseph 38
BEACHANT Sarah 88
BEACHLAND Elizabeth 9
BEAIHAN Susan 54
BEATIE Emma 122
BECK Sarah 39 Wm 39
BECKLEY Katy 94
BELL Mary 131 Nora 109
BENNER Wm 100
BENNET Ann 3 Nancy 3
BENNETE Barney 3 Catharine 3
BENNETTE John 122
BENNIX Mr 13
BENT Florence 77
BENTON Virginia 7
BERRY Anna 24 Benjamin 24 Catharine 62 David 105 Fanny 105 Jane 10 105 John 62 Mildred 10 Patsy 46 Rebecca 24 Thos 33
BETTELL Jenny 47
BILL Joseph 101

BIRCH John F 44
BIRMINGHAM Thom 102
BLACK Ann 107 Catharine 82 Cecilia 90 Clara 51 Eliz 112 Emma 3 Fanny 68 Henrietta 109 Jane 90 Jas 125 John 101 Laura 68 Libby 44 Lucy 8 46 Mary 46 112 Sarah 13 109 Susan 24
BLACKLOCK Mary 12
BLADEN Georgana 83
BLAKE Jas 77
BLAND Nora 67
BLEURO Infant 55 James 55 Ross 55 Sally F 55
BLISH Henry 13
BLOGGER Barbara 130
BLOW Wm 60
BLOXAM Henry 3
BLYTHE Mary 55 Susan 55 W 55
BOLL Adolphus 105
BOOKINE William 15
BORFFEY John E 55
BOSEY James 64 Mary 64 Wm 64
BOTEMORE Elizabeth 46
BOTHERTON Lewis 100
BOULDEN Edwood 131
BOW Georgiana 44
BOWMAE Edwin 64
BOWMAN J C 86
BOYER Elizabeth 124 John 95 Susan 53
BRADFORD C H 8
BRADLEY Mark 29
BRADSHAW H R 131 Mary 81
BRADY Ann 66 Jas 66 Kate 66
BRENT A M 55 Florence 73
BRETT Sarah 21
BREWIS T A 48
BRICK Martin 35 Mary 35
BROADBECK Emily 88
BROADUS Saml 47
BROADWOOD Chris 131
BROCKETT John 106
BROOK Frances 125 Georgiana 114
BROOKS Rebecca 45 Sarah 23 63 Virginia 45

ALEXANDRIA VIRGINIA 1860 CENSUS

BROWN A W 16 Ann 120 Betty 105 Elizabeth 64 Emma 114 H C 120 Henry 52 120 Lizzie 11 Thomas 64 W Car 129 Wm 3 Wolff 105
BRYAN James 86 Jas 54
BRYANT John J 115
BUCKANAH James 27
BULGER Alice 75
BUNTNY Mary N 101
BURG Agnes 2
BURGIE Ann 42
BURKE Josephine 64
BURLY Jas 7
BURNS Mary A 83 84
BURRIS Fannie 8
BURUS Biddie 18
BUSHBY Joseph 84
BUTLER Anna 129 Henrietta 11 Infant 123 James 32 123 Jas.. Jarvis 123 Mary 31 Peter 80 Washington 123
BUTY May 6
CABIT Kitty 89
CALON Ann 104
CAMPBELL Alexander 103 Sarah 94
CANDLISS Zach 71
CANLY Thomas 28
CANNON Cassen 49 Catharine 36
CARRICK Godfrey 100
CARRIES Anne 8
CARROLE Harriet 126 May N 102 Thomas 126
CARROLL Frances 103 Mary 111
CARSON H C 81
CARSON John 96 102
CARTER Jenny 85 Lonaz 71 Martha 45
CASEY Milton 110
CASSEY. Charity 12
CAVIL Margaret 29 71
CAVILLEAR Jane 118 Joseph 118 Samuel 118
CAWOOD Andrew 110 Ann 83 Benjamin 110 Catharine 83 Daniel 119 Joseph 110 Mary 119 Robert 110 Robt 9 Samuel 48 Sarah 80 85 Thomas 110 Wm H 110
CHAC James 37 Rosana 37 Rubertan 37
CHAPMAN Sidney 91
CHASE Betsey 73 Geo 63 Maria 34 Mary 125
CHELDON Frank 127
CHESHIRE James 103
CHEW Francis 28
CHEWS Armes Ste.. 77 Ellen 77 Frank 77 Hector 77 John 77 Martha 77 Mary 77 Thom 77
CHICHESTER Sally 92

CHICK David 67
CHIM Jas 104
CHINN Emma 21
CHISMOND Cornelia 23
CHURCH Susan 77
CINGHLAND Thos 40
CLAGGETT P A 48
CLAPDORE Ada 15 May 15
CLARK Alexander 44
CLARK Bettie 44 Caroline 44 Elizabeth 120 Joseph 14
CLARKE James 114
CLARRIAGE James 94 Mary 94 May 94 Willie H 94
CLEGETT Ann 94 Kate 94
CLEGGETT E H 86
CLEW Maria 66
COACHMAN J 86
COARSON Joseph 67
COATES Sally 17
COE Henry 75
COGAN Margaret 22 Mary 22 Richard 22 William 22
COHEN John 87
COLDER Adona 118 Isabella 118 John 118 Willie 118
COLE Bella 63 Charles 63 Edgar 63 Emma 118 Henry H 14 Jane E 72 Jas 63 John 63 Laura 128 Louis 63 Martha 63 Mary 14 63 Phebe 44 William 63
COLEMAN Ellen 23 John 23
COLINS Joseph 129 William 129
COLLINS Arrina 71 Rosa 49 Sarah 48
COLTER Sarah 93
COLTON Hanna 3
COLTONE William 7
COMELY Alfred 44
CONARY Henry 52
CONNER Ann 102 Mary 86
CONNERS John 28
CONNIFFY John 107
CONSTABLE Kate 72
CONWAY James 10
COOK Angela 10 Ann 6 Eli 72 Ellen 124 Enoch 10 Jas F 121 John H 73 Margaret 45 Martin 38 Mary 121 Rose 121 Susan 73 Willia 11 Wm 35
COOKLY Rubin 99
COOMBS Elizabeth 66
COONEY Joseph 84
COOPER Matilda 102
CORBEY Lawrence 24
COURTWELL Enoch 57
COWAN Sally 118 Thomas 118
COX Andrew 3 John 40 Levis 109 Louisa 109 Lucy 109
COXTON Bridgett 56 Henry 56 Mary 56 Mathew 56

CRAIG Gotlieb 100
CRANE Peter 86 96
CREIGH Michael 35
CROSON Robt 72
CROSS James 55
CROSSINGER Mary 2
CRUPPER Boston 93 Elizabeth 93 Susan 24
CUBIT Kitty 87 Money 87
CUNNINGHAM Martin 52
CUPUYA Mary 2
CURTINE Patrick 18
CYES James 105 Maria 105
DADE Eliza 1 Jane 1 Mary 40
DAIE Georgana 94
DAILY John 3 William 28
DAINGERFIELD Eliza 109
DALLAS Geo 81
DANIELS Lucretia 15 38 Walter 38
DAUGHTNY Daniel 63
DAVIDSON Eliza 15
DAVIS Ann 47 Benjamin 8 42 Bordgett 48 Cawhuie 86 Ellen 48 Emma 77 Eugen 49 Frank 3 Georgianna 101 Jane 100 John Anna 48 Mammy 125 Mary 52 Melvina 63 Rosene 46 Sarah 94 William 114
DAY James 5 Jas W 121 John 122
DAZE John 103
DEITZ John 84
DELCHOY Julia 131
DELPH.. John 97
DENNIS Mary 4
DENT McGruder 82
DICKMAN Bettie 110
DIGGS Mary 105 125
DIREMUS Susan 37
DIX Corrie 32
DIXION Geo O 127
DIXON Ch 117 Frances 88 124 Samuel 16
DODSON Catharine 69
DOGAN Rose 59
DOGINS Caroline 65
DOGLE Garnet 60 kate 55
DONALDSON Atwalter 75 Sarah 75
DONALLY Ellen 93 Rose 102 William 110
DONELL Geo 65
DOUGLAS Alex 13 Elizabeth 13 Ellinor 13 George 13 Kate 41 Sarah 41
DOWNEY Julia 85 Laune 85 Mis 119
DOYAN Norman 14
DOZAN George 48

ALEXANDRIA VIRGINIA 1860 CENSUS

DOZMAN Geo 21 Helen 21
DRUMMOND Virginia 129
DUFFEY Patrick 4
DUMAS Margaret 51
DUNCAN Jas 129
DUNDAS Diana 8
DUNMEAD Henry 34
DUNN Anthony 53 Edward 76
   Henry 63 John H 92 Mary 53
   Rosa 76
DUVAL John 84 Robt 77
DWYER Cor H 15
DYER Esther 93
DYSON Ellen 111 Jame 127 Mary 114
EACHES Connie 40
EAGAN Samuel 96
EASY Charles 131
EDELIN Louise 114
EDMONDS Ephaim 34
EDMONDSON Gruel 28
EDWARDS Amy 126 Henry 74
   Sarah 71
ELDRED Harry 128 Hester 128
ELKIN John 107
ELKINS Laura 20 Mary 68
ELLIOT Chas 110 Fanny 110
   Lucinda 98 Margaret 110
ELLIS Ann 3
ENER? Jon 38
ENGLEBRIGHT Carrie 48 J C 48
ENGLISH Thomas 108
ENNIS Michel 40
ERUPT Henry 41 Rebecca 41
ESKRIDGE Thomas 100
ETHERIDGE Grace 85
EVANS Abner 61 Adaline 67
   Billy 30 Charlotte 85 Jas
   61 John 48 Martha 61 Mary
   61 Sarah 61
EWING Johanna 29 Michie 29
FAIRFAX Karissa 112
FAISONS Wm 101
FALLES Bessie 48 Jane 48 R W 48
FAR Susan 18
FAWCETT Edward 112
FEGUSON Alice 23 Catharine 23
   Ella 23 Henry 23 John 23
FELL C W 48
FERGUSON Polly 120
FERRELL Ellen 48
FIELD George 31 Ida 31 Sarah 31
FIFER Wm 37
FINNIGAN Mary 3
FISHER Annie 103 Betty 129
   Billy 126 Sally 58 Thomas
   33 WM 86
FITZHUGH Amily 7 John 7
FLARITY Andrew 102
FLETCHER Fanny 93

FLOTTINGHAM Geo 48
FLUIR Eugene 38
FOERTCH J C 48
FONCE George 119
FORD Louisa 111 Wm 3
FORDHAM Andrew 70
FORSYTH May 5 Monia 5
FOSSETT Henrietta 72
FOWLE Susan 48
FOX George 108 Martin 77 Mary 3
FRANK Georgia 119 Hannah 105
   Mr 119
FRANKLIN Sarah 57
FRAZIER Caroline 116 Ed 14 S
   A 116 Wm 25
FREEMAN Emily 93
FREIDLY Geo 110
FRENCH Ca.. W 110
FUGET Catharine 16
FULLER Jenny 91 Martin 48
   Ruth 23
GAHAGAN Mary 49
GALLAHAY M 3
GALLAHER Mary 112
GALLAKER Margaret 45
GALLIGAN David 29
GANT Agnes 49
GARDNER Chas 103 Frances 103
   Mary 103 William 103
GARNET Laura 3
GARNETT Muscoe 53 Sally 53
   Samuel 53
GARNETT E 60
GATES Eliza 117
GATFIELD Martha 38
GENTRY Malinda 94
GEORGE H 116
GERMAN Michael 3
GETTS Johanna 29 Joseph 131
   Lotta 30 Mary 30
GETTY Dominick 80
GIBEN Eliza 34
GIBEN Robert 34 Sarah 34
GIBSON Albert 41 Charlota 87
   Ellen 6 Henry 87 Lewis 111
   Matilda 81 Susan 41
GILBERT E L 48
GILLING Dominick 84
GILMAN James 100
GILPIN Fanny M 52 Rachael 52
GIVENS Caroline 50 George 50
GLASCOE Charlotte 84
GLEEN Wellington 70
GLENROY Peter 100
GLOVER Thos 12
GOINS Mary 77 79
GOLDSBOROUGH J M 48
GOLSOY? Cornelia 122
GOODMAN John 87 Robt 87
GOODS Elizabeth 46
GORAM Wm 43

GORDON John T 54
GORE Annie 6
GRACE George 48
GRADY F J 48
GRAHAM Mary 89 Sarah 94
GRANALE Emma 53
GRANT Catharine 58
GRAVES Henry 110
GRAY Mary 68 121 Susan 101
   William 68
GRAYSON Julia 67
GREEN Ada 52 C W 48 Geo King
   52 James 52 Laura 52 Martha 52
GREENWELL Geor 98
GREENWOOD Eliza 56 Jay 56
GREGG Cym 108
GREGORY Douglas 82 Hamilton
   33 Marion 33
GRIDLEY Ellen 26 Thomas 26
GRIFFITH Alfred 121
GRIGGS Frances 3 Michael 3
GRIMES Julia 85
GRIS Louis 25
GRIST A A 122
GROSS Jacob 126
GUEST Elizabeth 80
GURBER Ledia 118
GURTLE J L 55
HAGAN Eliza 28
HALL Annie 15 Catharine 3
   Frances 15 James 26 Jane 63
   Mary 15 96 Rachel 26
   William 15
HALLS Margaret 4
HAMEL Annie 57 Bemone 57
   Roberta 57 Robt 57 Sarah 57
HAMILTON Annie 13 Chas 13
   Henry 12 Isabella 21 Louise
   13 Lydia 9 Maria 49 Mr 12
   Mrs 12 Sally 44 Will 70
HAMMOND John 16
HAMPSON Joseph 52 Julia 52
HAMRON Margaret 9
HARE Bridgett 42
HARPER Alice 118 Emma 118
   Frank 118 Jane 118 Kate 41
   W A 118 Willie 118
HARRIS Eliza 125
HARRISON C 27 Elias 77 John
   110 Robert 9 Robt 108
   Virginia 110
HASIN Patty 14 Wm 14
HASKEY Mary A 18
HASKIN Dennis 52
HASLIP Mary E 48
HASS David 105
HATHAWAY Maria 3
HAUSBY Lucinda 40
HAUVER William 28
HAWKINS Eliza 3
HAYS Lucy 104 108 Nora 112

137

ALEXANDRIA VIRGINIA 1860 CENSUS

HEALY Alexander 100 Pat 131
HEART Jno 55 Thos 115
HEBBNER Henry 45 Louise 45
HEBNER Joseph 13
HEINDAY Margaret 24
HEKEUDAFFER Frederick 123 Mary 123
HELLMUTH Peter 55
HENDERSON Lauretta 89 Louisa 69 Sarah 9 Wm 9
HENDRICK Frank 37
HENING Basil 125
HENNESSAY Jas 60
HENRETTY Francis 90
HENRY Adalvie 80 Amanda 37 70 Emma 70 Euman 37 Hugh 8 Jane 62 John 70 John Lecher 37 Polly 62 Robert 70 Robt 37 Wm 14
HENTON Isaac 101 R H 55
HERNDON Mary 50
HERRISH Jane 101 Mary C 101 Wm T 101
HERRSING Awdrey 56
HESS Elizabeth 3
HEYMAN Catharine 8 H 86
HIBBINS Maria 116
HICKEN John 116
HICKS Mary 3
HILCRULIN Rose 93
HILL G P 48 H J 48
HILLCOLME Billy 116
HIRTE Hugh S 84 Kiddin M 84
HISTER Wm E 86
HOBSON Ambler 10
HODGES Elizabeth 118 Mary 123
HOFFMAN P E 55
HOLLINGER William 40 95
HOLLOWAY Mary 67
HOLLY Fanny 78
HONESTY Lavinia 109
HOOE Augustus 125 Margaret 4 117
HOOPER Mary 71
HOPKINS Daniel 49 John 53
HORN Lizzie 129
HORNER Robert 119
HOSKINS George 115
HOUGH Susan 59
HOWARD David 119 John 119 Louise 110 Mary 119 Robert 119
HUDSON Robert 97
HUGH Mary 100
HUGHES Mary 114
HUMPHREY Lucy 99
HUMPHREYS A 48
HUNT Albert L 20 D 55 Danl 86
HUNTER Mary 93
HUNTINGTON Elizabeth 111 120
HURTLE Thos 110
HUTCHINS Cornelia 93

HUTCHINSON Mary 50
HUTCHIS Catharine 12
ICHBECK J 55
IKE Albert 18
INDLE Wm 28
INGALLS Edward 121 John 121 Monia 121 Sally 121
INS... May 21
IRVING Mary 129
IVEN James 50
JACKSON Ada 74 Alice 74 Camp 74 Christena 74 Damdiste 86 James 74 Julia 61
JACOBS Amanda 81 Amelia 81 Fanny 81 Thomas 81
JANNEY I J 48
JANNY A D 53 Eliza 53 Sallie 53
JEFFERSON John 3 Tom 61 Wm 27
JEFFRIES Annie 34 Cecila 34 James 34
JELIFF G D 87
JENKINS Geo 41
JENY Mary M 48
JESPER Andrew 98
JETTET Maria 49
JEWELL Hanna 130 Hannah 128
JOHNSON Jno 34
JOHNSTON Alice 125 Anna 32 Bill 39 Caroline 54 Fanny 131 George 54 Louis 76 Lucinda 13 Margaret 16 Maria 53 Mary 54 112 Wm 94
JONES Ann 127 Bertha 35 Kitty 97 Margaret 113 Mary 3 Sarah 3 William 86
JOURDAN J P 55 Susan 41
JOYEL Robert 9
JULIUS Elizabeth 97
KANE Patrick 68
KEATON David 70
KEITH David 29 Mary A 29
KELL Arthur 124
KELLY Aurosa 93 Catharine 93 Edward 93 Jack 34 Lawrence 63 May 112 Thomas 101 William 112
KEMPF Amanda 97
KENNEDY Bridget 91
KERR John 131
KEYS Alexander 87 Millie 129
KIDWELL Agnes 35 Caroline 1 Harriet 1 64 James 1 64 Jane 1 64 John T 34 Robert 1 Sarah 35 William 1 64
KIESLING Noah 10
KIGGING Mary 92
KINCAMM Kate 37
KING Albert 65 Annie 18 81 Chas 110 Fred 66 James 18 Margaret 114 Mary 66 Mattey H 83 Patrick 18 Sally 25 30

KING (continued) Sarah 66 Wm W 114
KINKAID Isabella 34
KINNER John M 67
KIRBY John 106
KLINE Geo 26
KRONS Arty 84
KULER E S 104
KULON Frank 110
KUTCHER Anna 113
LAFERTY Chas 68
LAFETTE Fanny 59
LAIN Abner W 16 Rosam..ol 16
LATCHFORD Cath 42
LATHROP Barbara 17 Bryan 17 Florence 17 J H 17 Mary 17 Minnie 17
LAURENS Catharine 111
LAVINE Elizabeth 71 Mary 71
LAW Mary 1
LAWLER Dennis 84
LAWRENCE Virginia 16
LAWS Laurena 13
LEADLY Amelia 98 Dan 98
LEE C(assius) F 121 Elizabeth 51 Henry 37 Infant 68 Maretta 66 Rebecca 127 Ritta 130 Rose 68 Sally 74 Willia 66
LEEF Wm 15
LEONARD Maggie 56
LEVI Amanda 14
LEWIS Selima 81
LI...MCH John 5
LINDSAY Emma 63
LIPPEL John 121
LOCKLAND John 131
LOCKRELL J 18
LOGE John 100
LOUDLEY Michael 93
LOVEJOY Francis H 34 Isaac B 34 Mary 34
LOVELACE Jane 19 Mary 72
LOYD Mary 83
LUCAS Ger 3 Monica 39
LUCKITT William 87
LUCY Henry 55
LUGANBEEL James 27 Mary 27 Prince 27
LUGANBELL Emma 31 Martha 31
LURUES Ellen 105
LUTHER John 60
LUTHERN Frances 75 Richard 75
LUTRELL Thos 93
LYLES Emily 93 Jane 68 William 68 Wm 68
LYNN Charley 87 M D 55
MADDOX Elizabeth 55 J E 86 Jane 55
MADISON A 9 James 60 Rosana 60
MAHANDX Wm 108

138

ALEXANDRIA VIRGINIA 1860 CENSUS

MAHLER Catharine 104 108
MAHONY Josephene 114 Susan 114
MAITLEY Johanna 31
MALORY John 79
MANING Margaret 69
MANKIN Ann D 37 Bertrand 101 George 101 Virginia 101 William 101
MANKINS Jno 13
MANN W H 55
MANSFIELD Johana 76 Robert 43
MARREY James 80
MARRIOT John 57
MARSHALL Charles 85 John 55
MARSTON Frances 75
MARTIN Bridgett 86 Clara 83
MASON Helen 34
MATHERS Hannah 45 Norman 45
MAY Alexander 3
MEAGHAN Ed 18
MEHT Frances 53
MELBOURNE Charlotte 64
MELCHOR Julius 84
MELVIN Jennie 40 95
MERCER Sarah 101
MERCHANT Thomas 51
MERTIN Mama 77
MEYERBURGH B 8
MILES Amelia 126 Mary 126
MILLER Edward S 20 Lucretia 53 William 38
MILLS Ada 126 Chamberlain 126 Clarence 47 Frances 26 Harvey 122 John 122 Nancy 4 Wm J 14
MIRRETT Mrs 119
MISER Geo 107
MITCHELL Dolly 54 Geo 52 Joseph 127 Juith 108 Julia 109 Kate 107 Lucy 127 Matilda 118 Robert 16 William 115 127
MITCLIFF Catharine 3 West 3
MITZ Geo 3
MOLAIR Bettie 87 James 87 Luther 87 Roze 87
MONAHAN ___ 81
MONROE John 57
MONTJOY Cloa 37
MOONE Clarence 34
MOORE Alvin 88 Roxie 17 Roxise 15
MORCIS Bashful 43 Wm 43
MORGAN Daniel 86 Elizabeth 10 Wm 99
MORRON Annie 83 Jas 83
MORTIMER Chas 7
MOULDER Christina 16
MUDT... David 43
MUIR Elizabeth 124 Jane 124 Mary 124

MULLICAN Saml 99
MULLIGAN David 77 Mary 43 117
MUNKINS Edgar 58
MURPHY Ann 15 John 29 35 Susan 37
MURRAY Charles 37 Edward 100 George 37 Jane 84
MURTOUGH Peter 42
MYERS May 49
McCARTY Jere 67
McBLOOD Biddie 44
McCAIN Margaret 127
McCARRIE Julia 125
McCARTY John 77
McCAULY Mary 27
McCAY Catharine 3
McCLAIN R A 48
McCLANY Mich 75
McCLOSAND Michael 116
McCLUSKEY J 3
McCULLIN Sarah 3
McDEVITT Thos 93
McDON Alexander 3
McDOYAL Sarah 52
McELLEGAN Margaret 9 William 9 ___ 9
McGEE Mary 90
McGIZZY J 3
McGRAW John 29 Mary 68
McGUIRE M G 55
McHENRY Virginia 79 Wm 41
McKINDNER Mary 128
McKNIGHT Mary 96
McMAHAND Wm 104
McMANN Mary 88
McMULLEN Sarah 27
McMULLIN Sarah 5
McNALLY P 80
McNEAR Jane 56
McNENERY Owen 20
NALLS John 59
NALORY James 95 Mary 95
NEUKINS Jane 63
NEULIR Elizabeth 131
NEVELL Bridgett 48
NEWFIELD May 3
NEWMAN Effin 93 John 93 Lena 93
NEWTON Ann S 77 Joseph 77 Margaret 87 Mary H 77 Virginia 77
NICHOLLS Thos 41
NIELSON Emma 12
NOKES MARY 18 ___ 18
NORMAN Thomas 72
NOVALL J B 48
NOWLAND John 84 Mary 14
NUTCH Charles 96 John 21 William 21
O'BRADY Mary 86
O'BRIEN Thos 67
O'FLANNAGAN Betty 85

O'HEARA John 40
O'NEAL John 50 Mary 50 Thomas 122
O'SULLIVAN Kate 63
OGDEN Elijah 26 George 49 Mary 49 Sarah 26 49
OVEAR Annie 96 Charles 96 Wm 96
OWENINGS Carrie 53 Jesse 53
PADGETT Georgia 102 Harriet 58 Lucretia 111 Sarah 111
PAGE Thomas 3
PARIS Rebecca 99
PARISH Ella 119 Frances 119 Mary 119
PARKE Kity 33
PARKERSON J 55
PARKS Sarah 44
PARSONS Franklin 57 John 84 Joseph 16
PASCAL Rebecca 54
PAYNE Cecilia 130 Helen 105 Jas R 102 John 2 Louis 117 Matilda 40 William 71
PEARL Thomas S 96
PEARSON Fanny 124
PENN Ada 65 Joseph 65 Mary 65
PERRY Thomas 48
PETERS Fanny 73 Lucy 73
PETTITE Robt 63
PETTY Geo 6 Mary E 5
PETTYMAN Mrs 119
PEYTON Jas 13
PHILIPS Ann 78
PHILLIPS Ann 93 Laura 93
PIERSON Joseph 87
PILES Benjamin 58 Kitty 58
PITMAN Vincent 37
PLACIDE M P 48
PLAIN Beryman 69 Caroline Amy 69 Catharine 69 John 69 Mildred 69
PLAINE John 50
PLANEL Benjamin K 66
POITOZE Victor 93
POSEY Ann 58 Martha 25
POTHAM Mary E 48
POTTER Nancy 130
POTTS Martha 66 Mary 66
POWELL John 1 Mary 1 Sidney 1
POWER G F 55 Julia 55
PRICE Edgar 72 Fanny 93 Jas E 6 Marrion 72
PRITCHARD A P 48
QUAID Elizabeth 26
QUANDER Gracie 29 71
QUEEN Rebecca 27
QUENZEL C 44
QUISAIL Chris 3
RABE A I 86
RAINE John 80 82 Mary 80 82
RAMB Edmond 82

ALEXANDRIA VIRGINIA 1860 CENSUS

RAMBURGH Henry 70
RAMSAY Christina 75 Edgar 75 Sarah 28
RAMSEY Jane 12
RANDALL Hester 86
RANKIN Margaret 75 William 75
REAVES Robt 59
REDD Charles 131 Josephine 131 Alice 83 Edwin 127 Ida 83 Martha 110
REESE Balak 112 Elizabeth 5
RHOAN Sally 52
RIARDON Rachel 79
RICE James 40 John 107 Mary 102 Owen 107
RICHARD George 54
RICHMOND Daniel 34
RIDGWAY Maria 118
RIGGS Townsby 65
RILEY Miron 29 Wm 3
RILL Mary 33
ROACH Adalaie 47 James 26 Johanna 26 Mary 3 109 Wm 39
ROADMAN Christian 23
ROADSTEIN Dan 107
ROBBS Jeremiah 127
ROBERTS Washington 20
ROBINS Elizabeth 26 John 5 Mary 5
ROBINSON Emma 81 John 38 Mary 11 R H P 55 Robert 38 Wm 3 _____ 105
ROBY Uphennia 32
ROCK Wm R 118
ROGERS Henry 63 J C 86 Jane 48 Julia 63 Mary 63 Monie 48 Pendleton 48 William 48
ROHAN John 52
ROLLING Julia 11
RONALD Lucinda 105
RONE Latita 28
ROSE Drucella 4 W F 55
ROSENFIELD Mike 125
ROSENTHAL E 55 J 55
ROSS John 28
ROTCHFORD Philip 37
ROWLAND R 92
ROXBERRY Mary 74
RUDD Harriet M 30 John A 30
RYAN Cornelius 93 James 18 Kate 52 Timothy 93
RYE Jane 3 Jane E 3 Jesse 3 96
S.. Tim 104
SAILAIN Abbie 129
SAINT Joseph 81
SAMPSON Julia 52
SAMUEL Susan 93
SANDERSON Samuel 75
SANDS Thomas 58
SANFORD V 86
SARTAM James 123

SATERFIELD Fanny 61
SAUL Emma 93
SAULS John 90
SAULSBERY Hugh 72
SAUNDERS Margaret 86 S L 86
SAVAGE Julia 49 Mary 82
SAWLER Edward 75 Johanna 75 Joseph 75
SAYLOR Chas 104
SAYRES Matilda 99 Virginia 99
SCEDMORE John 63
SCHWARTZ Emma 104 Mary 107 Rosannah 107
SCOLS William 131
SCOTT John 15 87 May 15 Sarah 114 Thomas 15 _____ 87
SEALS Namei 131
SEWELL Edward 69
SEYMOUR Charlotte 26 Lucinda 26
SHANK Mahallock 59 Mat... 57 Susan 59
SHAP Anna 91 Eddie 91 Susan 91 Virginia 91 Wm 91
SHAY David 70 Eliza 38 Robert 38
SHEARS Sarah 111
SHERDEN Patrick 63
SHERWOOD John 95 John A 46 Joseph 57 Joshua 46 Maria 88 Mary 46 Thomas 46
SHINN Elizabeth 23 Robert 23
SHIPLY Ensley J 52
SHIRKS John 89
SHIRLEY Anna 18 Chas B 18 Edward 18 Franklin 10 Minnie 18 Noville 18 Sallie 18 Sarah 18
SHONE Jane 129
SHREVE Richard 75
SHUMAN Franklin 3
SIDES Geo B 75 Wm H 75
SIGHT George 105
SILLS John 44
SIMMS Louis 3 Sarah 63
SIMPSON Adaline 55 Ann 28 Margaret 42
SIMS Caroline 118 Rosalena 118
SKINNER Ann 92 Jane M 92 Thos 92
SLAWOOD Maria 90
SLAYMAKER H 128 130
SMALL Henrietta 122
SMATHERS Lucy 98
SMITH Alan S 99 Baky 94 C 39 Catharine 99 Chin 84 Dalia 96 David 119 Dick 99 Geo 99 Griffith 96 John 96 John C 48 Joseph 55 56 Josephine 11 Larinia 101 Louise 6 Margaret 116 Mary Violet 6

SMITH (continued)
 Matilda 76 Richard 17 Samuel 99 Sarah 57 Sarah K 63 Wm 80 William 10 Wm 6 80 Wm M 86
SMOOT Adalaide 97 Florence 97
SNOWDEN Mary 16 William 16
SOLMER Caroline 125
SOLOMAN Eveline 105 Mary 105
SPADEU Ada 6 Edgar 6 Marion 6 Theodore 6 William 6
SPEDENS Wm 37
SPICER James 3
SPINKS Alice 44
SPOLDING Elizabeth 71
SPOTTS Wm 33
SQUEAR Ann 97 Emily 97 Geo C 97 Perkins 97 Rocetta 97
STABLER Rebecca 112
STALLY Andrew 47 50 Louise 47 50
STEDCROPH Sarah 21
STEELE M Spring 93 Mary C 93
STEELL Ann Spring 71 Margaret 71 Mary 71
STEPHENSON Emma 3 John 3 May 3 Sarah 3
STERLING Wm 28
STEUART Frank 48 Mrs 48
STEVENS Harriet 51
STEWART Geo L 48 Mary 116 Susan 48
STICKLEY A S 86
STIMSON Wm 79
STOUTENBURG Maria 127
STRAP Jackylin 10
STRIDER Alice 72 Eveline 72 James 72 Jas E 72 John 72 Phoebe 72
STUART Miss 119
STUCKLEY Fanny 62
SUFTWICH J 48 Julia 48
SULLIVAN Catharine 42 Edward 16 John 29 Mary 42 99
SULLY Robert 94
SUMMERVILLE Geo 70 M C 70 Robt F 70
SUTTON Fanny 100 George 121
SWAIN Samuel 69
SWAM Mary 9
SWANN John H 85 Wm 83
SWOPE John 45
SYPHAX Adalaide 62 David 62 Edith 62 Frances 112 Margaret 62
TALBOT Frank 27
TALIFERO H D 55
TATE Columbia 99 Daniel 103 Jas 86 Maj 17 Mary 103
TATSAPAUGH Richard 63
TATSPAUGH Richard 118
TAYLOR Ann 94 Caroline 108

140

ALEXANDRIA VIRGINIA 1860 CENSUS

TAYLOR (continued)
  Chas 104 Chas M 23 Eliza 22
  George 22 George W 22 J C
  55 John 22 117 Josephene 22
  Moses 31 Rose 117 121 Sally
  14 Sarah 22 Susan 47
  William 22
THAS? William 67
THEUWELL Mrs 48
THOMAS Charles 3 Edward 120
  John 14 107 Lucy V 120
  Martha 99 Mary 93 Richard
  108 Robert 3
THOMPSON Amanda 105 Bob 12
  Bridgett 38 Caroline 77
  Elenora 89 Elizabeth 3
  Elmira 89 Elyabeth 29 Ida
  89 Joseph 83 Millard 12
  Sally 15 Samuel 127
THOMSON Amos 44 Massachusetts
  44
THORM Clay 3
THORNTON Frances 47
THORTON Mary 61
THROP Rachel 3
THURSTON Sarah J 50
TIMBERLAKE J M 104
TOB Phoebe 83
TODD David 113 Emma 54
TOLBERT Elizabeth 131
TOMS Clement 61 Joseph 61
  Louise 61 Moran 61
TOTLE Mary A 79
TRACEY Margaret 69
TRAVIS Henry 118
TROFIT Jacob 114
TRUMAN Geo 5
TUNNING John 85
TURLEY Sarah 26
TURNER Barbara 130
VERMILLION Alice 59 Nelson 58
VERNION James 65 Mary 65
  Sarah 65 William 65
VERNON Susana 36
VINCENT Lenora 108 William
  108 Wm 108
VINE Danl 35
VIOLETT Jno 122
VIRSON Mary 53
WADDY Amanda 130 Walter 130
WADE Susan 60
WAGG H... 106
WALKER Ann 33 Dan 120 Harriet
  102 John 37 71 73 Samuel
  132
WALL Conrad 3
WALLACE Adam 97 John 97
WALLOCK Maggie 77
WALLS Ellen 12
WANTON Hannah 98 William 52
WARD Chas 72 Frances 75 Geo C
  27 H C 48 James 72 John 3

WARE Adaline 87
WARNER Mary 129
WASHINGTON Mary 32
WATERS Adelide 7 Anthony 7
  Charlotte 7 Daniel 7 Helen
  6 Marjarietta 7 Phebe 20
WATSON James 19 John 70
  Matilda 19 Sarah 19
WATTLES Sarah 110
WEADEN Geo W 66
WEBB Mary 21
WEBSTER Caroline 10 Jas 124
WEEKS Ellen 47
WEIPHEG Anne 75
WELLS George 123 Joe 34 Julia
  115 Kate 123
WELSH Annie 46 Ellen 108
  Joseph 108
WESBERY Franklin 94 Ida 94
  John 94 Martha 94
WEST Asma 95 Chas 56 Fannie
  11 Harriet 7 John 95 Mary
  112 Rebecca 112
WHARTON ... 48
WHEAT H K 20
WHEATLY Wm 47 50
WHEELER Josephine 90 Mary E
  90 Mattie 8 Ray 3
WHISKEY Georgana 65
WHITE Amy 61 Ben 106 Frances
  57 Maria 44 Mary 45 Mary H
  44 May 43 Nuttin 31 Ellen
  129 Fred 129
WHITELY Ellen 129 Fred 129
WHITFIELD Sarah 56 Thos 56
WHITING Ella 93 Jane 105 John
  58 Mary 105 Mrs 42
WHITLEY Eli 79
WHITNEY Elizabeth 88 James 88
  Jane 88
WHITWALL Anna 77 Mary 77
WIBERT Garret 96
WIGGS Betty 90 Caroline 90
  James D 90 Jas 90 Mary V 90
  Richard 90 Ryner 30
WILEY Andrew 17 Mary 17
  Pendleton 17
WILKINS Elizabeth 36
WILLERSON Bettie 103
WILLIAM Sophia 108
WILLIAMS Emily 25 George 117
  James 96 Jas 25 Jas E 110
  Martha 117 Mary 81 Wm 3
WILLYTON Mrs 48
WILSON Eliza 25 41 Ethan 7
  Frances 53 John 3 Kate 11
  Margaret 99 Mary 25 41 107
WINDEL Jas 28
WINDSOR Wm 72
WINE Ellen 20
WINSSELL Helen 83
WINSTON John 92

WISE Alice 92 C J 55 Margaret
  70 Susan 70
WITHERS John 48 Littleton 48
  Margaret 90
WOK May 59
WOOD Andrew 34 Ann 14 Ella 30
  Frank 112 Jno 54 Juda 61
  Laurson 115 Malissa 61 Mary
  93 Nancy 58 Robt L 61
  Samuel 68 Willia 37
WOODHOUSE Wm 105
WOODY John 18 Sally 18
WOOLS William 77 79
WORTH Wm H 61
WORTHLIFFE A J 55
WREN Harmon 60 Infant 60
  Martha 60 Robt 60
WRIGHT Anna 94 Francis 64 Wm
  86
YOUNG Lizzie 129
ZIMMERMAN Adaline 125 Alice
  125 Dora 125 J R 86 Martha
  39 Mary 125 Walter 125
  William 125
_____ Haywood 105

www.ingramcontent.com/pod-product-compliance
Lightning Source LLC
Chambersburg PA
CBHW081133170426
43197CB00017B/2844